IMAGES
of America

JUNIATA'S RIVER VALLEYS

I0806151

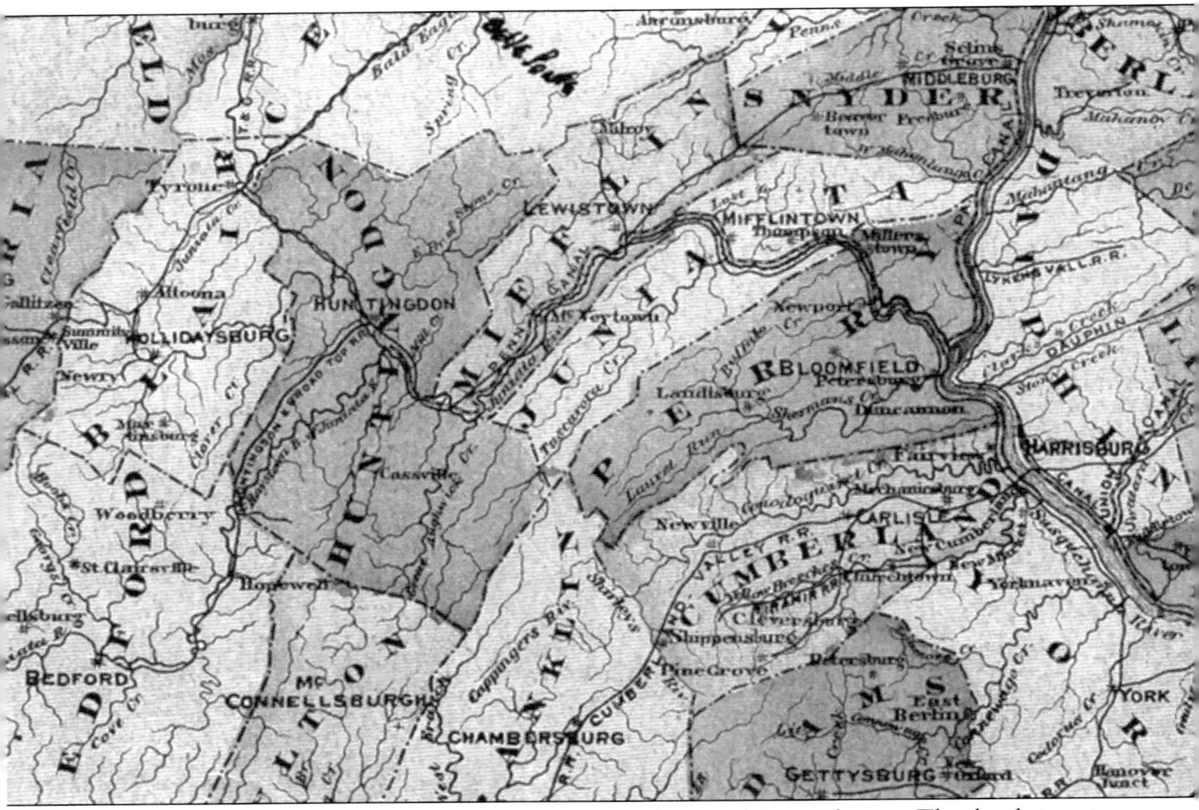

The Juniata region is shown on this 1871 map of Central Pennsylvania. This book is written with the perspective of traveling from the Susquehanna River inland along the Juniata River through the counties of Perry, Juniata, Mifflin, Huntingdon, Bedford, and Blair. When this map was drawn, the Pennsylvania Canal was included. However, it had ceased to operate in many places. The Pennsylvania Railroad led to its demise. (Author's collection.)

On the Cover: At the far reaches of the Juniata River System, more than 100 miles from the Susquehanna River, three generations of a family pause for the photographer during a barn raising. For this family, this is a moment of celebration. The grandparents ventured west to build a log cabin on the land to which they laid claim. They can now rejoice in seeing their grandchildren enjoy the results of a lifetime of hard work. (Author's collection.)

IMAGES
of America

JUNIATA'S RIVER VALLEYS

Jeffrey Adams

ARCADIA
PUBLISHING

Copyright © 2011 by Jeffrey Adams
ISBN 978-0-7385-7419-6

Published by Arcadia Publishing
Charleston, South Carolina

Printed in the United States of America

Library of Congress Control Number: 2010934334

For all general information, please contact Arcadia Publishing:
Telephone 843-853-2070
Fax 843-853-0044
E-mail sales@arcadiapublishing.com
For customer service and orders:
Toll-Free 1-888-313-2665

Visit us on the Internet at www.arcadiapublishing.com

This book is dedicated to the memory of Rhoda Burns Adams,
a true lover of the written word and a perfect mentor.

Contents

ACKNOWLEDGMENTS

In the course of assembling the images used in this book, I found it necessary to consult the pages of the individual historical societies of each county to verify the accuracy of my information. I realized that it is these groups that need the praise and support of all who live in the Juniata Valley. They are the ones preserving our heritage and celebrating our lives. All of this is to give future generations a true picture of the struggles and accomplishments their forbearers experienced.

It is with this in mind that I want to thank Nancy Smith of the Tyrone Area Historical Society for her dedication in recognizing that each fact and notion may have an importance to some individual in the future. I also want to acknowledge the memory of Frances Jone, educator and librarian, who contributed greatly to my photographic collection.

My hearty praise goes to Dennis P. McIlnay, author of the book *Juniata, River of Sorrows*. I thank him. Reading his book pushed me to get my act together with this project. His historical and colorful account of our beautiful river is the best on record. For once, he describes the Native Americans factually and in a way that humanizes them far better than others who have tried and failed in doing so.

Also, a special mention goes to Judith A. Heberling, Ph.D., of Heberling Associates, Inc. Located in beautiful Alexandria, HAI has completed comprehensive studies of lost treasures in the Juniata region. This team of archaeologists has painstakingly uncovered canal locks, mills, and work sites. The published reports they produce are worth a fortune in knowledge. Judith Heberling provided me with valuable research information.

All images appearing in this book are from the collection of the author.

INTRODUCTION

For more than two-and-a-half centuries, many tales have been told of the first Juniata Valley settlers' trek into the wilderness along one of America's most scenic waterways. The age-old trees and fertile fields were shadowed by the rolling hills and occasional lofty peaks. The ancient pathways used by the Native Americans trailed closely to the Juniata waterways. These same paths were rebuilt as successive generations introduced newer modes of transportation.

The valleys of the Juniata occupy the very heart of the state of Pennsylvania. They snake eastward toward the mighty Susquehanna and provide an outlet for mountain water across the Allegheny Front. This ecosystem is a major contributor to the great Chesapeake watershed that drains a major portion of the continent. The river cuts through several southwest-to-northeast ridges, mostly of sandstone sandwiched with limestone valley floors. Several spectacular water gaps are encountered when traveling the valleys.

Three distinct branches of this river combine in Huntingdon County to form the main branch of the Juniata River. The Little Juniata River meets the Frankstown Branch near Petersburg. Past the Borough of Huntingdon, the winding Raystown Branch blends with the Frankstown and a full river is born. The Juniata system crosses eight counties and takes in water from some nine other counties by tributaries. By damming the Juniata River on the Raystown Branch, Pennsylvania's largest inland lake was formed in 1973.

After 1730, European immigrants of mostly Scotch-Irish, English, and German descent were attracted to the bountiful wildlife, seemingly endless forests, and flat lowland for farming. They were astounded by the plentiful produce that grew here. It was not like that found in their homeland. But in this beautiful new territory lurked an unfathomable danger. Three governmental bodies—Pennsylvania, Great Britain, and France—all had plans for this region. The French, to secure their holdings in the New World, incited the natives to commit terror and genocide on the unwary settlers in the Juniata Territory. The British did likewise. This period of the mid-1700s has come to be known by some as the "Sorrow of Juniata." Eventually hostilities ended and migration resumed. The Native Americans ultimately headed west for new lands.

With the American Revolution taking place throughout the colonies, the Juniata became a land of exploration. Lead was discovered and became valuable for munitions in the 1770s. It was hauled over rough terrain back east, where it was announced that iron ore had also been found in abundance within a short distance of the Juniata River. This important discovery helped usher in the Industrial Revolution in America as "Juniata Iron" furnaces soon dotted the landscape and lit up the sky at night.

The completion of the Erie Canal through New York State in 1825 sounded an alarm with the Pennsylvania Legislature. It was as if Pennsylvania had been trumped. The battle to gain a foothold in the commerce of the vast mid-section of the new territories had been won by New York. To challenge New York in the struggle for economic supremacy, the monumental task of canal building began across Pennsylvania in 1826. The Juniata Valley would be an important segment of this system. Work commenced here in 1827. In 1832, with great fanfare, the 127-mile Juniata Valley Division of the canal was opened for navigation. A total of 86 locks were required to overcome a change in elevation of 584 feet over the full length of the canal. The public works project of the Pennsylvania Canal did not garner the profits expected in the Juniata region. The impediment of crossing the Alleghenies was a major factor. Boats had to be lifted from the water and transported over the mountains by a series of locks and train cars on the Old Portage Railroad. This costly process did, however, become recognized as a wonder of the age. Frequent flooding along the Juniata River also contributed to costs.

Needless to say, the conquering of the inner waterways had a benefit that changed America. Innovations made to locomotives and improvements in rails now permitted trains to travel great distances. The endless forests of Pennsylvania could be used as fuel to power these dragons. With this in mind, officials of a proposed railroad company rode the canal and took notes. Maps were drawn and the legislature was convinced that the unthinkable could be done. In 1846, the infant Pennsylvania Railroad was launched. This new companion to the Juniata River eventually became the standard railroad of the world.

The Pennsylvania Railroad made the Juniata Valley the most traveled route in America and used symbols of the Juniata in its advertising. The largest locomotive repair and construction operation ever conceived was located in the Alleghenies at Altoona and was named the Juniata Shops. Photographers the world over, as well as sketch artists, traveled to these valleys by rail and shared their impressive views in travelogues and published weeklies. This enticed travelers to journey here and enjoy the beauty firsthand.

With road building for automobiles in the 20th century, highways followed much the same path as their predecessors. The Juniata River soon experienced a growth in tourism, since those in cars could plan their own trips along the waterways, at their leisure.

This photographic history of the Juniata Valley primarily demonstrates how evolving modes of transportation and the use of the river system shaped the world as we know it. Also shown is how the heavy industry of mechanized transportation and manufacturing can share the same environment with those who enjoy exploring nature using the river systems as a form of relaxation and pleasure.

Today, new generations have developed hiking trails on the industrial footpaths of our forefathers. The same river trails that led our ancestors to these hills are now enjoyed by weekend vacationers and fishermen who want their children to experience nature. The unusual stone formations, the endless variety of plant life, and the magnificent river with all of its opportunities for adventure await all who come for a visit.

One

Juniata Meets the Susquehanna, Perry County

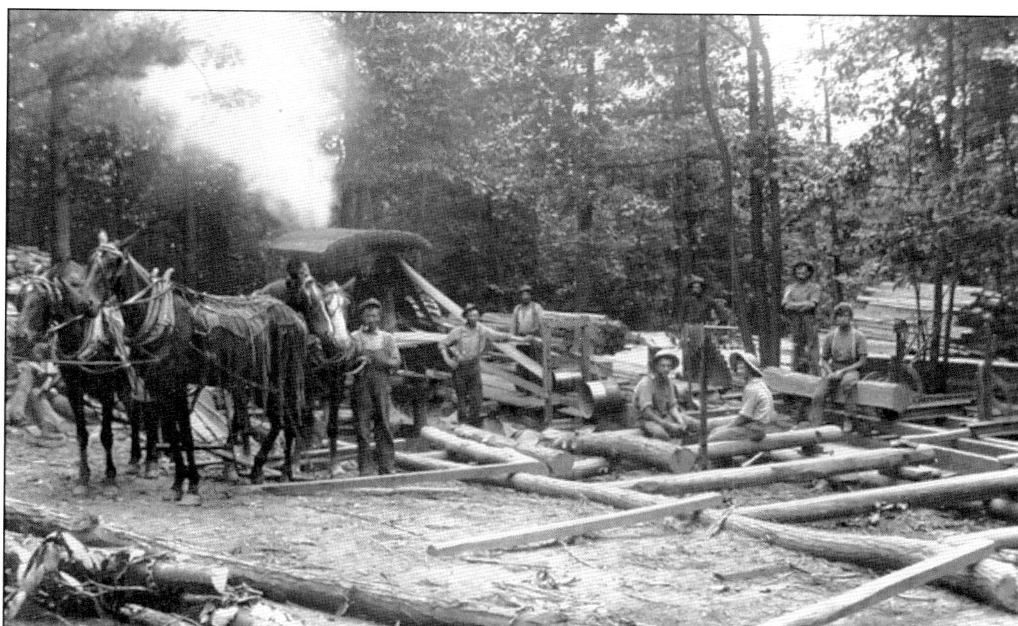

The lumber industry in Pennsylvania was a vital part of the economic development of the commonwealth. Scores of lumber towns popped up in the northern parts of the state after 1840. Here at Duncannon, logs rafted from the upper reaches of the Susquehanna were gathered from the river and processed for use in the Juniata Valley.

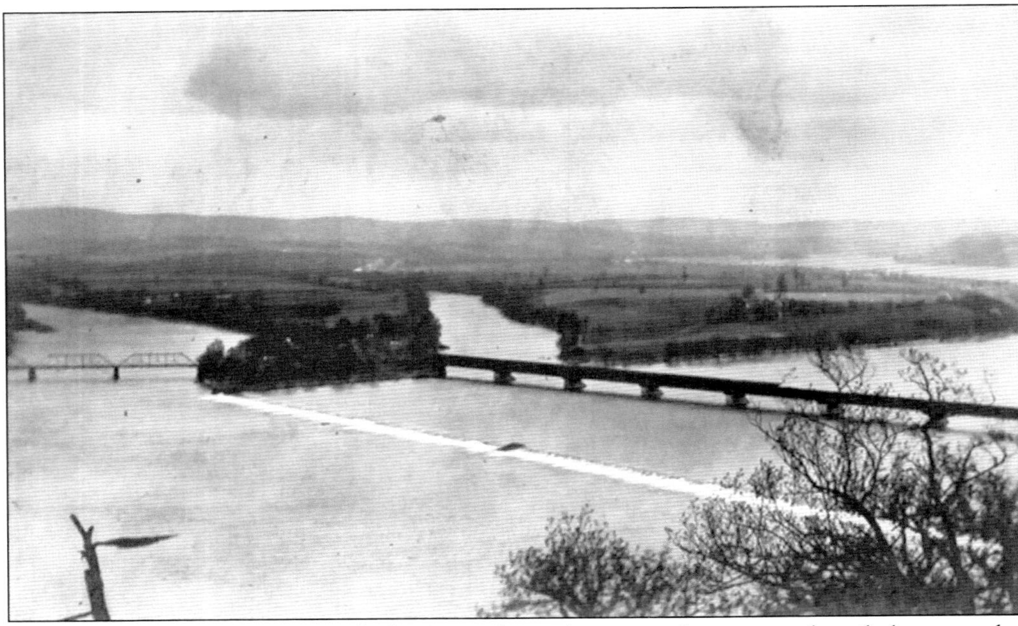

Connecting Duncan's Island with the Susquehanna's eastern shore, a nearly mile-long wooden bridge was constructed in 1829 at Clark's Ferry. Using the Burr design, this elegant structure resembled a number of others on the river; however, it featured a unique double towing-path as part of its architecture. A dam just below the bridge created a pool to guide canal boats across the Susquehanna to the Juniata.

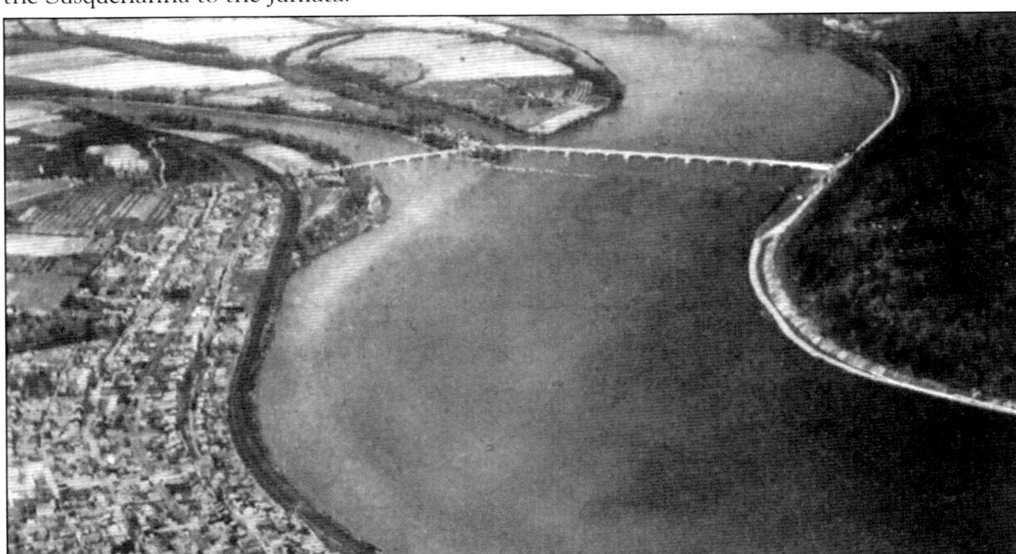

Clark's Ferry is actually in Dauphin County. The shore, just beyond, is the Perry County line. The William Penn Highway (US Route 22/322) crossed the Susquehanna River on this concrete arch toll bridge constructed by the Clark's Ferry Bridge Company in 1925, replacing the near century-old covered bridge. Prolific bridge designer Ralph Modjestki was the consulting engineer on the project that produced these twin spans. A ferry was located here, operated by Robert Clark beginning in 1785.

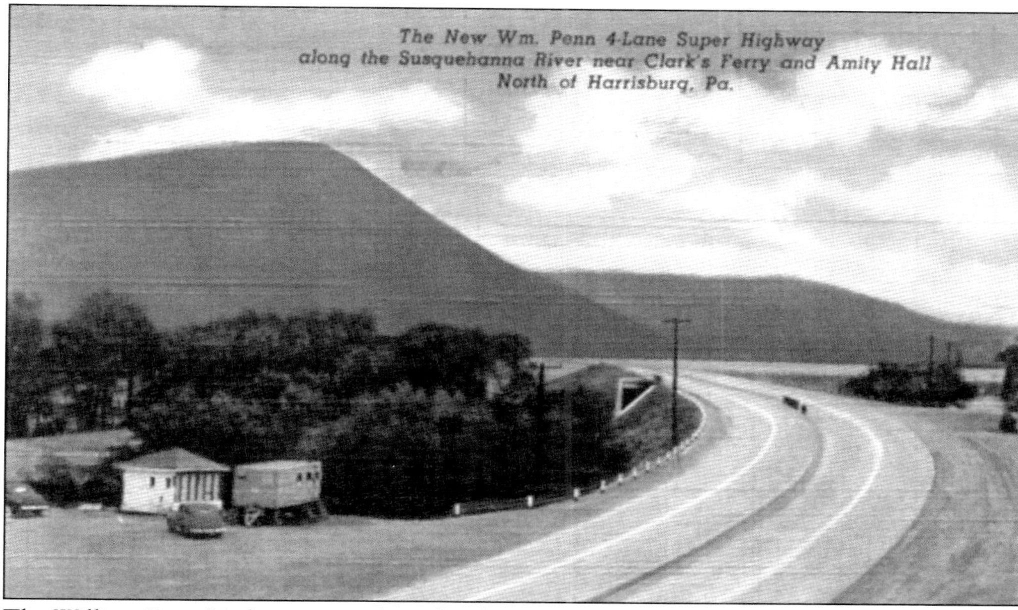

The William Penn Highway was enlarged to four lanes in the 1940s. The approach to the Clark's Ferry Bridge gave a nice view of Peters Mountain on the eastern shore of the Susquehanna River. This is the place where the Appalachian Trail crosses the river.

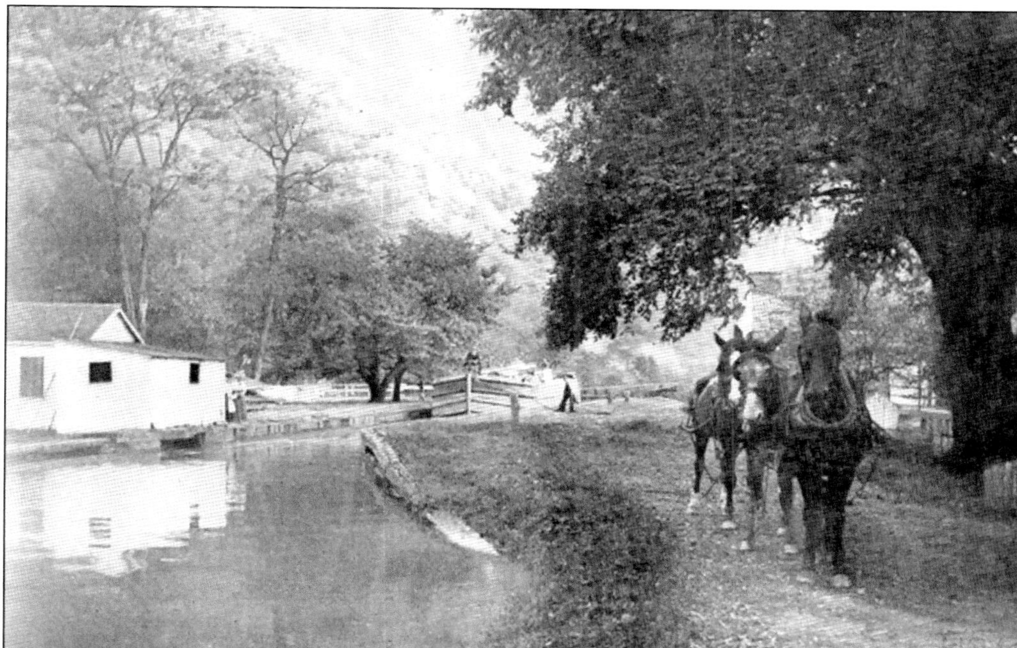

A packet boat approaches on the Dauphin County side of the river, preparing for a Susquehanna crossing. Three mules are puzzled by the photographer. Larger boats contained a room on deck for two resting mules. Daytime tables converted to beds at night for passengers. Separate quarters with a dressing room were provided for ladies. The average passenger packet could comfortably accommodate 30 passengers and travel between four and six miles per hour.

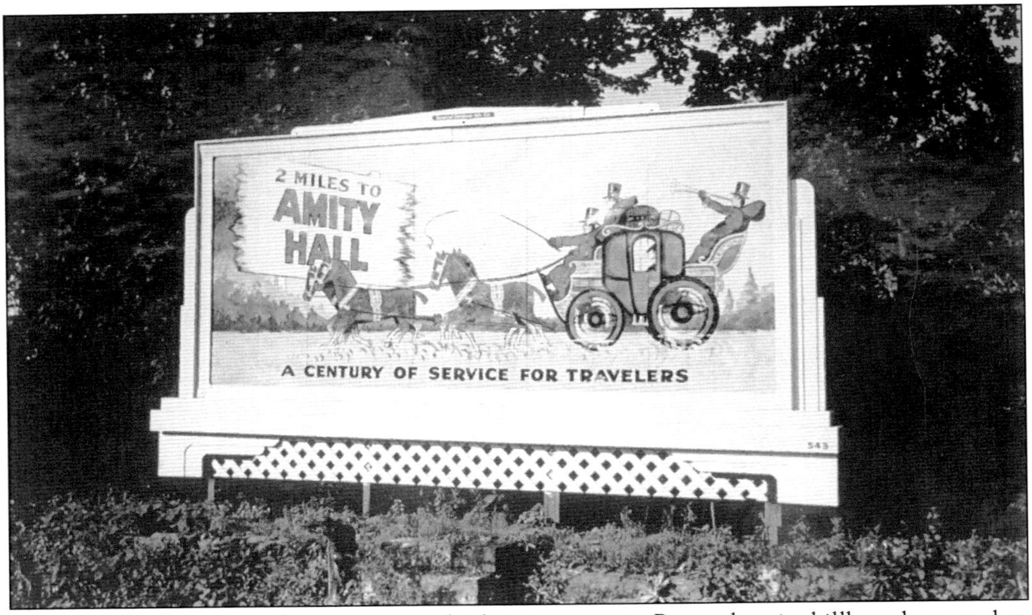

With the development of the new state highway system in Pennsylvania, billboards started to appear on the landscape. Increased automobile speeds required that larger signage was needed to convey the message. This classic logo for Amity Hall greeted travelers as they approached Duncan's Island from the west. This streamlined creation was typical of the many boards seen along the way in the 1930s.

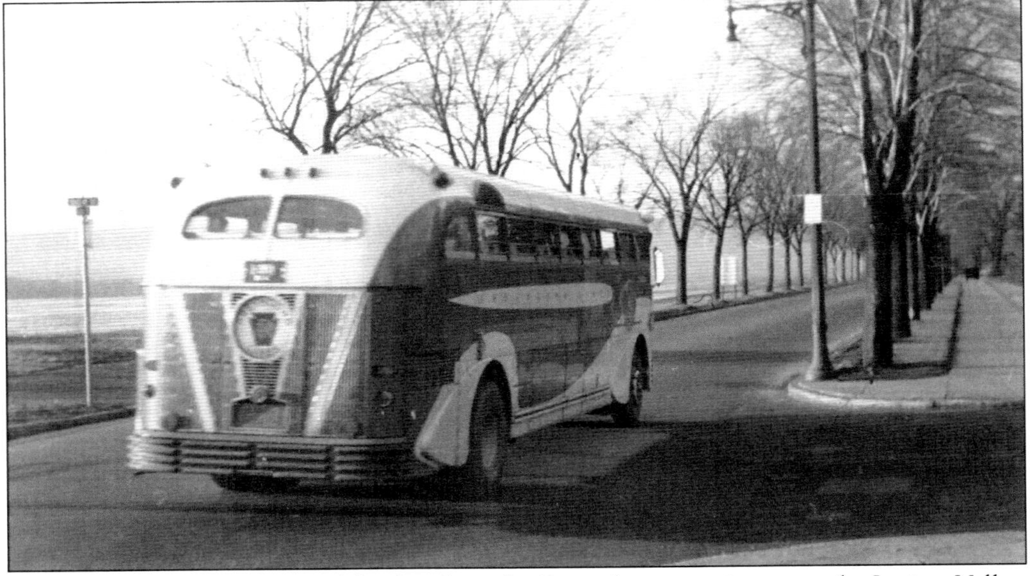

A Pennsylvania Railroad (PRR) bus heads up the Susquehanna on its way to the Juniata Valley. The Pennsylvania Railroad acquired a number of smaller transit concerns beginning in the late 1920s. This gave it the ability to better serve passengers within cities and provide transportation to communities via routes that had no rail connection. Peoples Rapid Transit consolidated into Pennsylvania Greyhound lines in 1936. The PRR had partial ownership of this company through 1954.

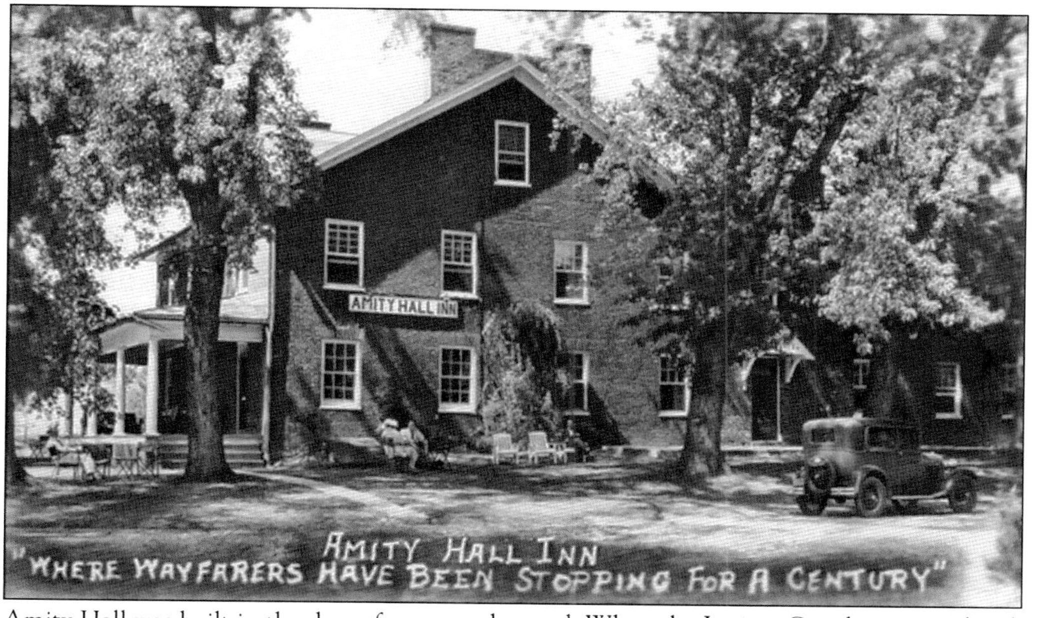

Amity Hall was built in the days of stagecoach travel. When the Juniata Canal was completed, it crossed the lucrative north-south Susquehanna Canal where Amity Hall stood. Amity Hall became the most famous inn in the state. Steam locomotives took the traffic off of Duncan's Island and the inn became a private residence in the late 1800s. The coming of the automobile made possible its reopening in 1922.

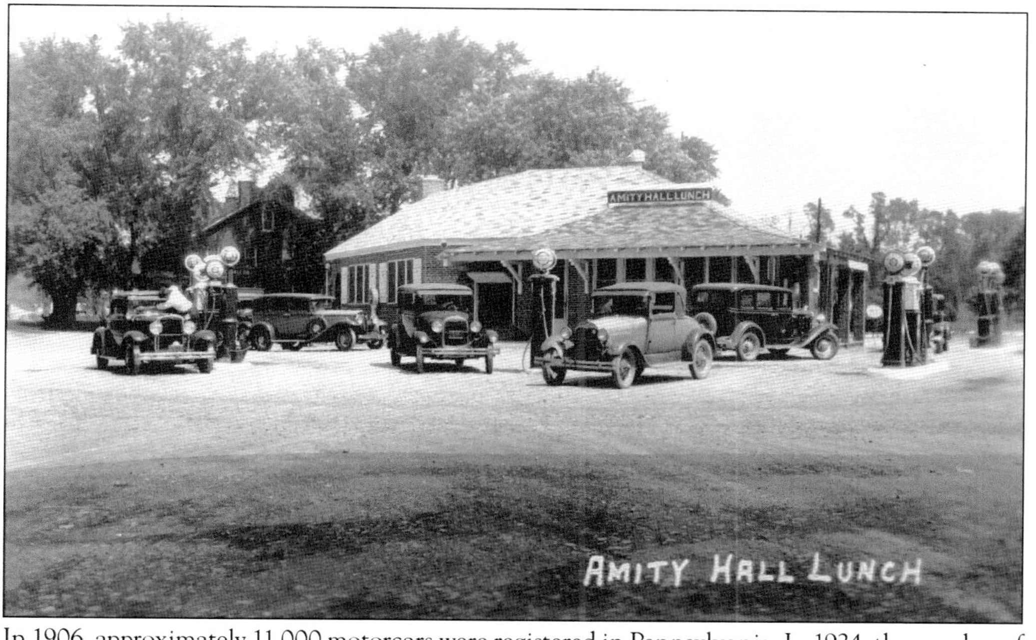

In 1906, approximately 11,000 motorcars were registered in Pennsylvania. In 1924, the number of cars fitted with plates exceeded one million for the first time. By the 1930s, the ribbons of concrete crossing the state were showing a full flow of traffic on weekends. At Amity Hall, the William Penn Highway (US Route 22/322) and the Susquehanna Thruway (US Route 11) intersected.

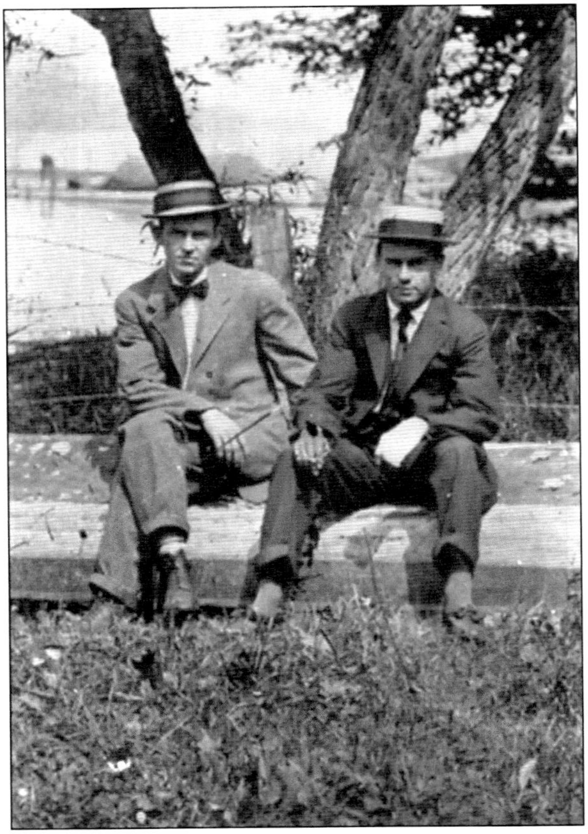

This old tintype shows two business travelers from Harrisburg at Amity Hall. They took a canal boat as opposed to the train just for the experience. The Pennsylvania Railroad ran its line on the opposite shore, running through Marysville and Duncannon and then along the Juniata River. Duncan's Island became a quiet place to enjoy the rivers.

When the early settlers began occupying the Juniata Valley, they were puzzled by the basket contraptions set up in channels where the waters flowed swiftly. Native Americans had long ago learned to fashion fish traps. These elevated baskets quickly guided fish propelled by the water's current up a wooden pathway with no return. The settlers improvised the design, and soon were catching eels, catfish, perch, and other types of the plentiful fish of the Juniata.

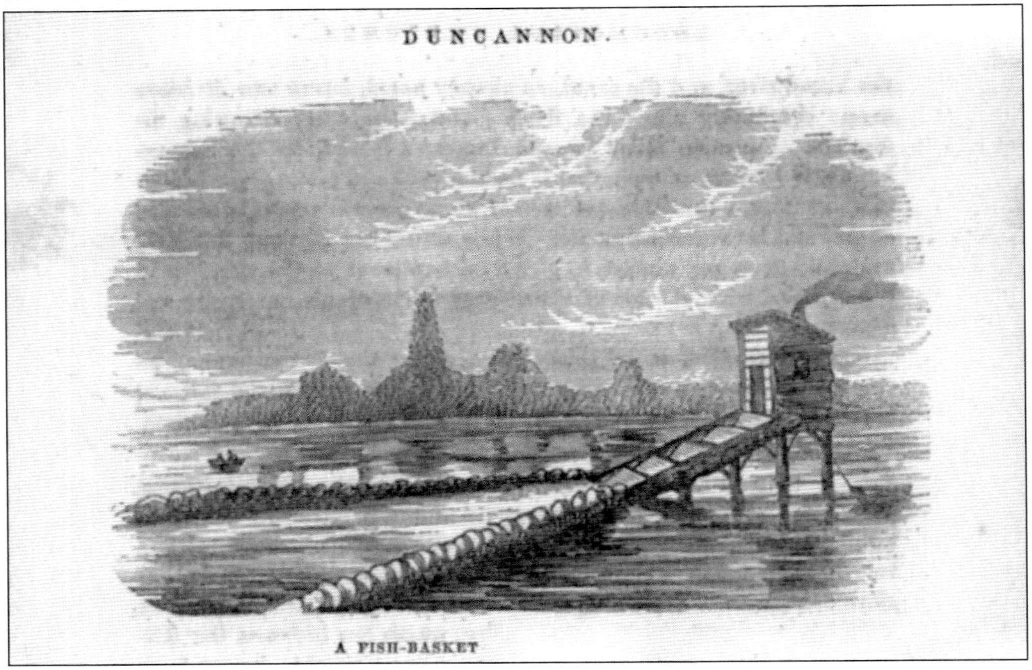

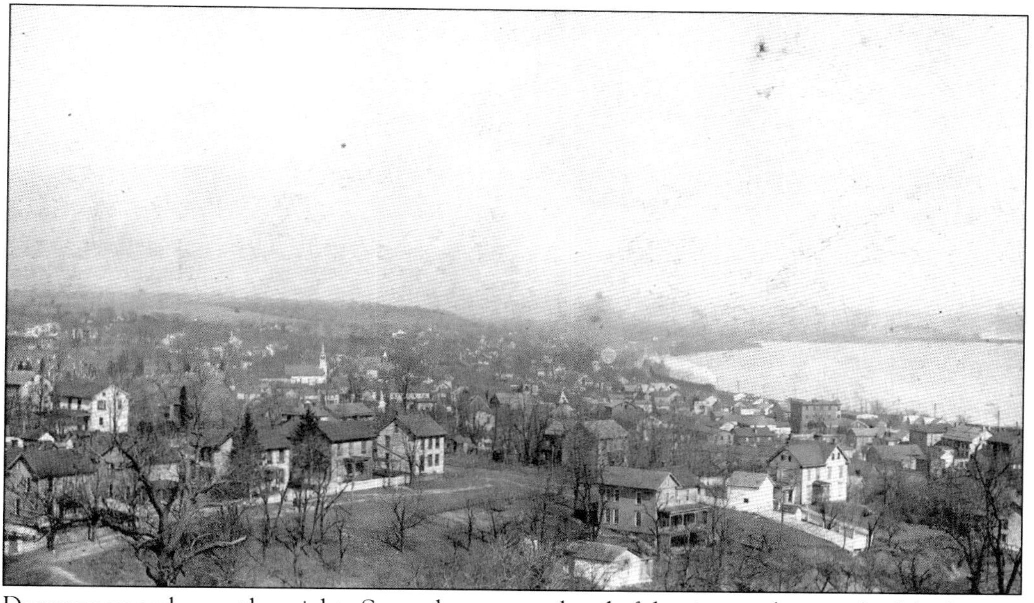

Duncannon embraces the mighty Susquehanna on a bend of the river at the mouth of the Juniata River system. Iron brought here by packet boats and later railcars created an important industry. A claim to fame in the 20th century for Duncannon was the unique manufacture of Lightning Glider Sleds and wood products at the Standard Novelty Works. Found throughout the Juniata Valley are porch swings and coaster wagons marked Duncannon, Pennsylvania.

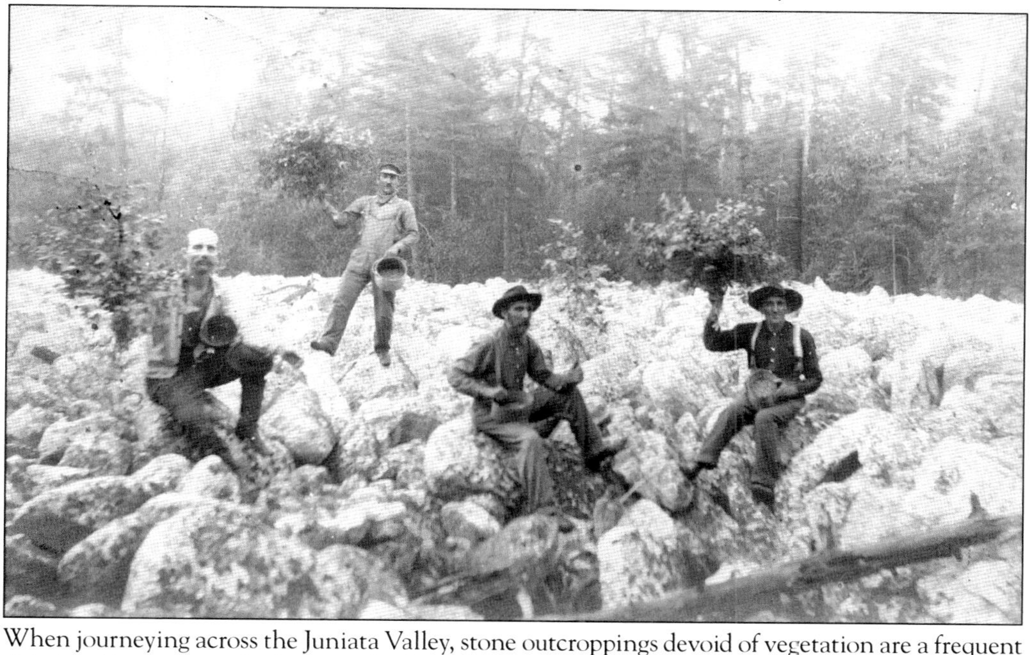

When journeying across the Juniata Valley, stone outcroppings devoid of vegetation are a frequent sighting. Some are on hillsides and others cling to the river's edge. Near Duncannon, the three Summy brothers, Lucian, J.P., and J.M., along with their friend Robert Barninger, spend the day gathering huckleberries. The rocks provide superb drainage for a hearty plant. A photographer captured this whimsical image on his travels.

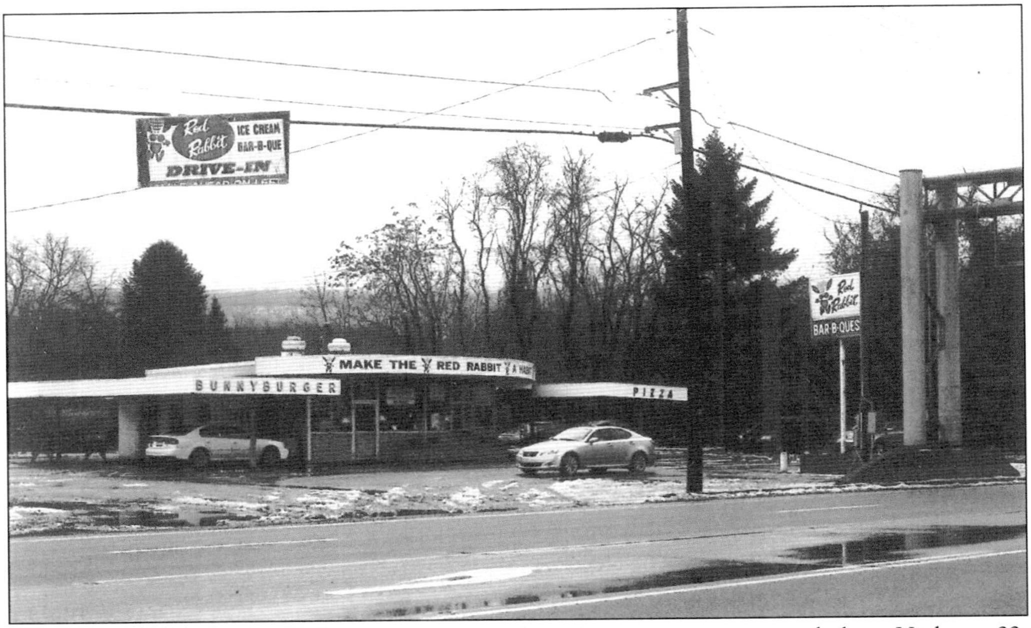

In the wake of the post-war drive-in craze, a truly unique restaurant opened along Highway 22, half a mile from the Clark's Ferry Bridge in 1964. Red Rabbit Drive In is a 1950s-style restaurant that still provides curb service bringing "bunny burgers" to customers' cars. A unique menu and quirky bunny logo add to the attraction. "Make Red Rabbit A Habit" is their slogan.

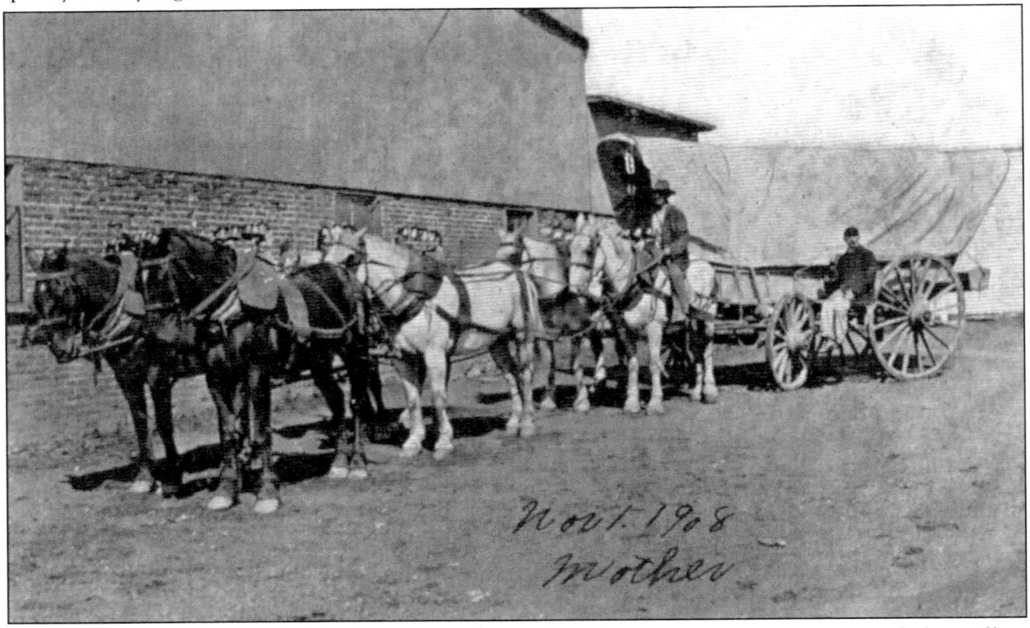

Period illustrations of the Juniata River indicate that Conestoga wagons traversed the valley. Built in nearby Lancaster County, this clever vehicle curved upward to prevent the contents from tipping and shifting. The wagons had tar waterproofing to protect them from leaks. Special high wheels were shod with iron straps. The Conestoga was the primary overland cargo vehicle crossing the Appalachians until the development of the railroads.

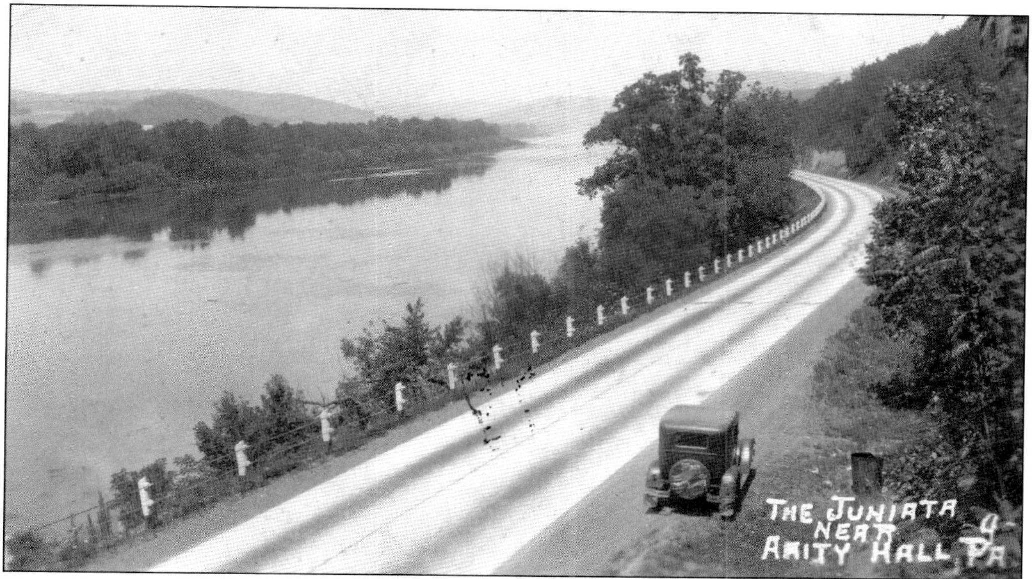

The 1920s witnessed the replacement of the earlier-style wooden guard fence that had become familiar along Pennsylvania highways. With increased automobile speeds, it became apparent that heavy-gage cables mounted on deeply driven poles would help to encourage an out of control motorist to right his vehicle. Here a touring car pauses on the roadside west of Amity Hall next to an ancient mile marker. The wheel cover advertises automobile supplies.

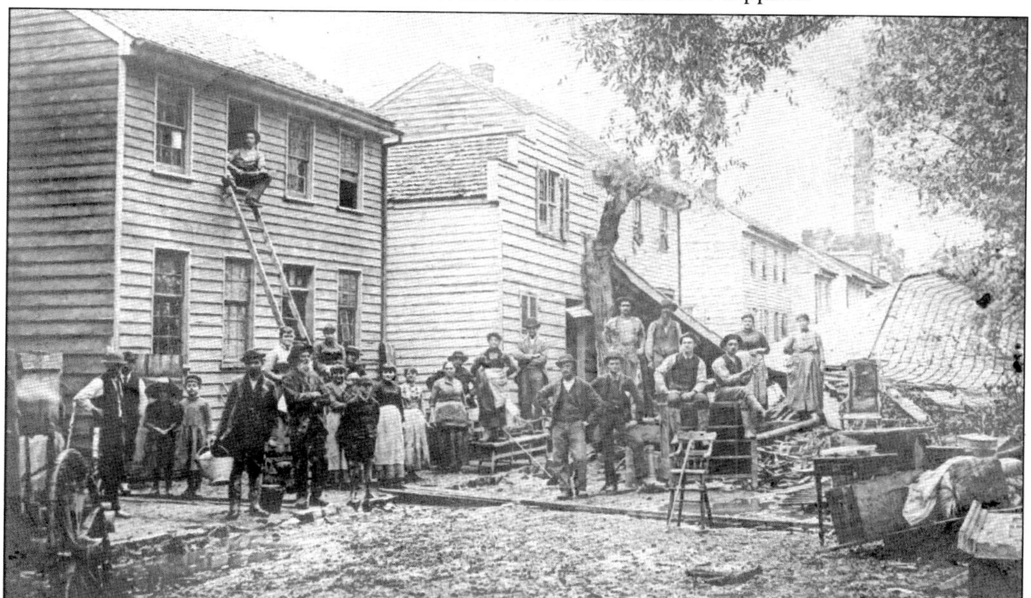

The citizens of Newport, Perry County, gather in the street to assess the damages resulting from high waters. On March 1, 1902, the Juniata River began cresting and eventually reached more than 25 feet. Townsfolk huddled in attics and others sought higher ground. A few brave souls waited out the deluge in trees. This event was just another on a long list of floods that plagued the Juniata Valley.

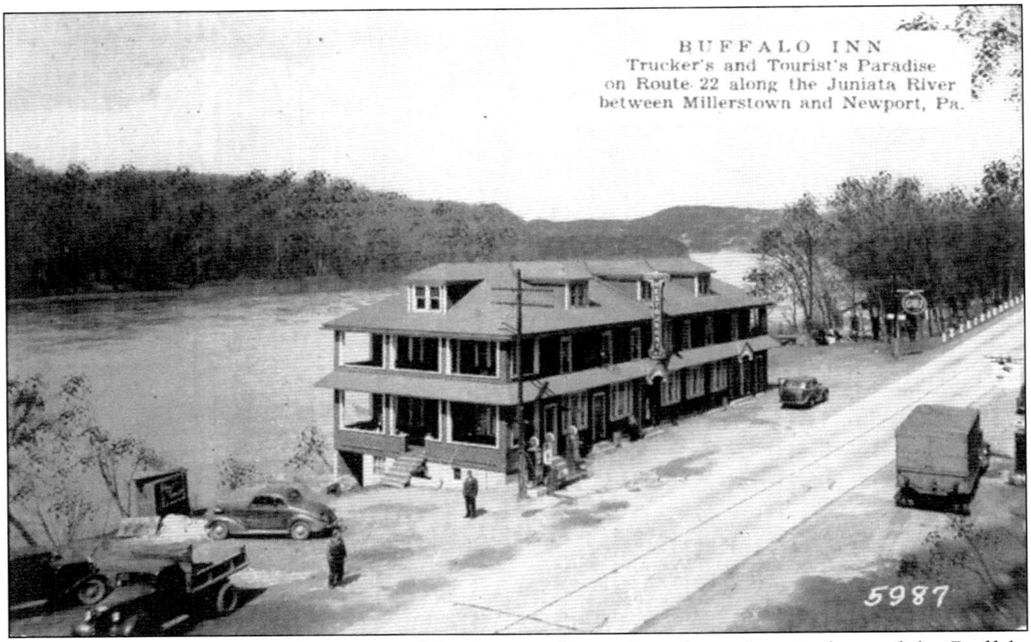

It would be hard to find a finer view of the Juniata River than from the windows of the Buffalo Inn and Restaurant. This roadside tavern was a popular stop along the stretch of highway between Newport and Millerstown. The Buffalo sold Gulf Gasoline, while a rival Mobilegas outlet opened on the opposite side of the highway.

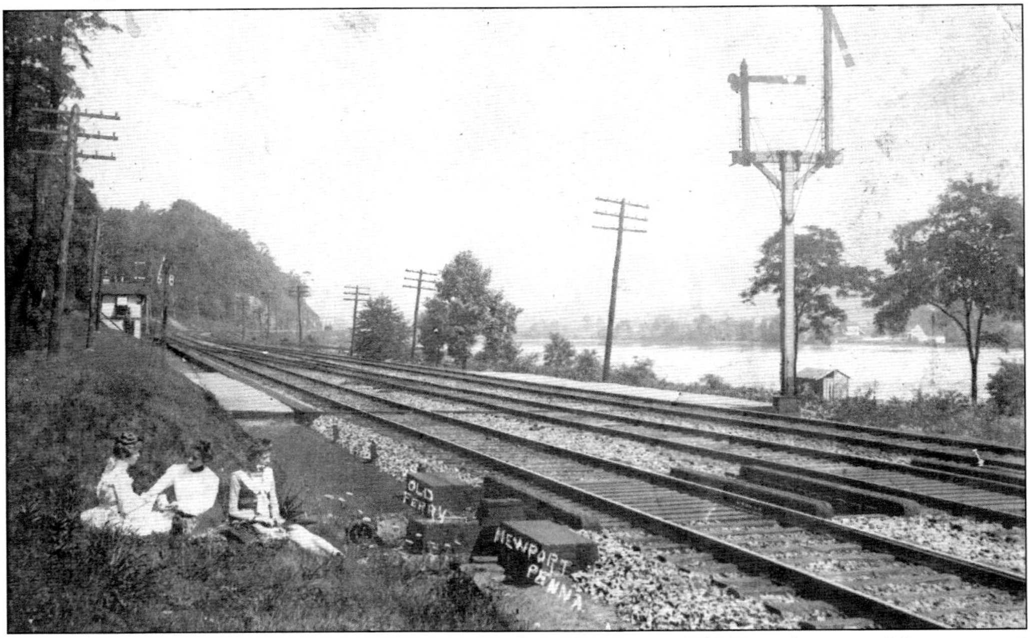

Three young ladies enjoy a view, around 1909, of the Juniata at Old Ferry between Newport and Millerstown. The Pennsylvania Railroad (PRR) creates a barrier between this grassy knoll and the river. Although there is no depot, it is evident by the developed siding that some boarding was scheduled at Old Ferry. Note the recently patented safety signal arms installed at this location by the PRR.

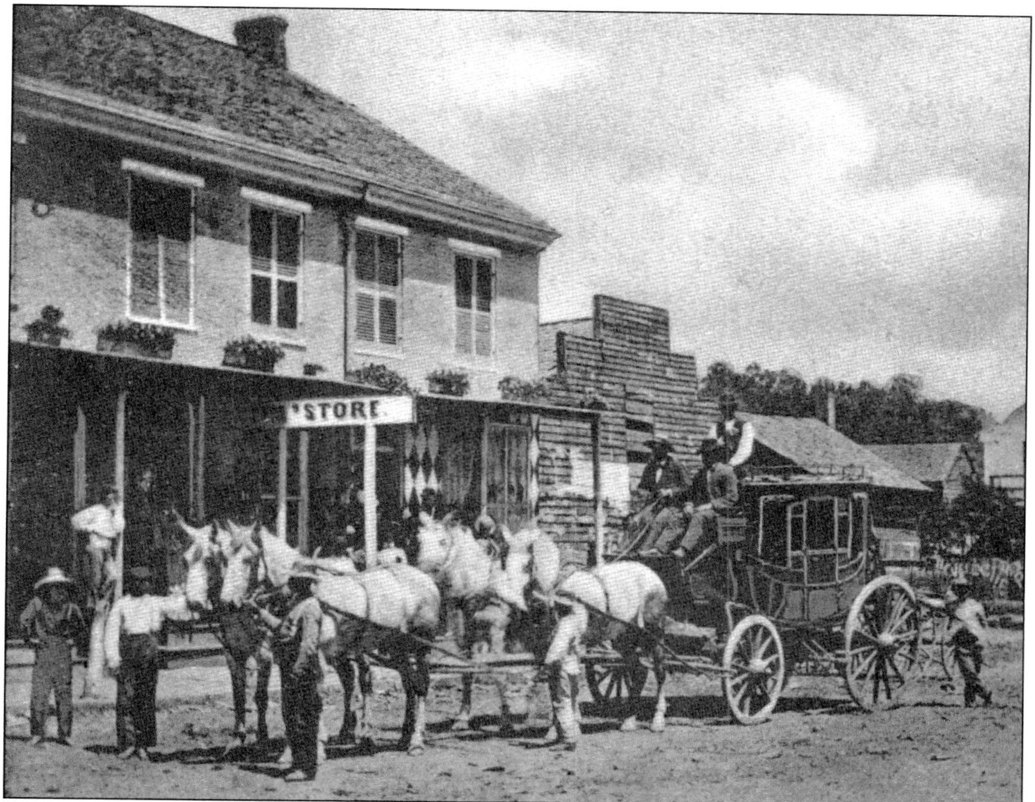

The old pike crossed the Blue Mountain between Carlisle in Cumberland County and Newport, Perry County. Resting in front of the landmark Gantis Hotel on the state highway of Newport's Fourth Street is this "coach and four," as they were called. The Rice family ran this stage route on the winding road. This mode of transportation, shown here in the 1860s, was once a common sight in Pennsylvania.

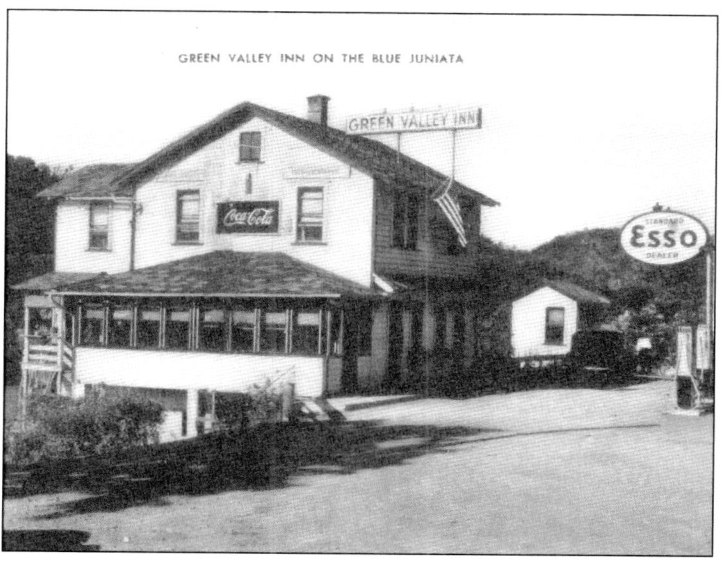

A popular stop on the old highway below Newport was the Valley Green Inn. The address is 344 Juniata Parkway East. In addition to selling Esso Gas and groceries, the rear of the property went down to the bank of the Juniata River. Small cottages were built and for many years this stretch of the Juniata continued to be a place for a relaxing weekend of kayaking and tubing on the slow-moving river.

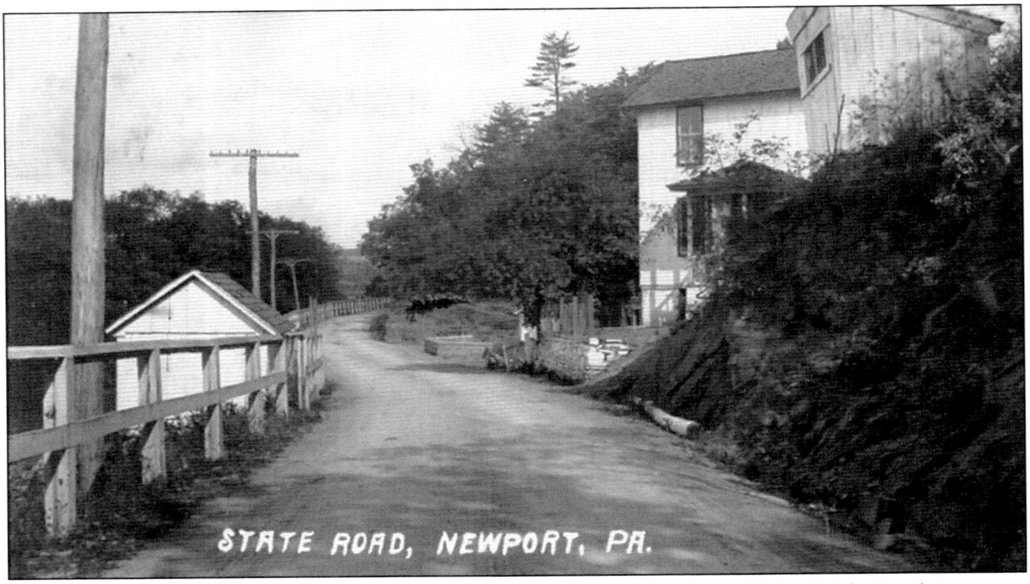

A winding footpath followed the Juniata before recorded history. Pennsylvania's Native Americans tramped the great valleys on this route. In the early 20th century, it took on the distinction of being a state road and was widened to accommodate increased use. As evidenced here in 1910, some property owners now found their domain divided by this new endeavor. The wooden guide fencing delineates the road.

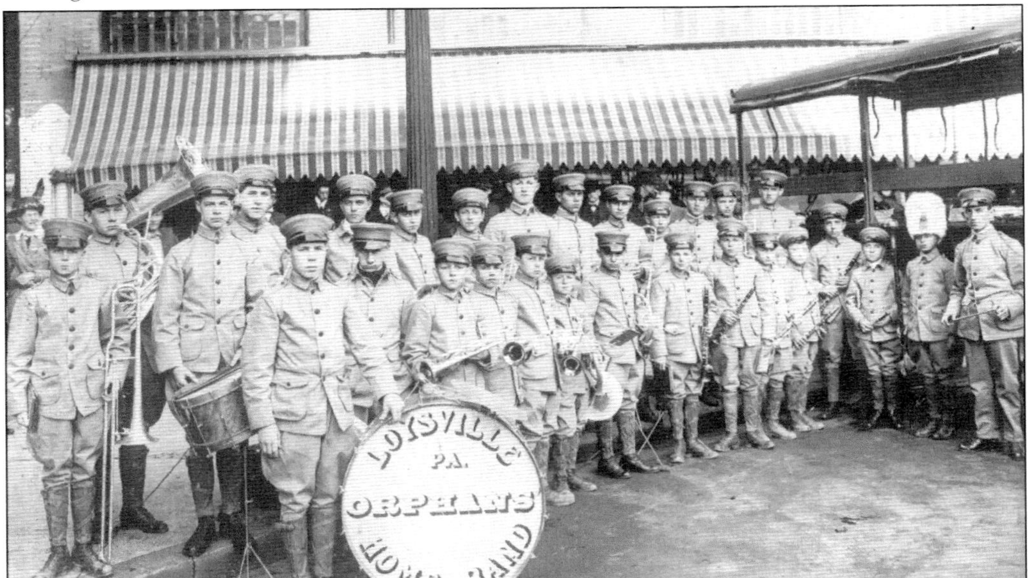

Many people in the Juniata Valley have had a young relative residing at Loysville. Opened in 1868, the Tressler Orphans Home, also known as Tresslertown, provided a home for poor orphaned children. The activities on campus afforded a wholesome and well-rounded guardianship. An academy on the grounds guaranteed a proper education. Beginning in 1890 and continuing through the 1940s, Tresslertown was represented at events far and wide by the Orphan Boys Home Band.

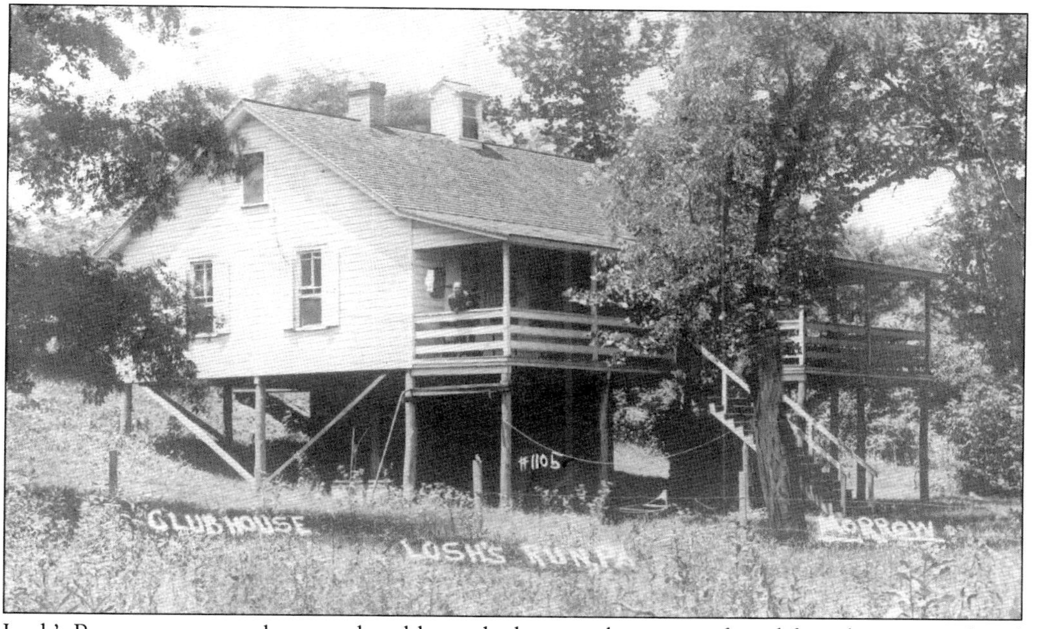

Losh's Run was once a place on the old canal where coal was transferred from boats to railroad cars. There was a large basin located here for turning and handling boats. West of here is Watts' Valley. Shown in this photograph is an old clubhouse. It was built elevated because of the possible change in the river's water level. The crow's nest on top allowed the cook to keep a lookout for returning fishermen.

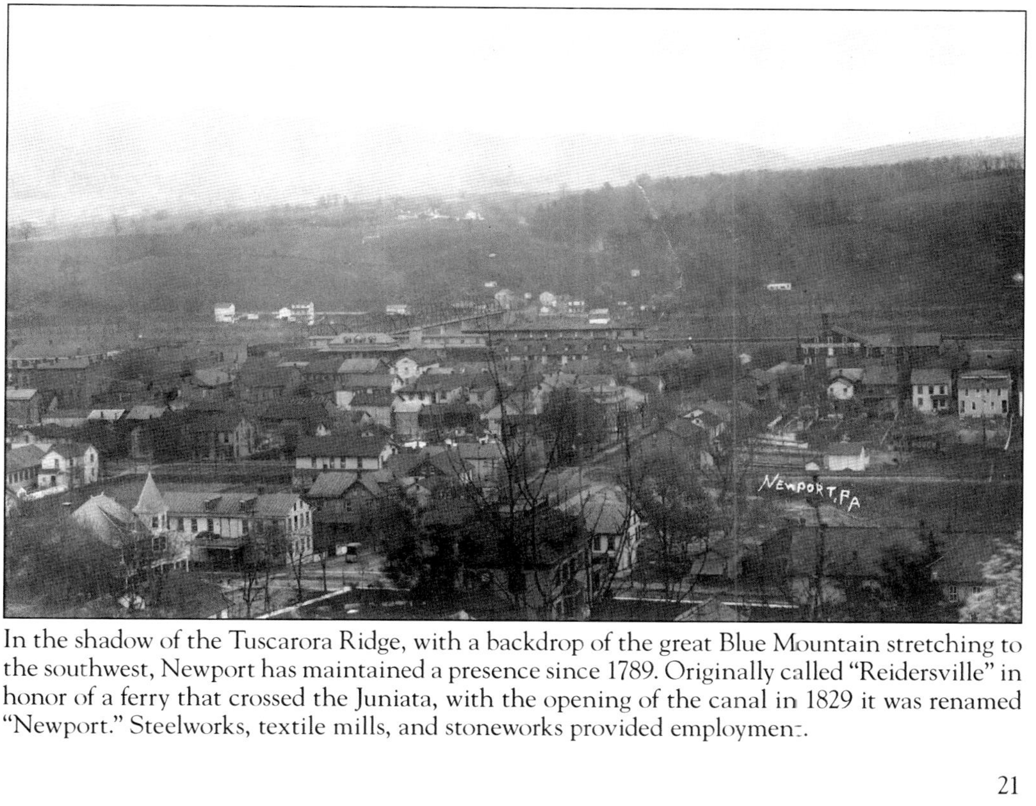

In the shadow of the Tuscarora Ridge, with a backdrop of the great Blue Mountain stretching to the southwest, Newport has maintained a presence since 1789. Originally called "Reidersville" in honor of a ferry that crossed the Juniata, with the opening of the canal in 1829 it was renamed "Newport." Steelworks, textile mills, and stoneworks provided employment.

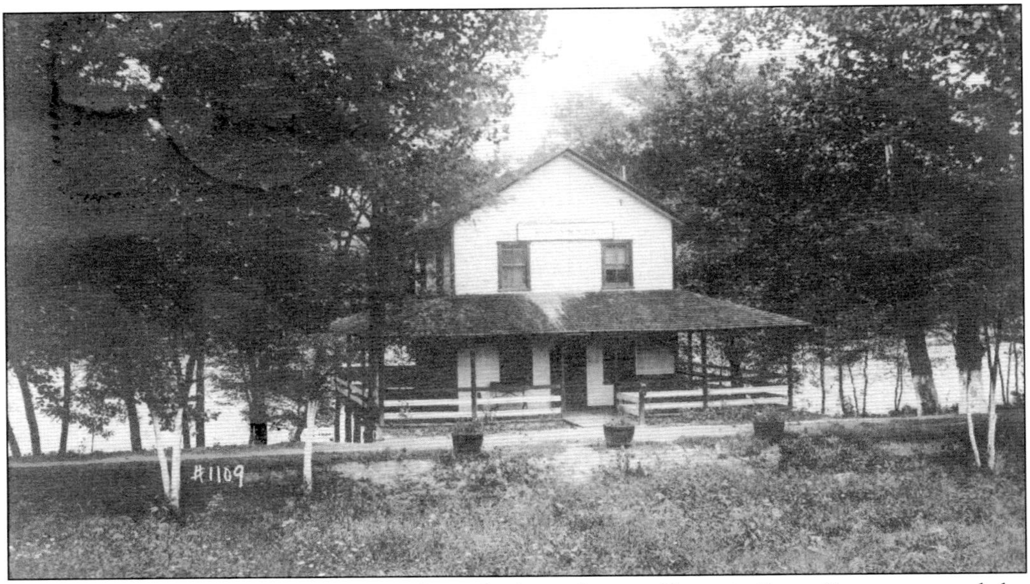

Cottages of all sizes began appearing along the lower Juniata River in Perry County around the turn of the 20th century. This one was dedicated as "Logania," the name of a small nearby village. The wide verandas caught breezes and might have been used as a screened sleeping porch. The lower portion facing the river was equipped with a boathouse. Sometimes this became a kitchen for preparing freshly caught fish.

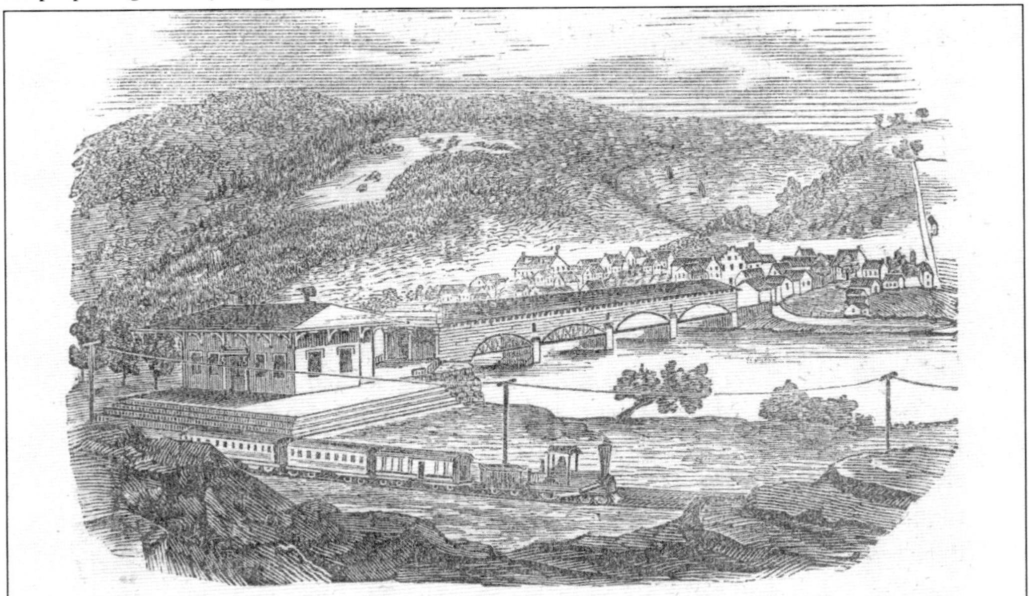

MILLERSTOWN, ON THE JUNIATA.

The Pennsylvania Railroad provided communities along the rail line with wooden Italianate- or Gothic-styled depots in the 1840s. Since the Millerstown depot was on the opposite side of the Juniata, a double covered bridge provided passengers access. A toll was charged to use the bridge. The canal still operated on the north side of the river. During the canal days, Millerstown was the most populated settlement in Perry County.

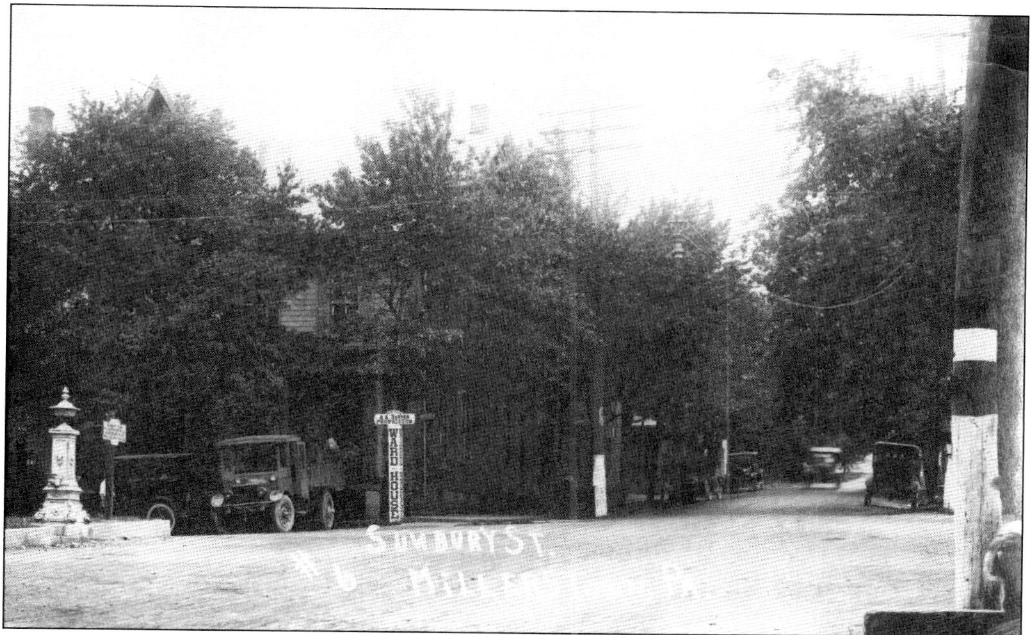

During the period that the Juniata canal was being built, Millerstown was the site of 17 inns. Its distinctive Market Street is to this day dotted with impressive buildings where the old stone hotels once stood. In the early automobile days, Highway 17 led northeast from this square following the old Sunbury Path. This route was a connection for 18th-century settlers, linking the Juniata River with the Susquehanna River.

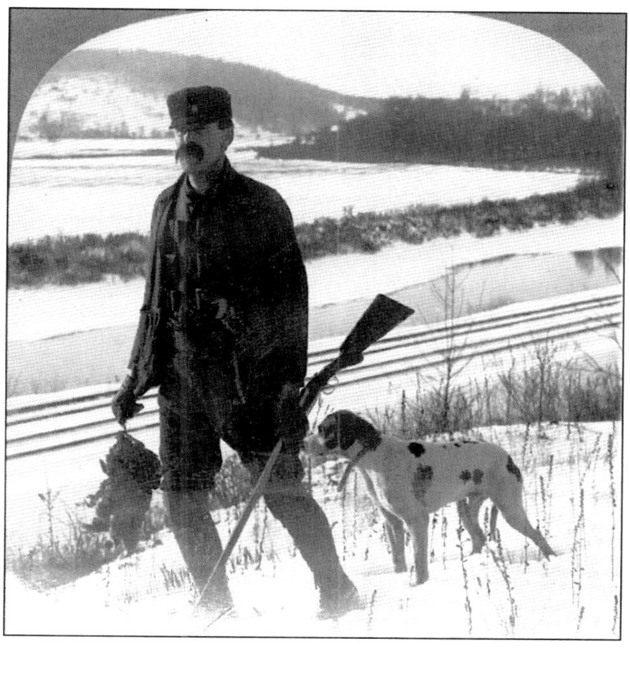

At day's end, a hunter is homebound clutching his quarry. His bird dog follows on heel. In the distance, the hills of Pennsylvania frame the icy river. Two rail tracks cleared of snow cross the photograph at midpoint. From the epoch of the native inhabitants through modern times, Pennsylvania's valleys have been home to a wide variety of wildlife.

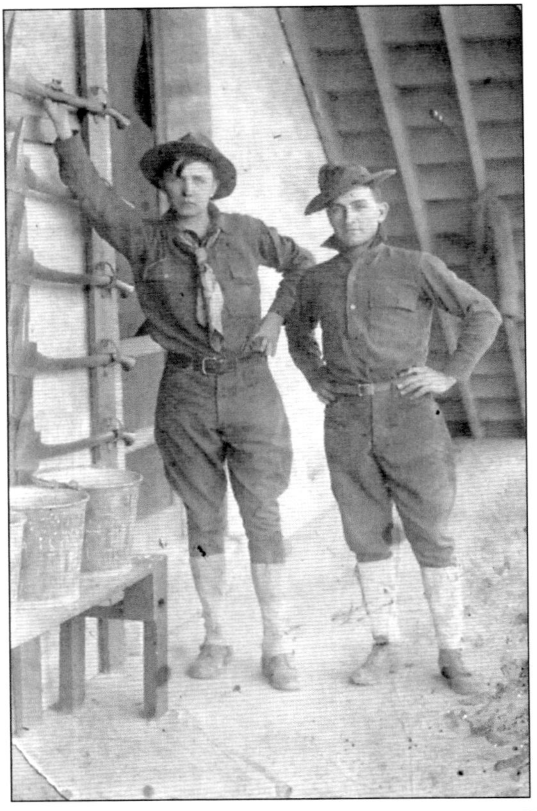

Two Boy Scouts fitted in their uniforms give a demonstration of emergency preparedness. Buckets of sand for grease fires and buckets of water for brush and paper fires are within reach. A display of axes is on hand for a quick rescue in the event of an unexpected disaster. The Boy Scouts, founded in America in 1910, quickly took a foothold in Juniata culture. Some towns had as many as four troops.

Here an early wood-burning passenger locomotive chugs along the Juniata in 1851. The Main Line of the Public Works chartered the Pennsylvania Railroad (PRR) in 1846 to build a line to connect Harrisburg to Pittsburgh. The railroad and canal corridor followed the Juniata River to the Alleghenies. In 1857, the PRR incorporated and took possession of both the rails and the canal. The outmoded Juniata Canal gradually ceased operation.

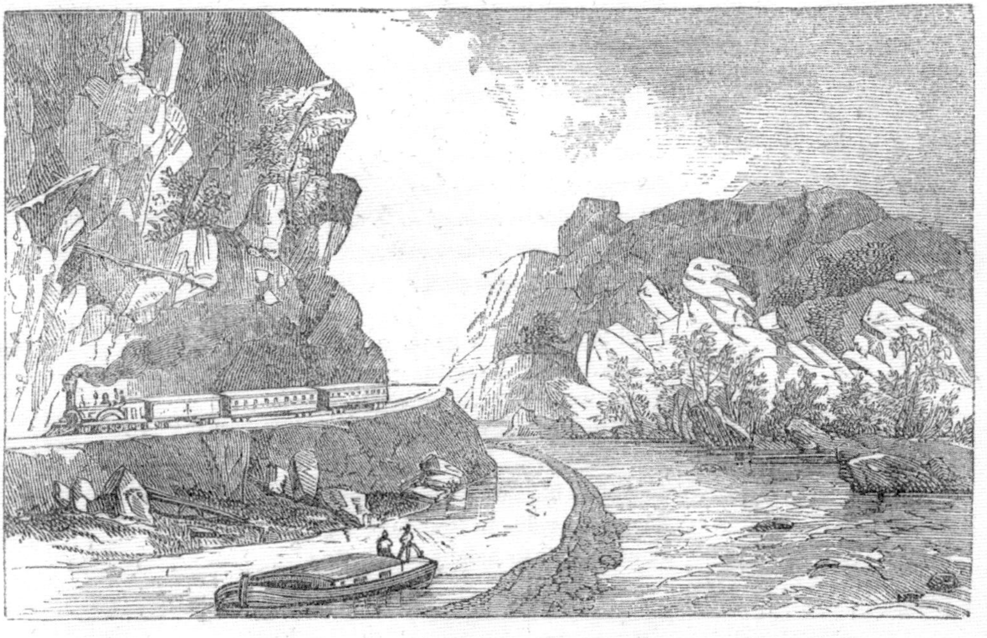

RAILROAD AND CANAL.

Two

JUNIATA, THE COUNTY

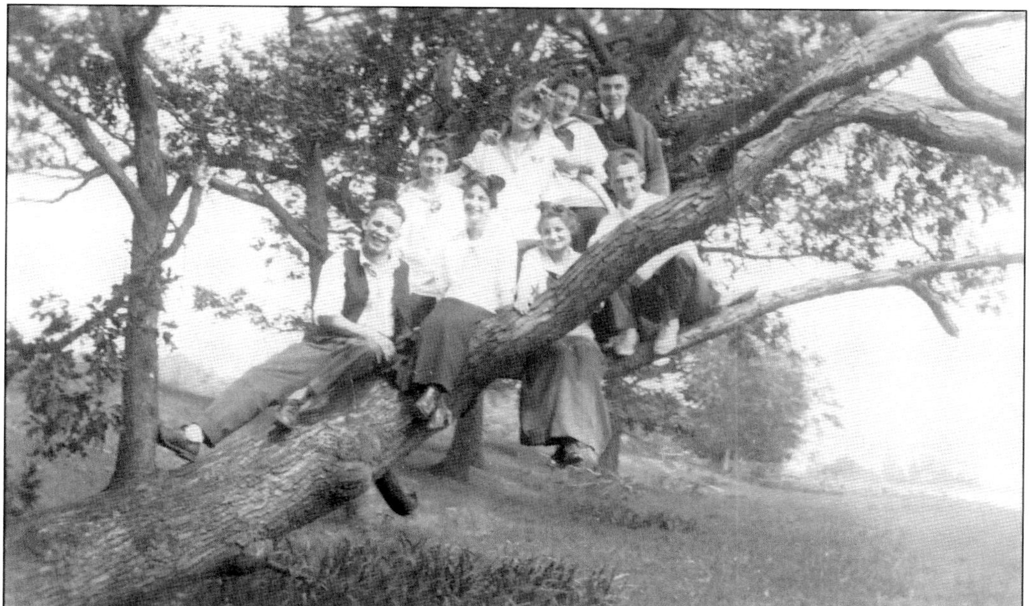

Brought down by a flood in seasons past, this oak survived to provide the ideal spot for a group of picnickers. Beginning in the late 1890s, cameras became available for amateur photographers. These could be carried to any gathering without the clumsy tripods and chemicals that required a skilled artisan. Because of this, photograph albums began to convey a more relaxed and sentimental feeling around the beginning of the 20th century.

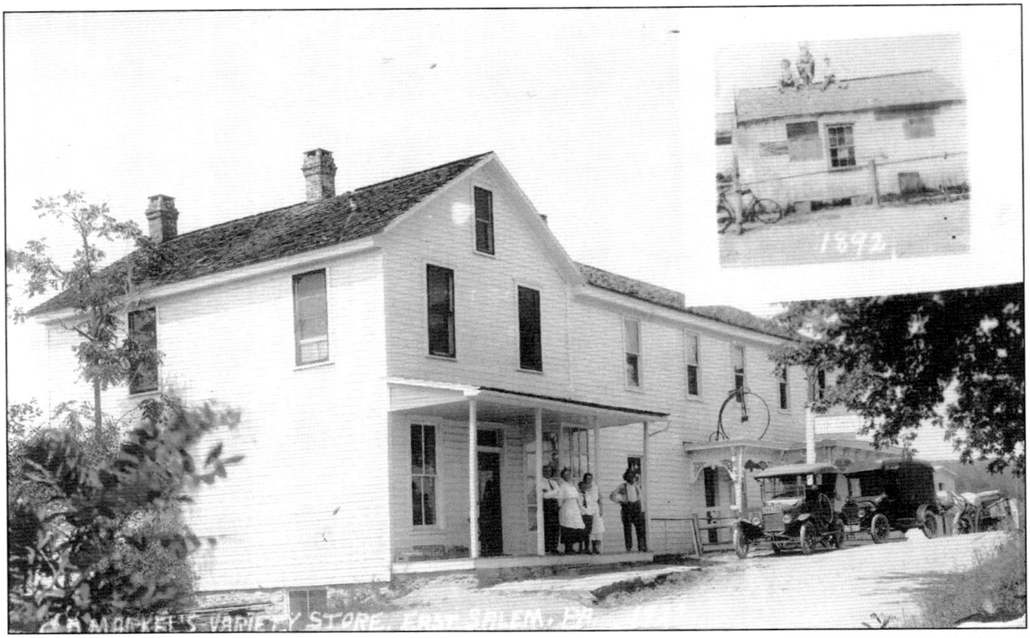

Before there were shopping centers and malls to draw shoppers away from town, C.D. Markel saw to it that his patrons had plenty to browse at his variety store in East Salem. In 1892 (inset), his establishment was not much more than a chicken coop. Over the ensuing years, Markel expanded and added gas pumps. Enclosing the front (below), there was now a place for books and magazines. Baked goods, hardware, and yard goods were stocked on site. Pickles, home canned provisions, and locally made candy were always on hand. Markel's wife even did mending. For many years, Markel's high-wheeled bicycle was perched over the door as a sign of stability.

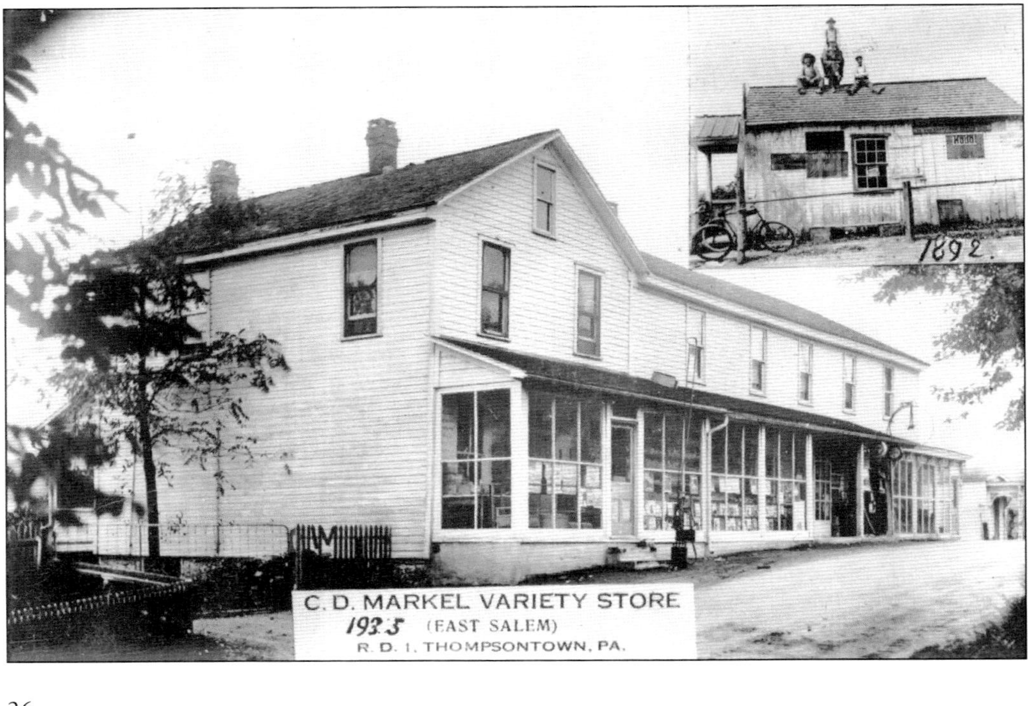

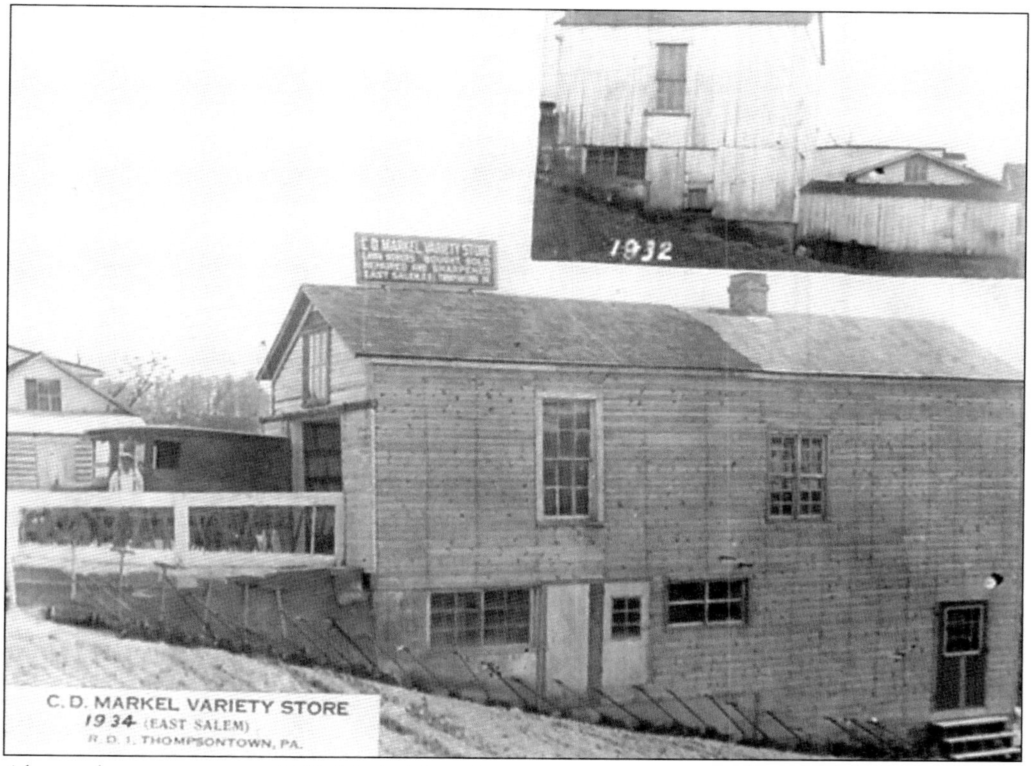

Always the entrepreneur, C.D. Markel found a load of salvaged lumber and transformed his former barn into a machine shop for repairing all types of small farm implements around 1933. He sold dozens of push lawnmowers each spring. His enterprise kept most locals from venturing outside of the county in search of merchandise. Markel had a gift for gab and was able to provide a solution for just about every mechanical dilemma.

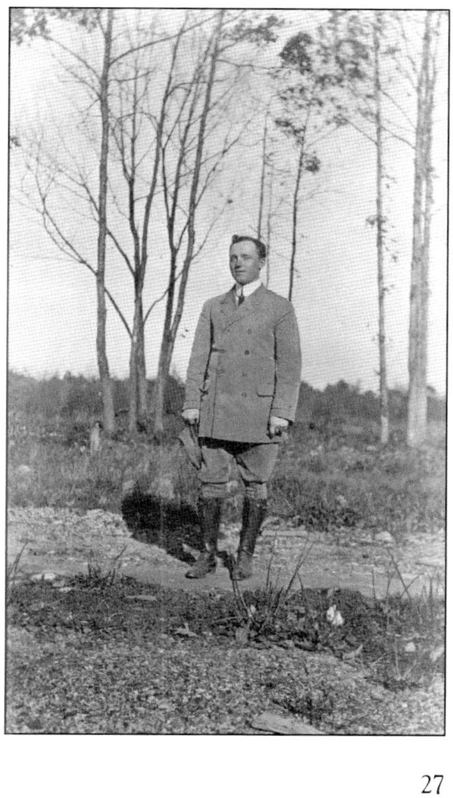

Shown in his uniform, Edgar Patterson of Thompsontown was a chauffeur for one of Pennsylvania's most unconventional politicians. Patterson drove for Gov. John Kinley Tener, 1911–1915. The Irish-born Tener was a professional baseball player who actually left the stands once to pitch at a game in Harrisburg while serving as governor. This photograph is dated November 14, 1912.

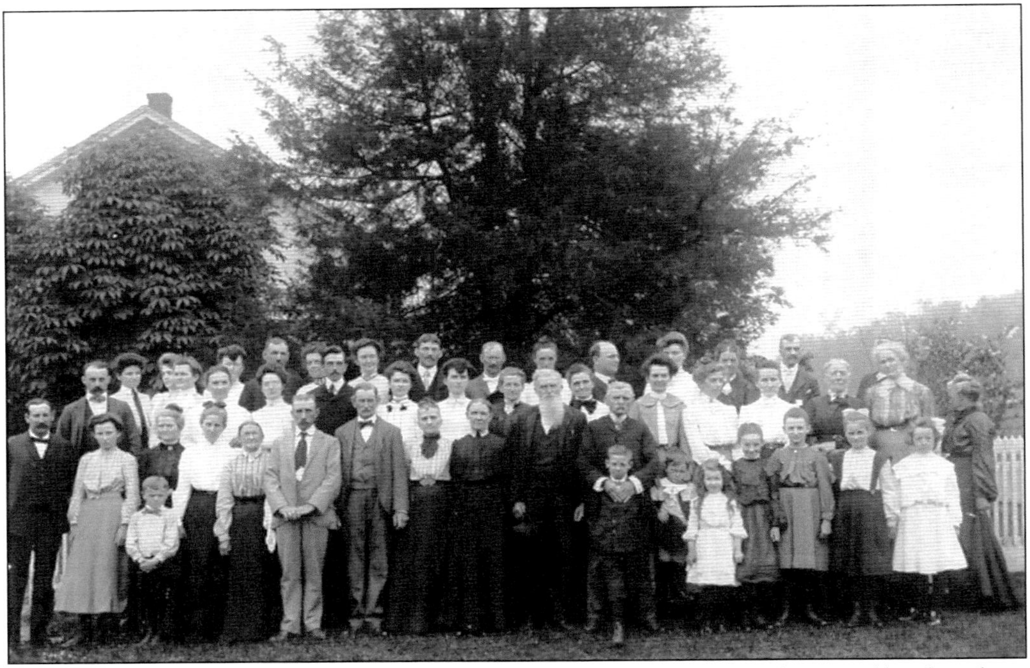

Juniata County split from Mifflin County in 1831, and was known for its farms and hard-working inhabitants. Many Juniata County residents trace their heritage back to the first settlers of the pre-American Revolution days. The Esh family has shared the land and the simple values of those of Juniata County and Mifflin Counties. A strong spirited family, they represented the many Pennsylvania German plain folk who populated Juniata and Mifflin Counties.

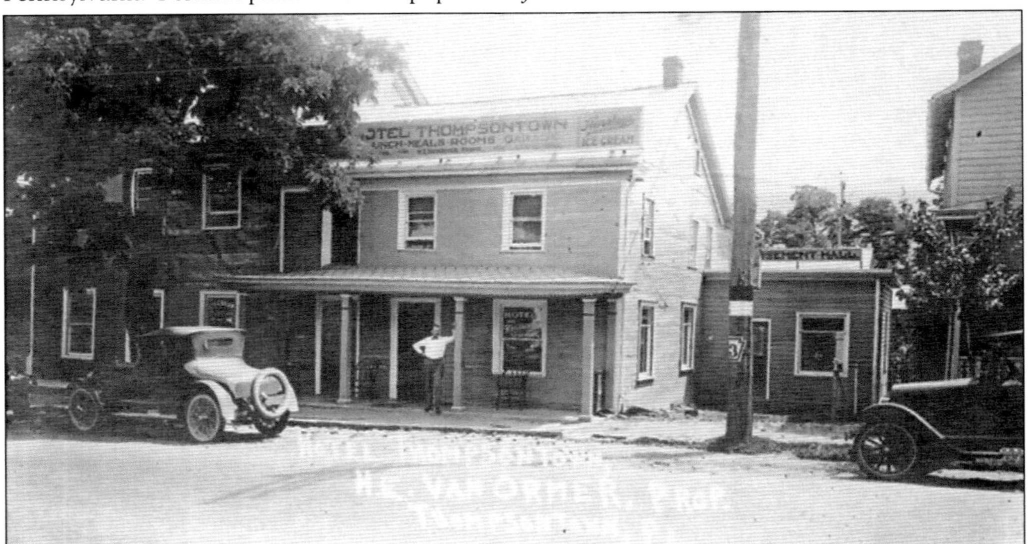

On the William Penn Highway, H.E. Van Ormer operated the Hotel Thompsontown. Increased motor traffic brought commerce to the Juniata Valley main streets. This hostelry was typical of similar establishments one would encounter while traveling cross-state. Van Ormer had a separate facility for amusements that undoubtedly contained a billiard table and dispensed cigars. Note the Highway 3 sign. The 1928 travel maps had it redesignated as Route 22.

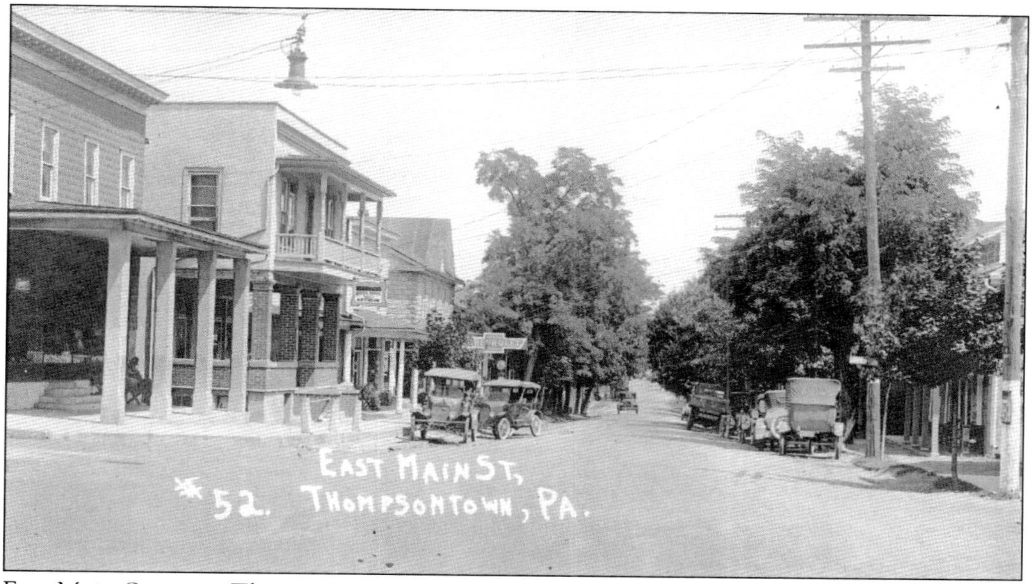

East Main Street in Thompsontown prior to 1920 was already showing the influence of the automobile. The extended porticos that were becoming the fashion along the highways of that era were a major presence at this corner. Just beyond the Russ Ice Cream Shop, a newly constructed Chevrolet dealer has installed his sign above the pavement at 10 East Main Street.

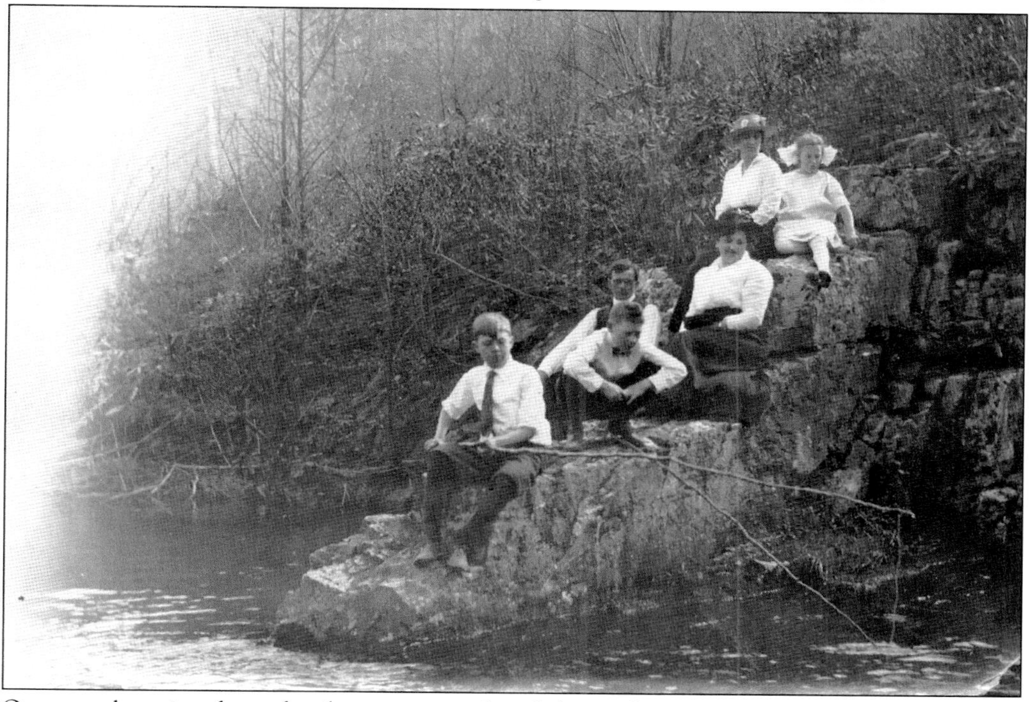

On an early spring day, a family on a picnic found the perfect stone formation for enjoying the Juniata River. The boys had fishing hooks and line tucked into their shirt pockets. After lunch, they fashioned fishing poles from clean-cut branches of nearby hemlock trees. Scenes such as this were common all along the river.

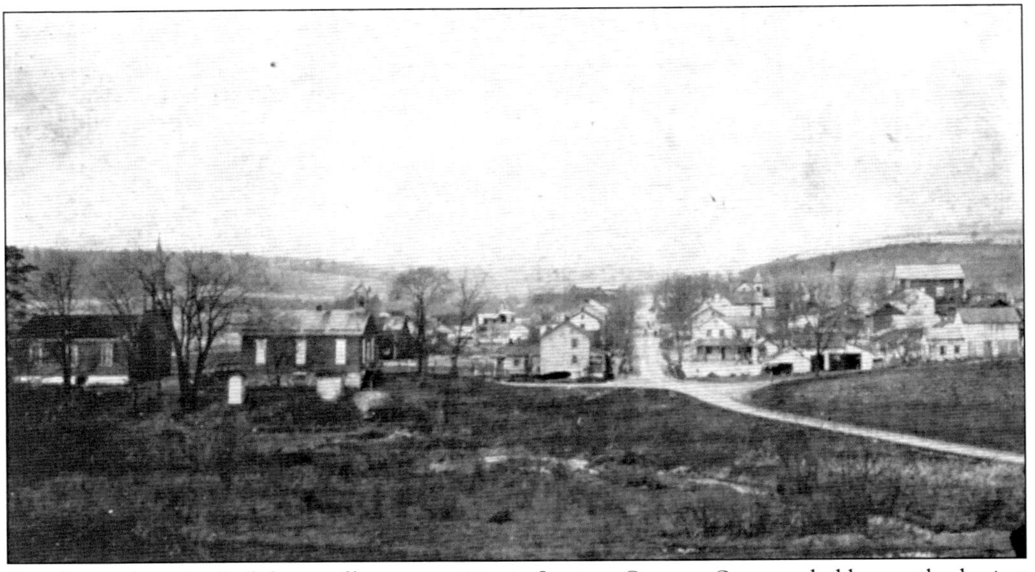

East Salem is typical of the small communities in Juniata County. Surrounded by gently sloping hills and farmland, the town lies picturesquely in a valley. The highway forms a wide main street on its way to Cocolamus. It is interesting to note that the church and the school shared a common yard. This was often the case in rural areas of Pennsylvania.

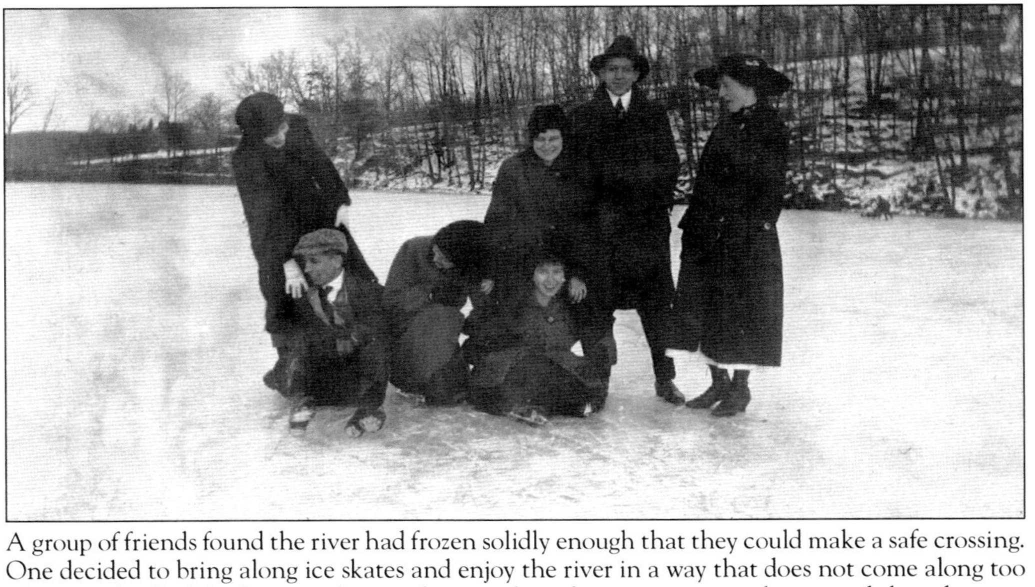

A group of friends found the river had frozen solidly enough that they could make a safe crossing. One decided to bring along ice skates and enjoy the river in a way that does not come along too often. With all of the lines in the ice, she must have been running circles around the others.

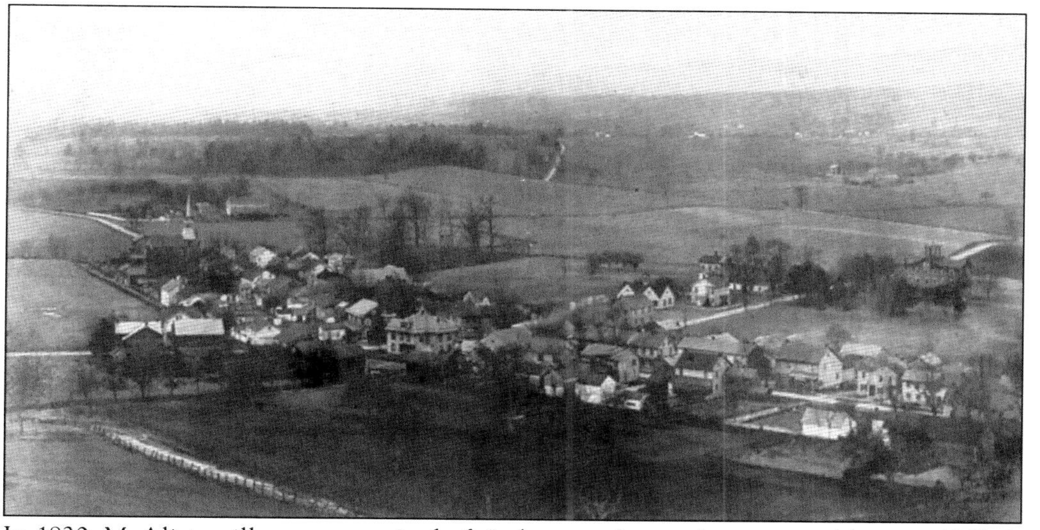

In 1830, McAlisterville was comprised of six houses. An academy opened here in 1855. It subsequently came under the charge of Prof. George F. McFarland. A call to arms during the Civil War prompted McFarland, and many of the students, to enlist. Suffering injuries at Gettysburg, Colonel McFarland returned to the academy and campaigned to provide education to the orphans of fallen soldiers. The school expanded to 30 acres and operated until 1899.

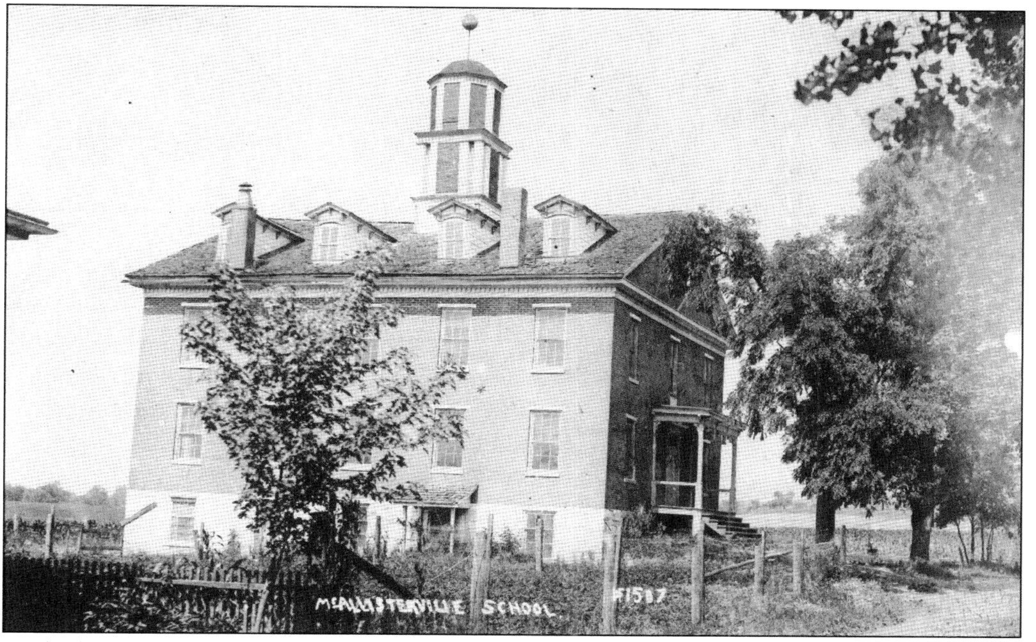

With the expansion of the McAlisterville Academy, a much grander administration building was erected. This is the original "old main" building that continued to be used. Prof. George F. McFarland eventually turned over control of the school and moved downriver to Harrisburg, where he opened a renowned plant nursery on the Susquehanna River. His son J. Horace McFarland, born in McAlisterville, was a founder of the conservation movement in America and an influential urban planner.

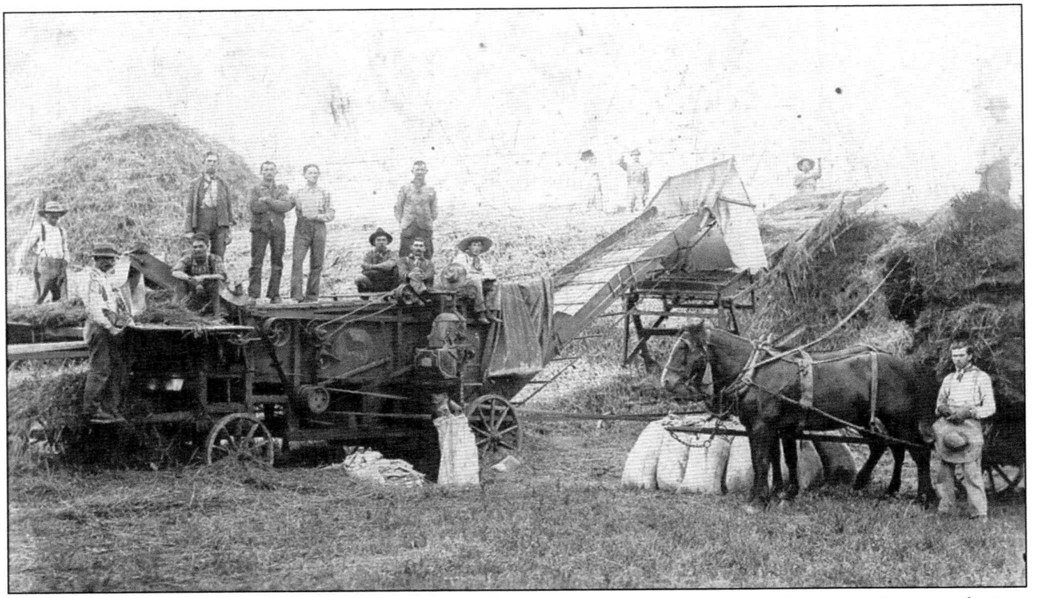

Juniata County has always depended on agriculture as its primary source of income. Its population of farm animals exceeds that of residents. Although the work is demanding and time consuming, the introduction of the thresher eased the way farms were run. This Russell combine performed many tasks, from separating grain to bagging and then ejecting the straw. Known as "the Boss," it was also shared by many neighbors as a co-op venture.

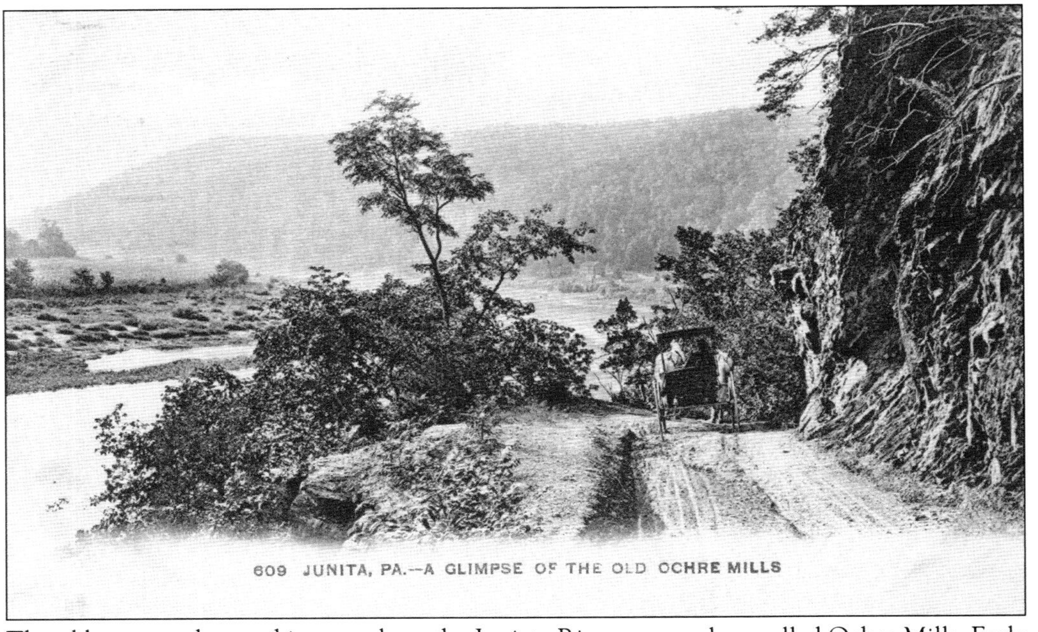

The old state road wound its way along the Juniata River near a place called Ochre Mills. Early settlers discovered naturally tinted clay containing mineral oxides in the loose rock hillsides. Ochre mined from the banks of the Juniata was hauled west over the Alleghenies to Pittsburgh. A growing paint industry was in need of this crucial ingredient. Potters in Huntingdon and Mifflin Counties found salts and other minerals for glazing their wares.

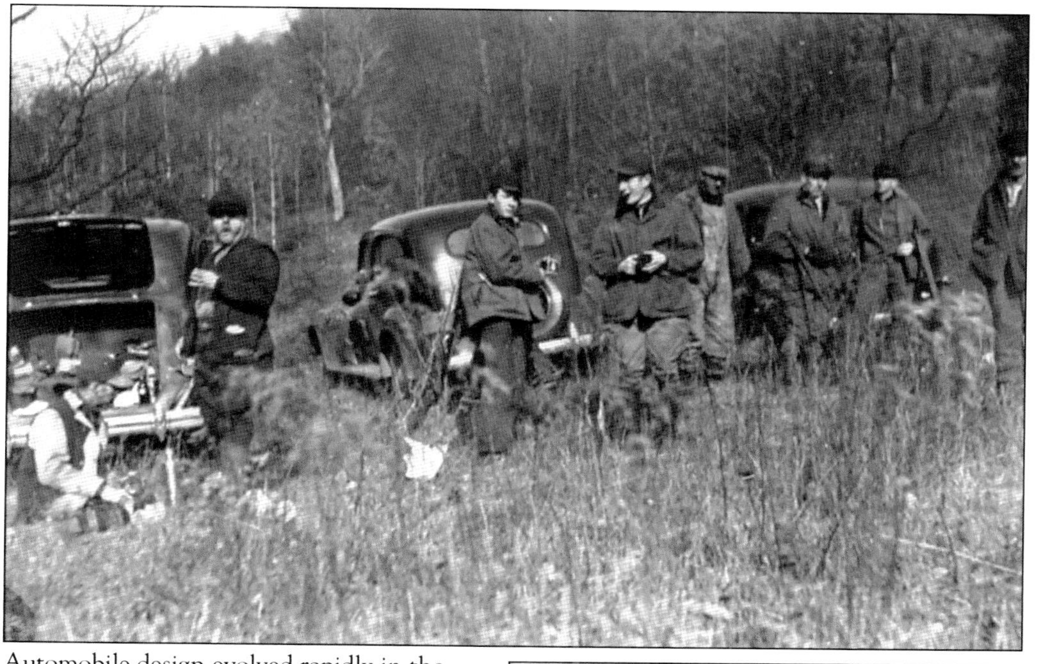

Automobile design evolved rapidly in the 1930s, resulting in a roomy coach with an ample trunk in the rear that could accommodate any load. Hunters found that the new sedans were not only adequate to sleep two passengers quite comfortably, but all gear and meal preparation facilities could be maintained from the same vehicle. A common sight in the Juniata Valley was hunting parties using their cars as makeshift hunting camps.

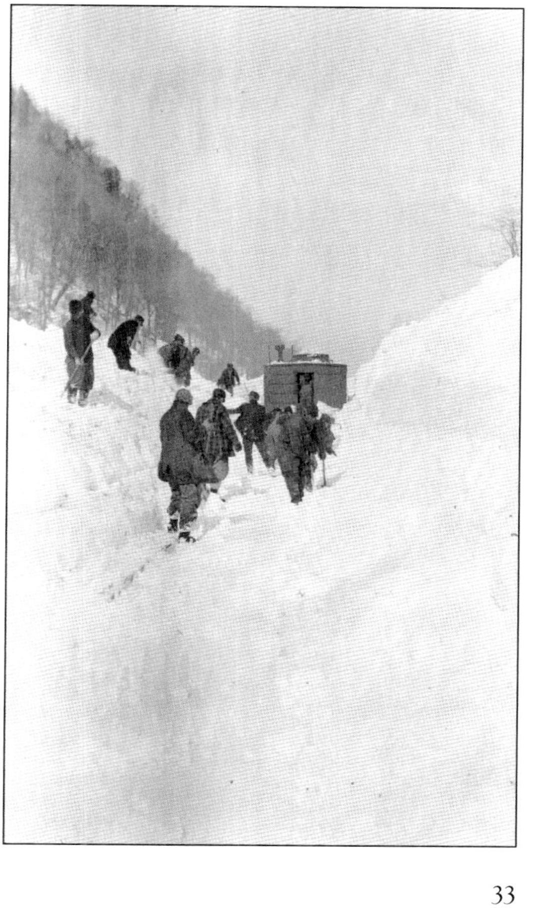

Throughout the Juniata valleys, numerous branch rail lines brought raw materials to industrial plants and farm products to market. Narrow gage lines went off to bituminous coal mines in distant hills and others hauled sand, clay, and finished refractory bricks. Occasionally, it became necessary for rail employees to dig out a locomotive that became stranded in drifting snow in one of the tight hollows that lead to the Juniata River.

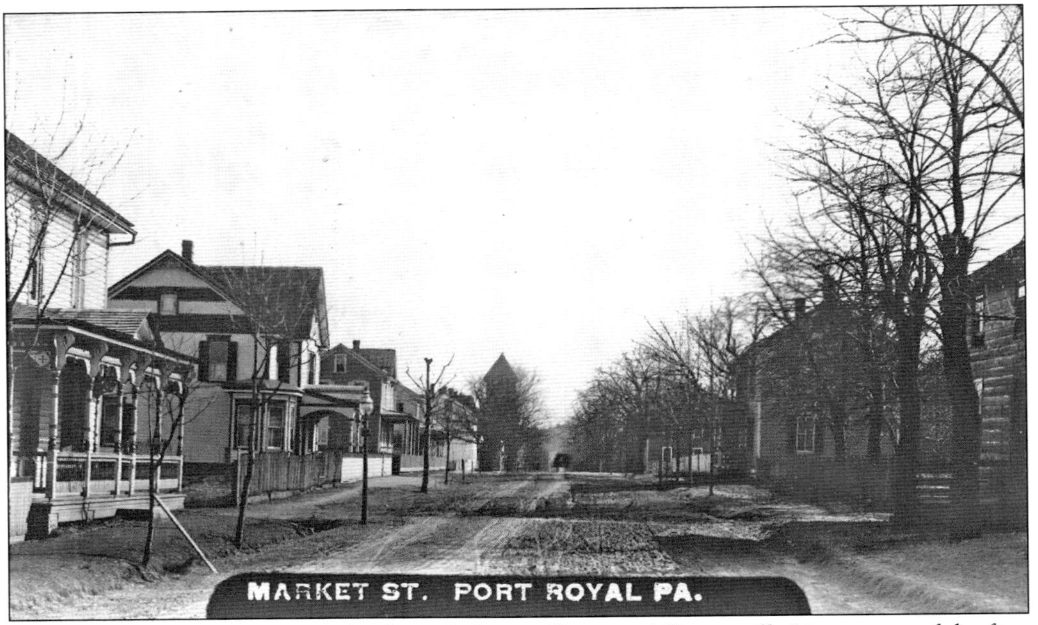

Port Royal has always been a hub of travel. Originally named "Perrysville," it was one of the first towns linked to the original Pennsylvania Railroad system in 1846. It was also the northern terminus of the narrow gage Tuscarora Valley Railroad, which was decommissioned in the 1930s. In the days of the Indians, the Juniata Path joined the Tuscarora Path at Port Royal and followed the river to meet the Kittanning Path at Mount Union.

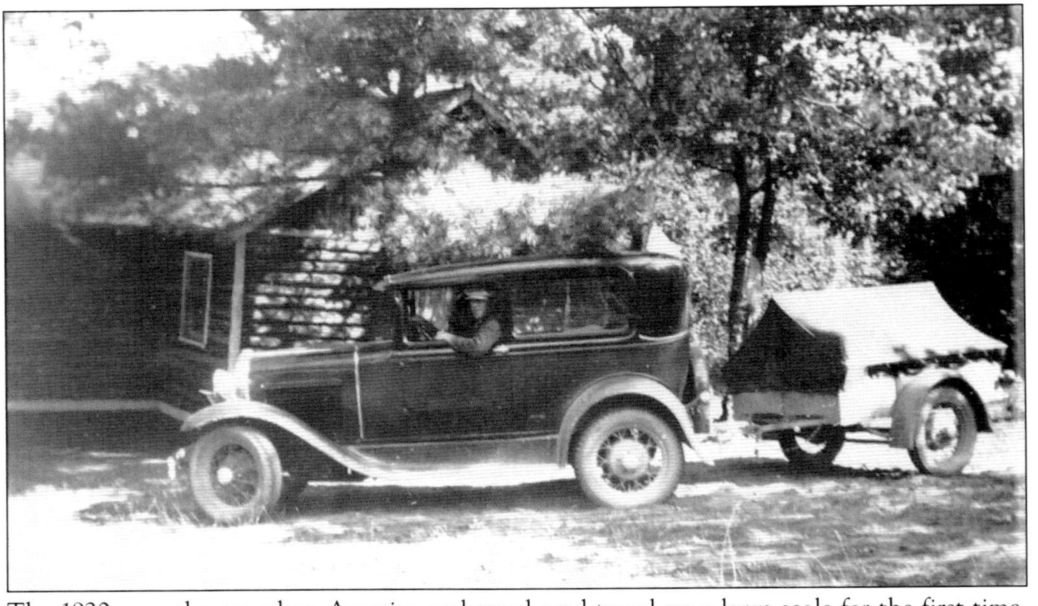

The 1920s was the era when America embraced road travel on a large scale for the first time. Millions of automobiles were manufactured during the Roaring Twenties. With improved roads and enticing travel advertising, it was only natural to take to the road. Travel trailers began appearing in numbers to bring along the comforts of home. Many of those pulled in the early days were constructed by the owner.

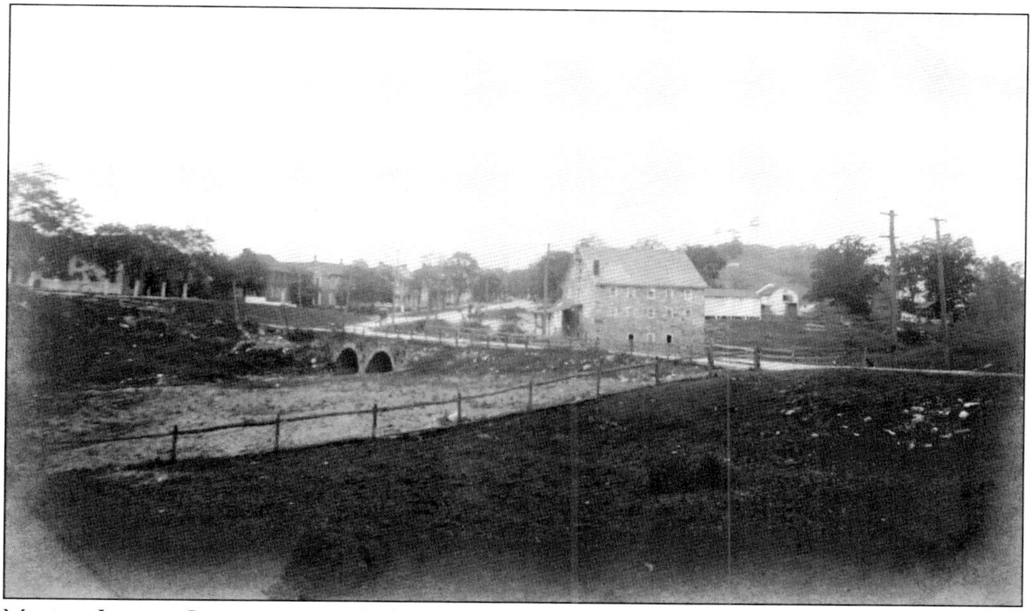

Mexico, Juniata County, sits on Cedar Spring Run, which empties into the Juniata River. The layout of the land was a perfect place for a mill. A picturesque double-arch stone bridge carried the roadway across the run. Mexico is just one of a number of foreign place names used in Juniata and Mifflin Counties. Peru, Macedonia, Cuba, and Jericho are a few other examples. Today's Buttonwood Campground is located nearby and is a getaway for water recreation.

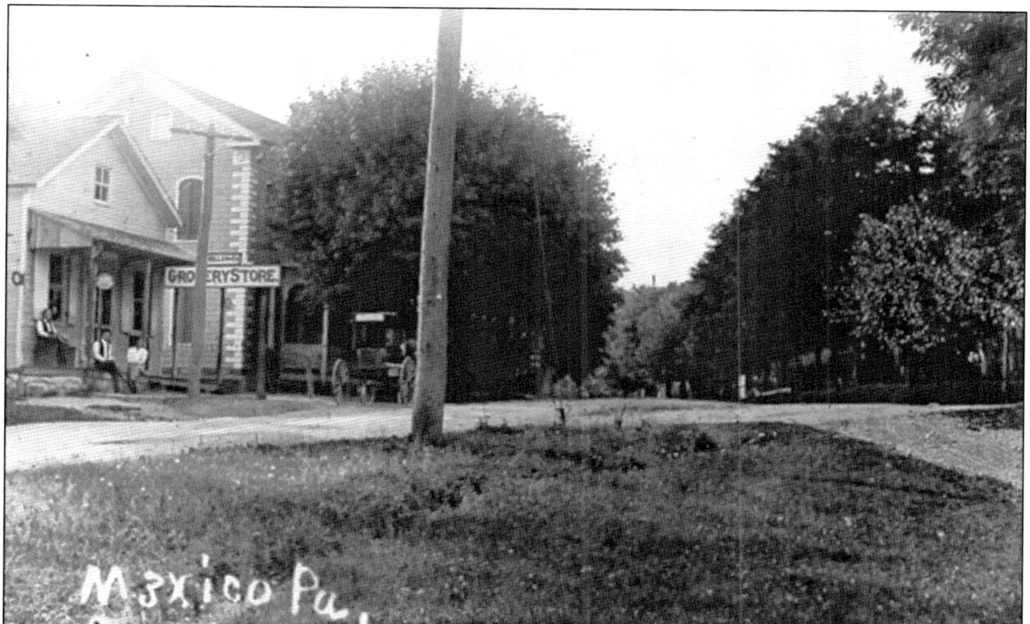

On the square in Mexico, a few folks sit on the porch of Weller's Grocery Store. Not much was happening that day. Although Mexico, Juniata County, never grew to be a large town, it is known for one interesting contribution to the Juniata Valley: the stones for the Juniata canal locks and bridge abutments were cut from a quarry outside of town.

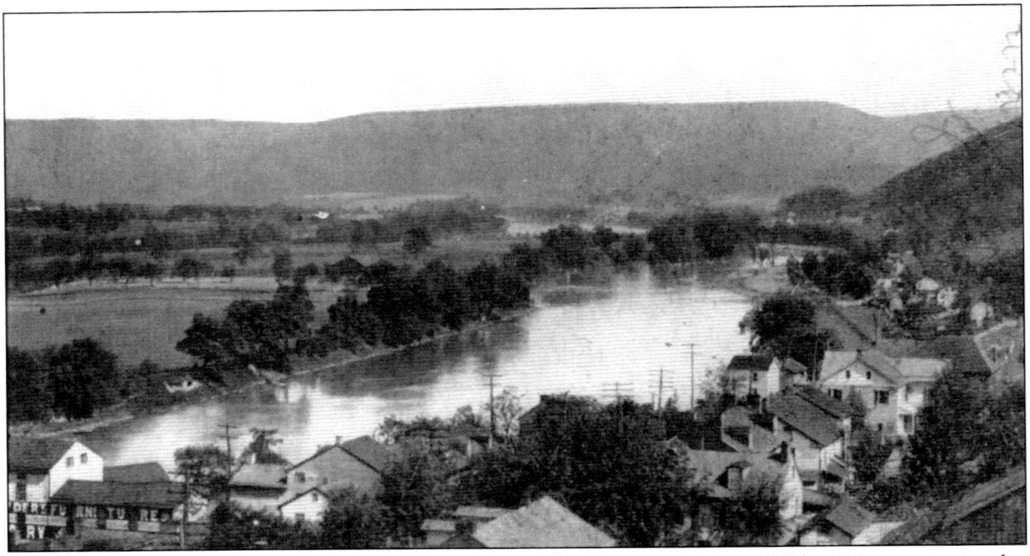

The Juniata River winds past Mifflintown with Shade Mountain and Blue Mountain in the distance. The river splits as it flows around Bell Island. In this photograph, William F. Snyder's Furniture Factory appears at the lower left. Snyder crafted thousands of chairs and fancy benches in the mid-1800s. Today, his highly decorative products are prized by collectors and represent some of the most sought-after Pennsylvania-made craftwork.

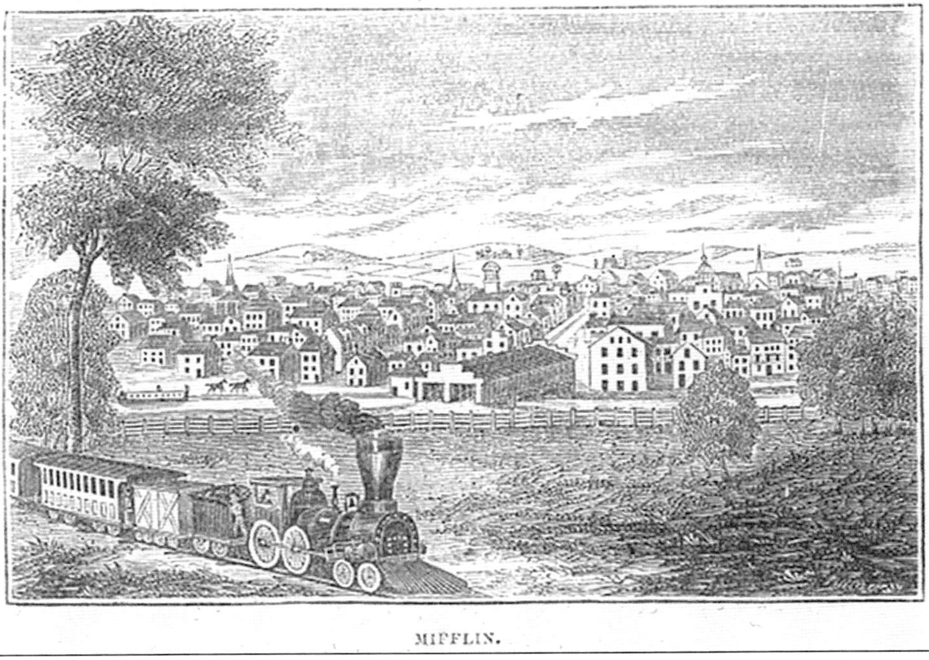

MIFFLIN.

The village of Mifflin was largely undeveloped in 1850. The railroad company stopped at Patterson House, which was a celebrated hotel named for a former president of the Pennsylvania Railroad. On the opposite side of the river, Mifflintown has grown to a sizable town. The courthouse is seen at the center. The canal runs under the bridge in the foreground.

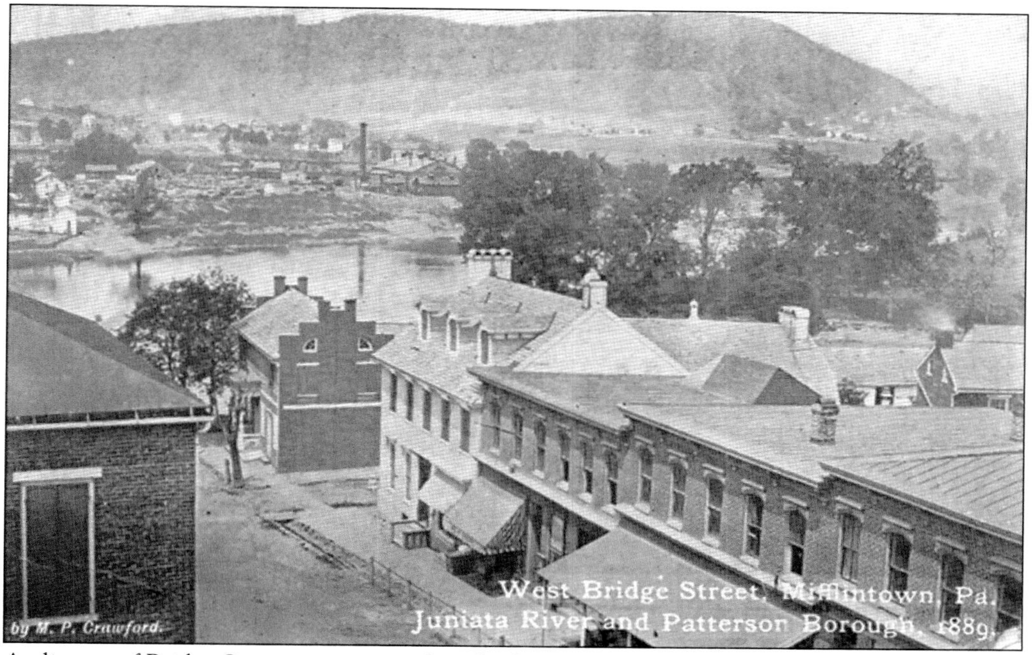

A glimpse of Bridge Street as it approaches the Juniata in 1889 shows Patterson Borough in the distance. Laid out in 1849, Patterson maintained a separate identity from the well-established Mifflintown. However, the railroad company had other plans and renamed this growing neighborhood "Mifflin." An important coal supplier, Mifflin also served as a repair location for locomotives. A few late Federal-style canal buildings still stand at water's edge.

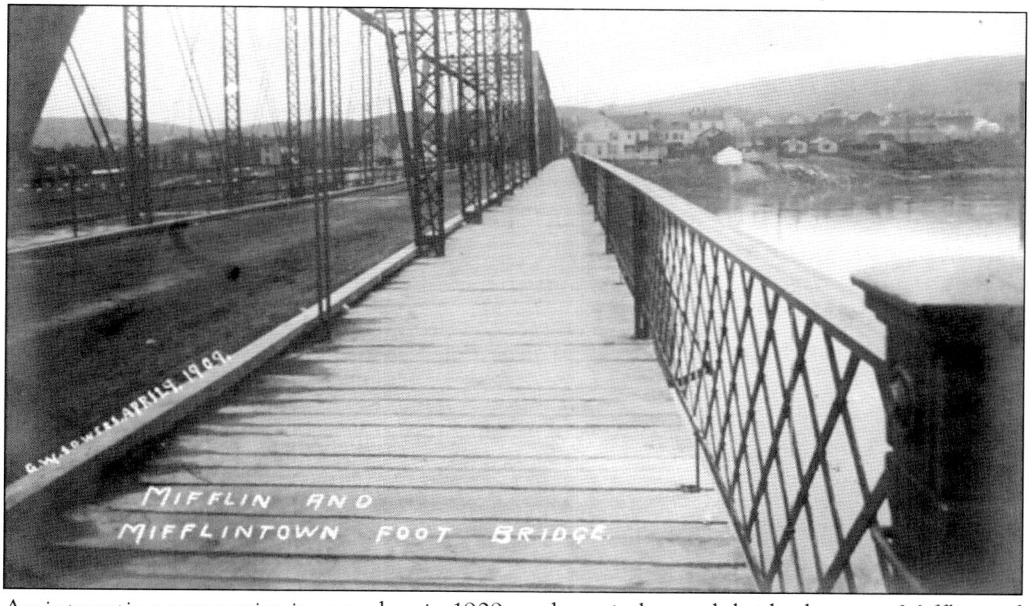

An interesting perspective is one taken in 1909 on the twin borough bridge between Mifflin and Mifflintown. The decking was made of lumber. In the distance, to the left of the railroad repair shops, can be seen a familiar sign. The E.E. McMeen department store operated here for many years. Shoppers arrived by train from other towns to patronize businesses in Mifflin.

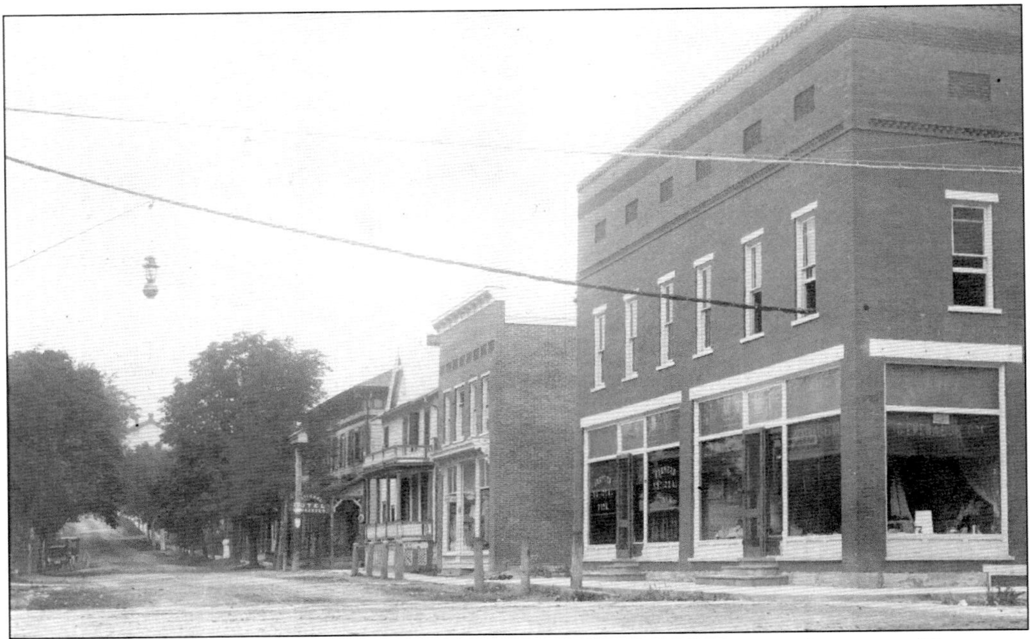

The photographer came out early one morning in Mifflintown to capture this image. The street is deserted except for one lone woman near Shawver's National Hotel. On the corner is a large general store that shares a building with Farmers National Bank. Beyond that is a military store. The birdhouse on a pole outside the hotel seems unusual.

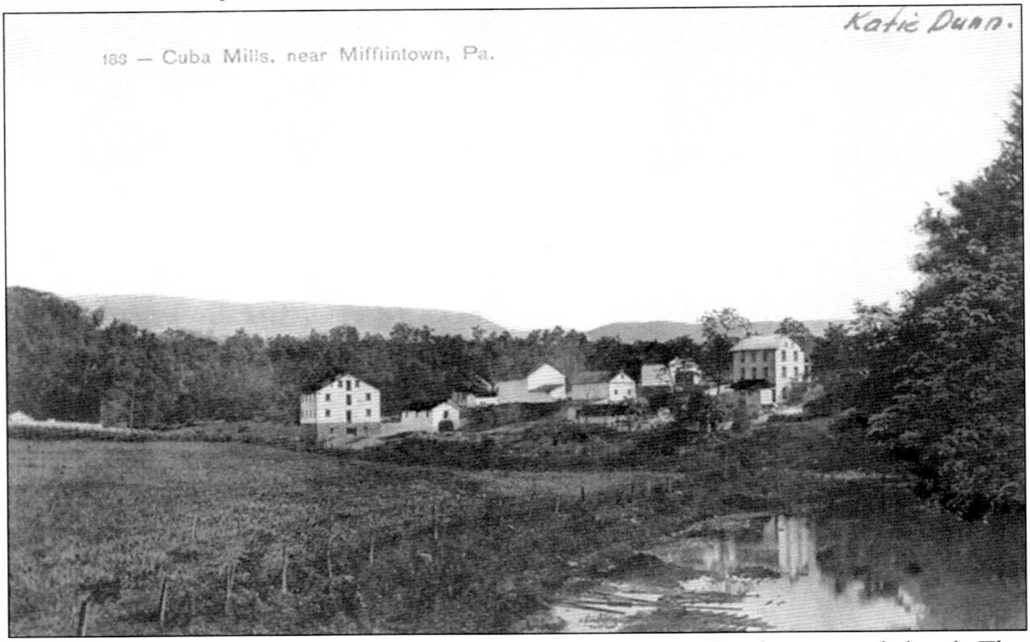

The old village of Cuba Mills as it appeared around 1900 is reflected in the waters of a brook. This grouping of mill buildings is located west of Mifflintown in Fermanagh Township where the Little Lost Creek enters the Juniata River in the shadows of Moyer Ridge. Mills were common throughout the valley due to the abundance of grain grown in the cleared meadows along the river.

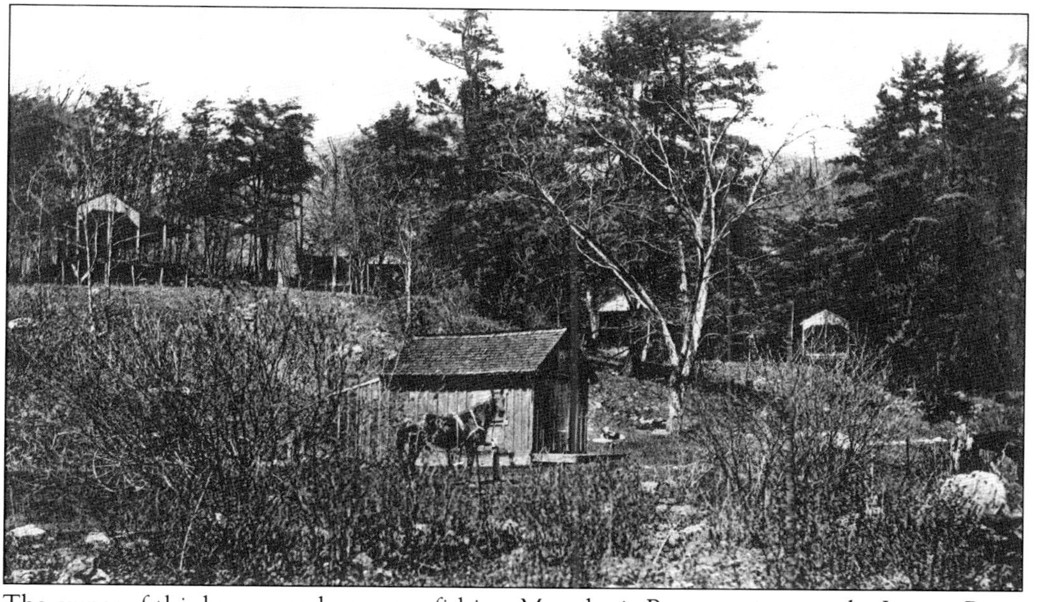

The owner of this horse may have gone fishing. Macedonia Run empties into the Juniata River near lock No. 13 of the old Juniata canal. An early picnic ground was laid out here. In the center of the photograph is the caretaker's cabin, next to the horse. In recent years, this spot became a centerpiece in the development of a canal park featuring hiking paths.

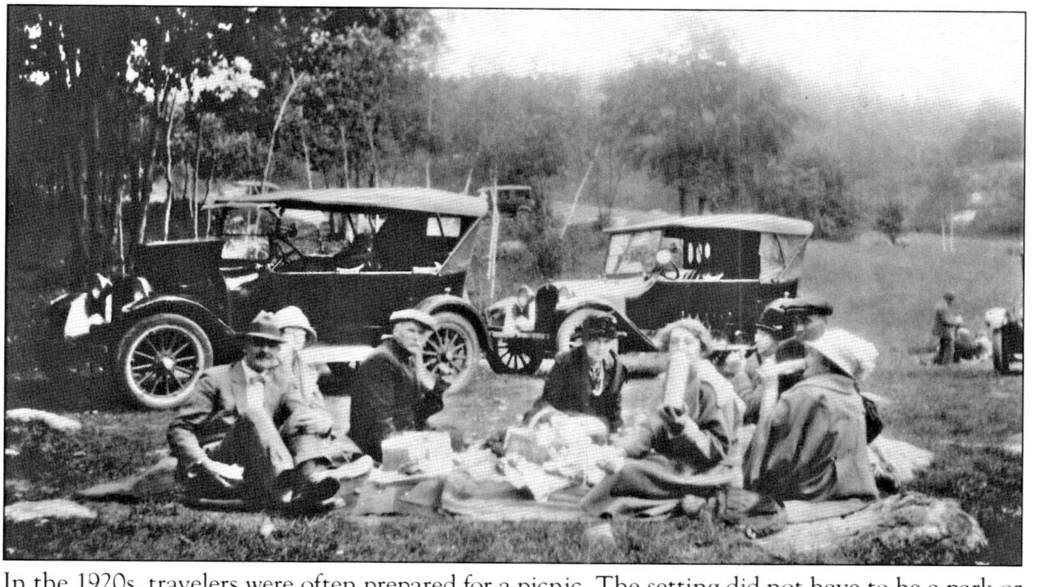

In the 1920s, travelers were often prepared for a picnic. The setting did not have to be a park or a campground. An open field along the way provided the perfect place to pull over and spread a blanket. The William Penn Highway along the Juniata River was an inviting place for Sunday afternoon travelers of the early motor age.

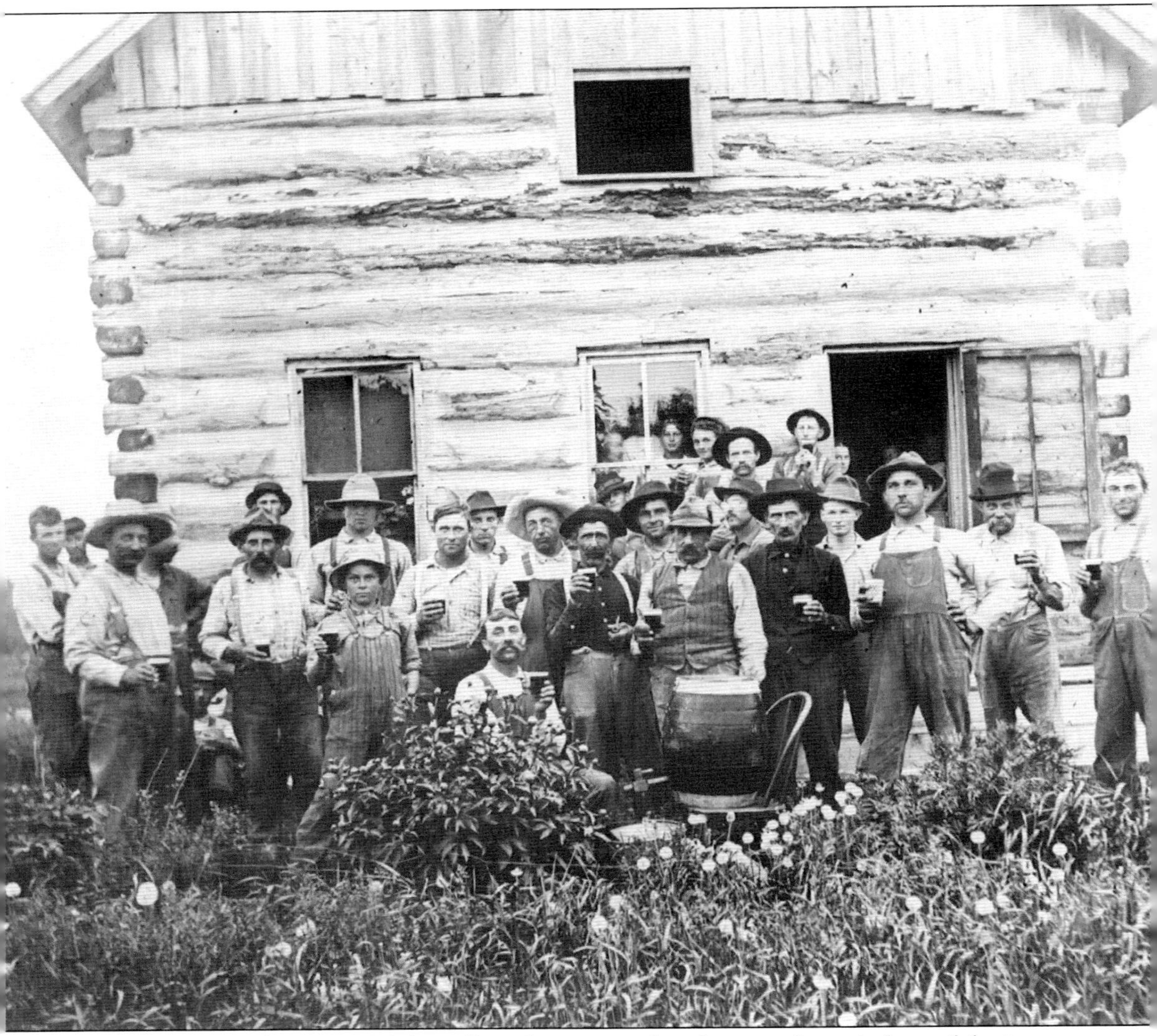

Simply labeled "Juniata Jubilation" on the reverse, this photograph reminds us of the important role that Pennsylvania played in the beer industry. Immigrants from Central Europe brought with them the knowledge of crafting beer and lager. They shared their German passion for good food and their heritage of lagering with their neighbors. Professional breweries were established in hundreds of towns in Pennsylvania in the late 1800s. Output was measured in barrels. While some produced hundreds of barrels a year, others were able to deliver tens of thousands. Some bottled their beer while others sent it to hotels and saloons in wooden kegs on wagons pulled by teams of horses. In Juniata towns and cities that had a high German population, such as Tyrone and Altoona, breweries sponsored singing societies where language, culture, and the food and drink of the German republics were celebrated.

Three

Mifflin, Juniata's Heartland

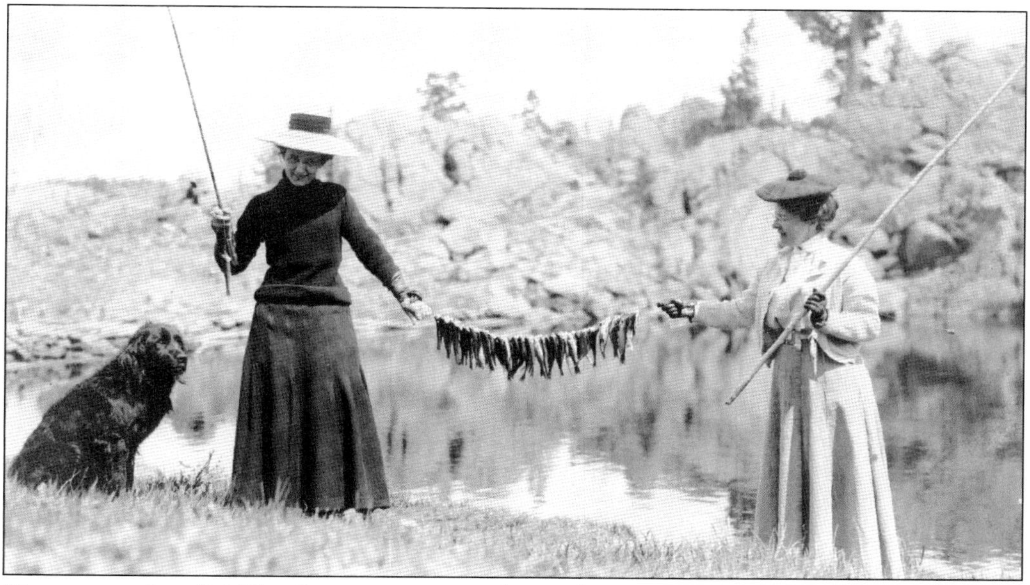

The topography of Mifflin County greets travelers with some ponderous scenery. In this county, the traveler can find spectacular water gaps. The river flows in all directions to navigate the hills. This confounded those who built the canal and laid the rails. The early settlers were awed by the fertility of the soil and made note of the abundance and size of the produce. Also, the streams were habitats for a variety of fish.

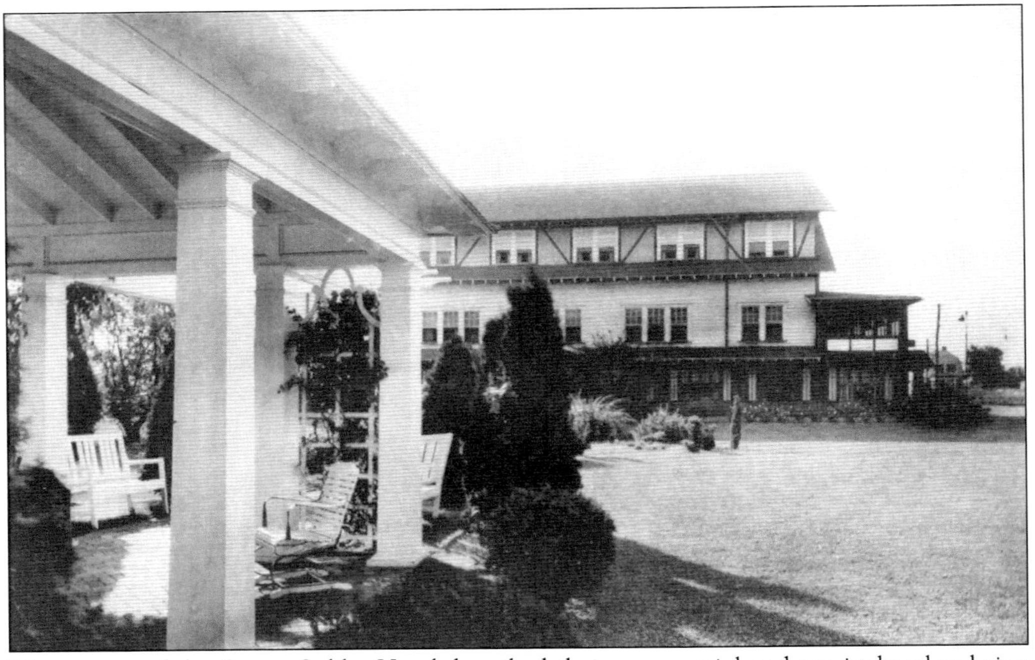

The owners of the Green Gables Hotel described their commercial and tourist hotel as being "unusually different." Opened in 1931, the main building, located at 900 South Main Street, is strategically located where the old William Penn Highway enters Lewistown after meandering through the tight portion of the Juniata Valley known locally as "the Narrows." Motor traffic brought travelers from all parts of the country. For those who stopped and spent time here, this would certainly be a memorable occasion. Sitting on the long, enclosed porch with comfortable furniture decorated in bright hues, a view of the water gap in the distance is a pleasant way to spend the visit. Few hotels are positioned to offer such an unspoiled view.

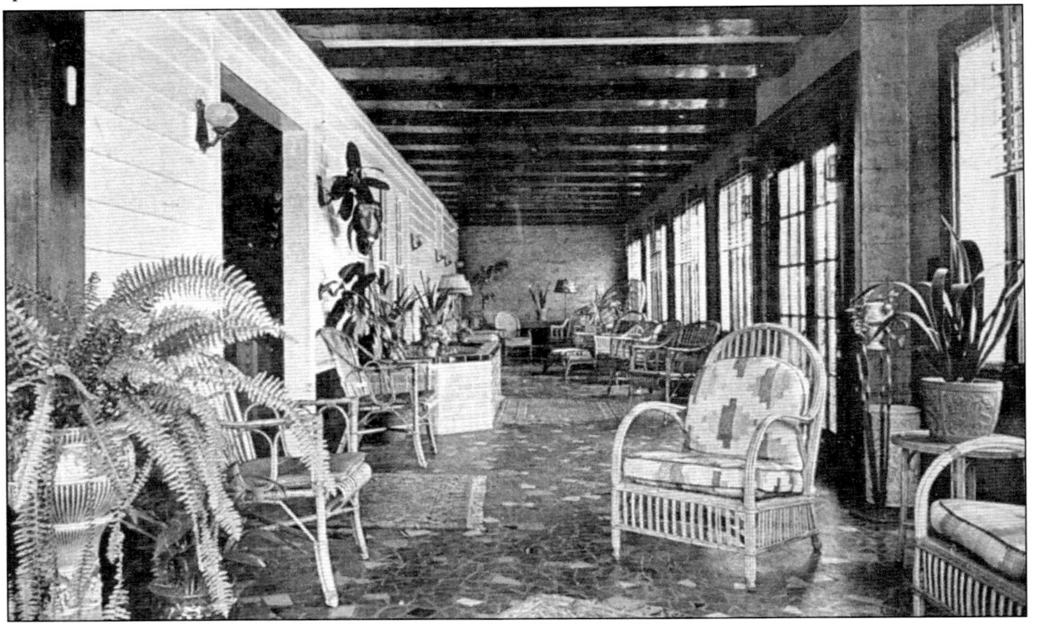

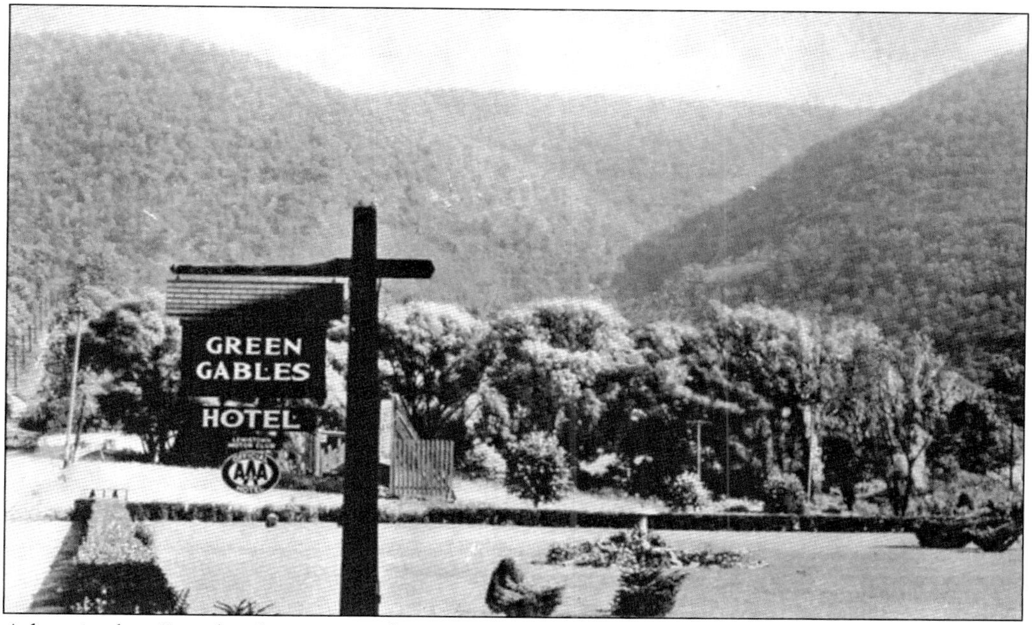

Advertised as "on the direct route from New York, to the West," the William Penn Highway passes directly below the expanse of the Green Gables Hotel. "The Narrows" winds its path in the distance. Blue Mountain is a backdrop to Shade Mountain on the right. Together, these two peaks squeeze the path so tightly that early colonists had difficulty finding a footing at times. Eventually, the canal, highway, and railroad all maneuvered this passage together.

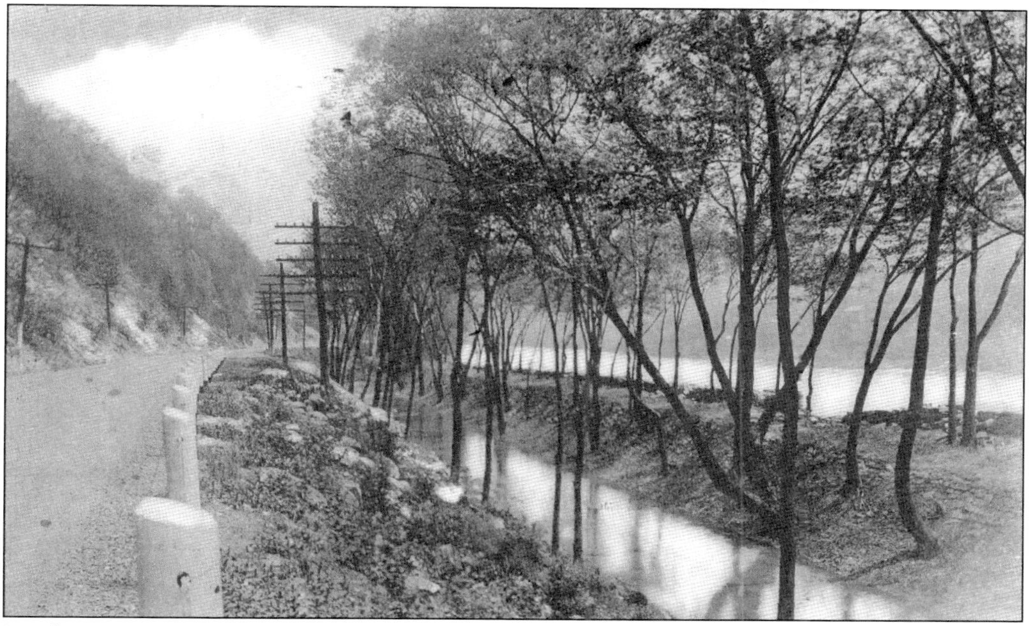
In "the Narrows," the old Pennsylvania Canal is still discernable in the 1940s, fifty years after it was abandoned in these parts. In complete running order in 1833, the canal brought prosperity to Lewistown. The major flood of 1889, known historically as the Johnstown Flood, hit all parts of Pennsylvania and dealt the final blow to the no longer funded canal.

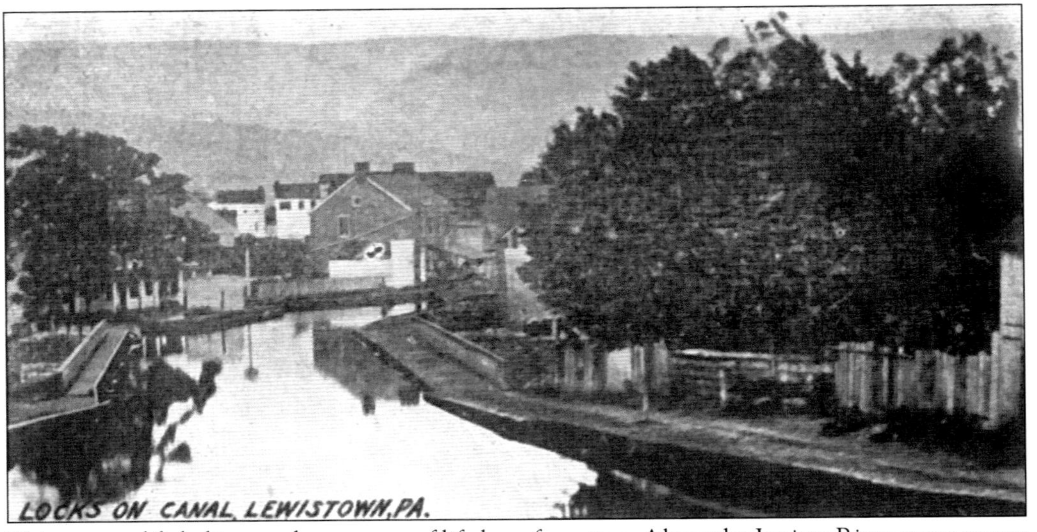

This rare and faded image shows a way of life long-forgotten. Along the Juniata River, some towns provided access for the canal to enter the community away from the river. At Hale and Elizabeth Streets, the towpaths skirted warehouses. Hotels, pubs, and merchandisers established businesses in town for travelers. Manufacturers and millers now had a way to expedite their finished products to market in other settlements without having to provide the transportation.

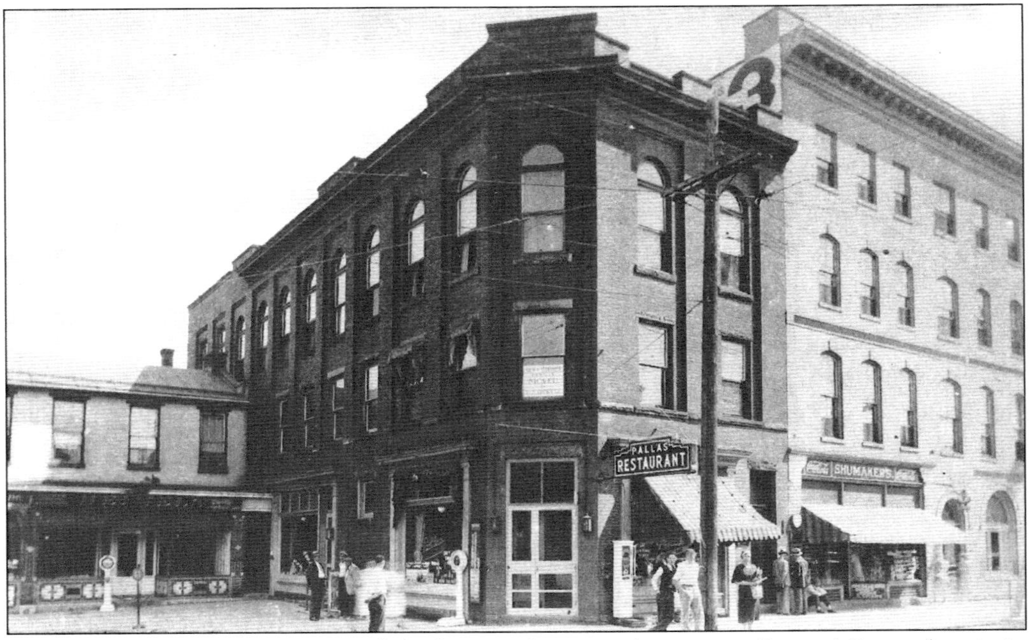

Downtown Lewistown was one of the busiest shopping districts in Central Pennsylvania in the 1930s. The Pellas corner was also the Greyhound Bus depot. Located right on the square, Pellas used the slogan "A Modern Restaurant at Moderate Prices." Note the three mechanical penny scales. Schumaker's Store is in the Coleman Hotel, which was built in 1893. A previous Coleman Hotel, destroyed by fire, occupied the same spot. In the days of the canal, the Red Lion Inn stood here.

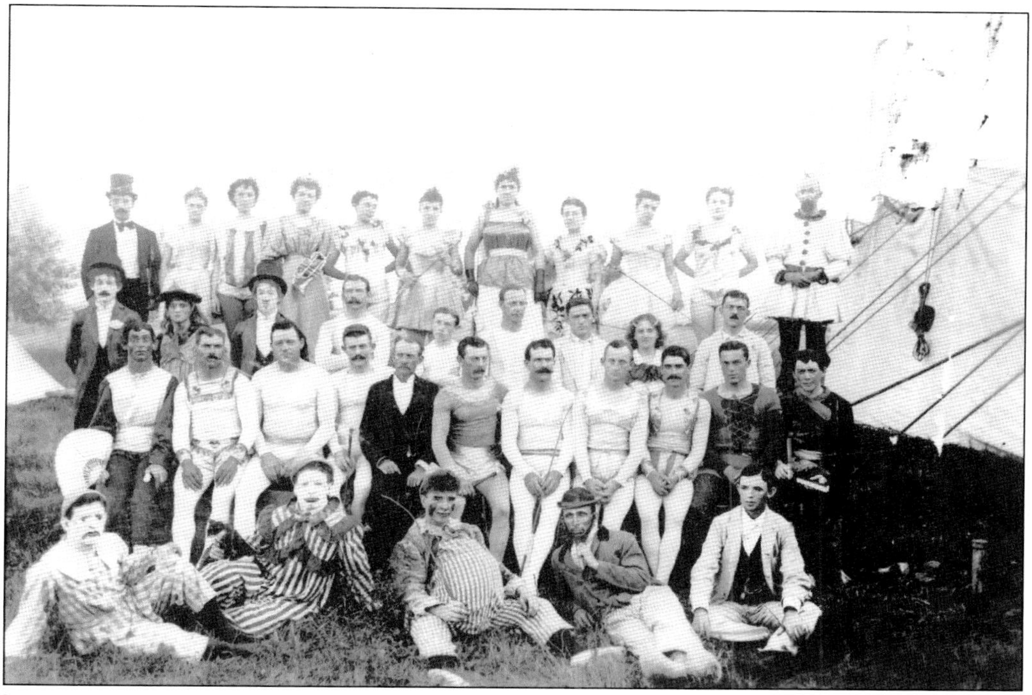

Lewistown anxiously awaited the Walter L. Main Circus in May 1893. Word was received on the morning of May 31, 1893, that the show was cancelled. On a steep mountainside descending to Tyrone from Houtzdale, the train carrying the circus members and animals lost control, resulting in the most complete destruction of a circus train on record. After convalescing and rebuilding at Tyrone, the Walter E. Main Circus was reborn. Here the clowns pose 10 years later.

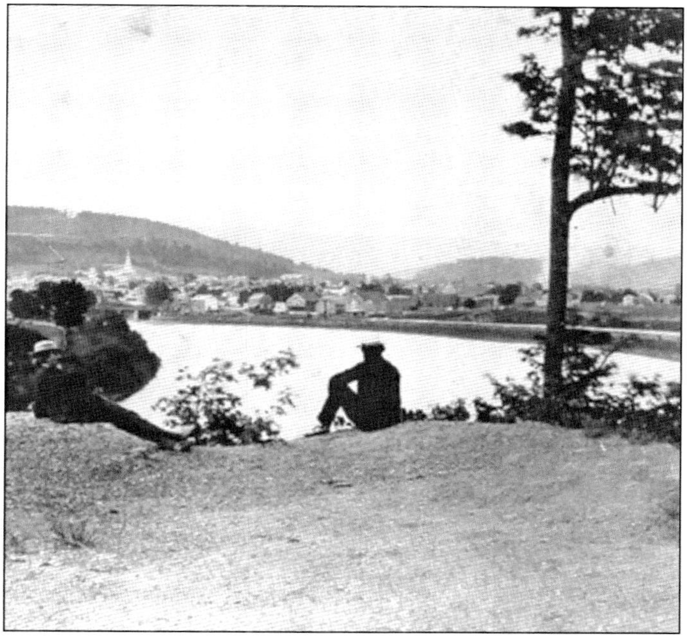

On the Lewistown Junction side of the Juniata River, two men relax with the town of Lewistown in the distance. The spires of the churches dot the landscape with a backdrop of the water gap where the Little Kishacoquillas Creek led to the Juniata. The full sweep of the Juniata canal can be seen as it follows the opposite shore on its way into Lewistown. This image dates to the 1870s.

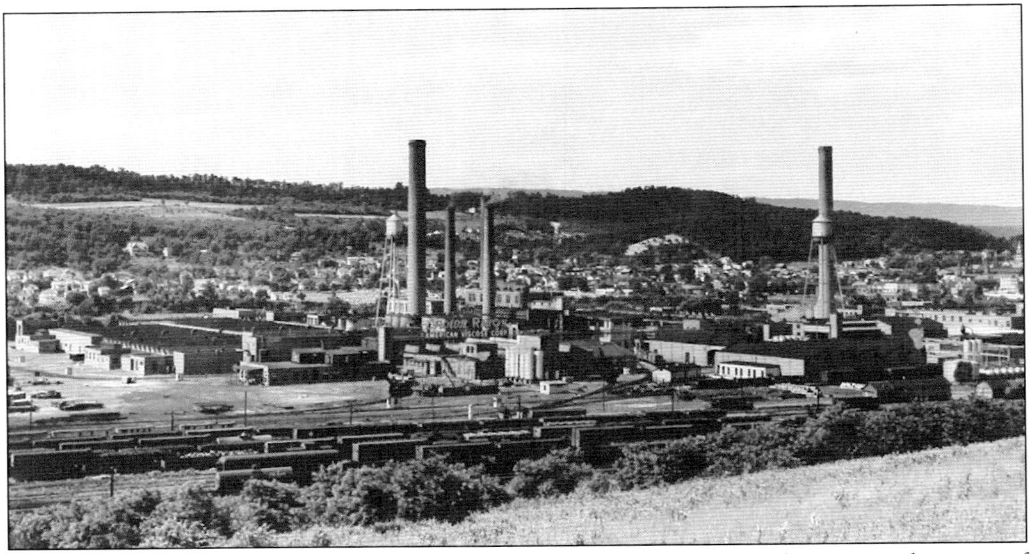

For more than 50 years, the American Viscose Plant operated on a bank opposite the town of Lewistown. Employing at one time as many as 5,000 workers, this manufacturer of synthetic silk built a planned community nearby for the workers and named it "Juniata Terrace." The plant suffered greatly from Tropical Storm Agnes in 1972, which caused it to cease operation permanently.

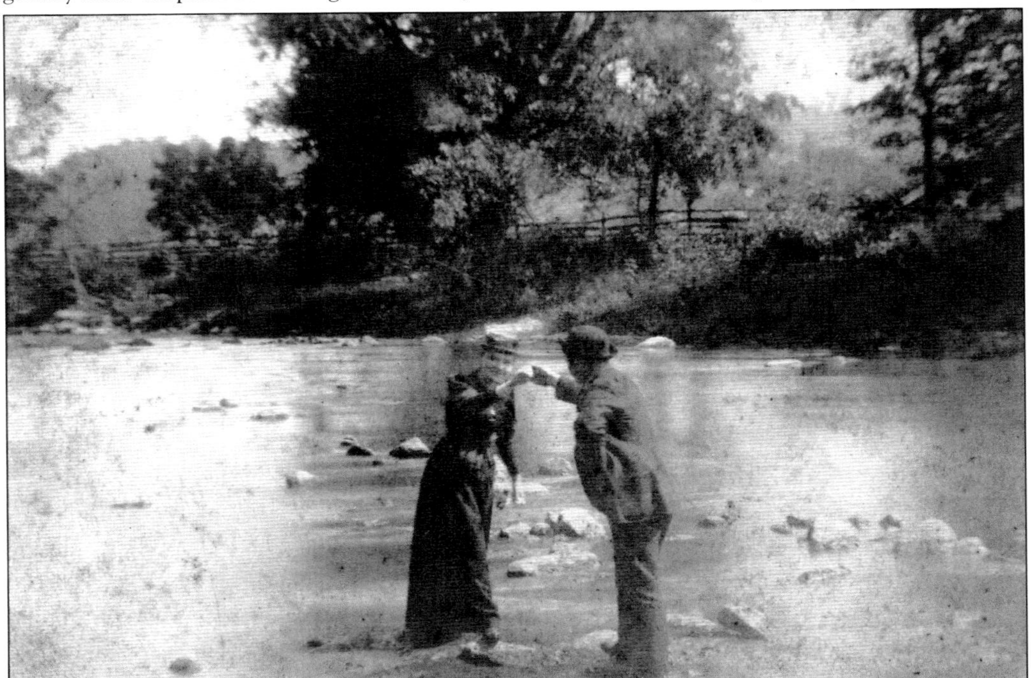

On the Little Kishacoquillas Creek, a photographer from Lewistown staged an outdoor artistic setting. The light was perfect and the background was a lush meadow. In this 1880s photograph, a young man offers assistance as a smiling lady, identified as Margaret Watson, navigates the rocks. The location was known as "Logan" when the photograph was produced. That name gave way to Burnham Borough in 1887.

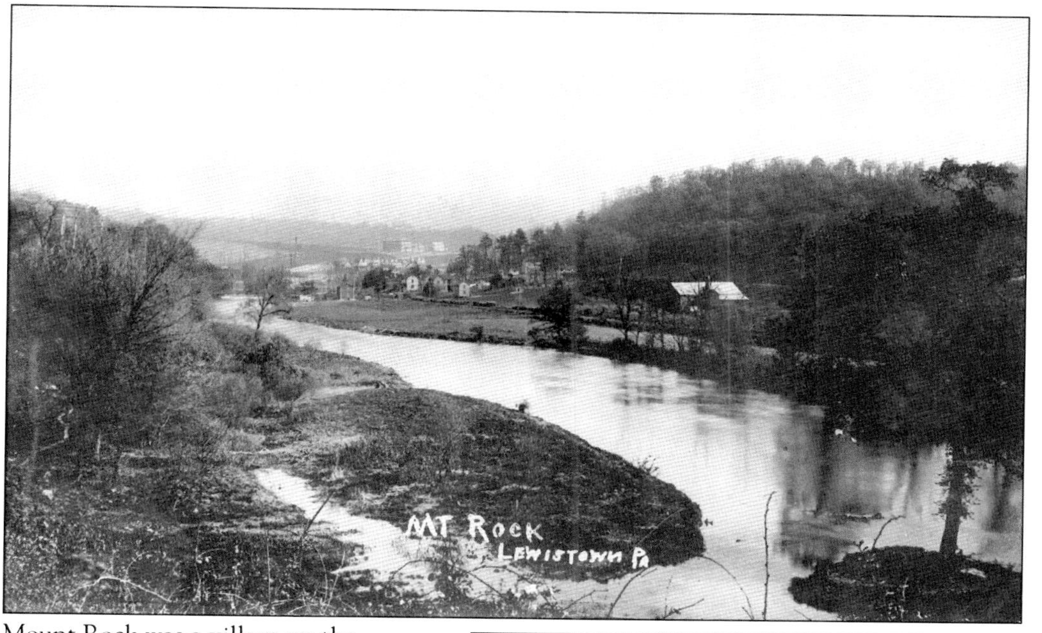

Mount Rock was a village on the Kishacoqullas set back against the hillside. An old pike passed through from Lewistown and continued up the valley. Eventually, the open spaces were filled in with new homes and highways, making the identity of "one stop along the way" history. Mount Rock was consumed by the progress and development of Lewistown and Burnham. Eventually it was not listed on the map.

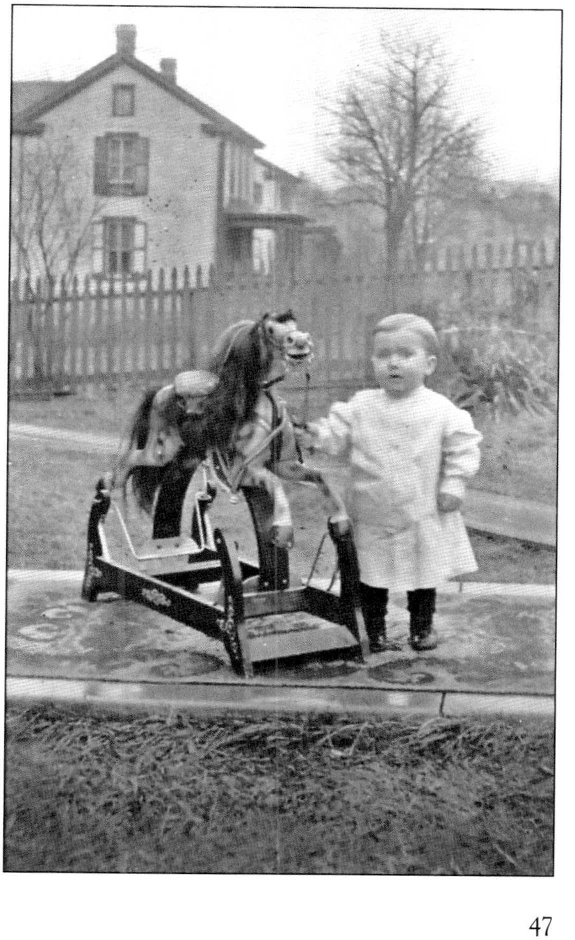

Christmas 1910 was a happy occasion for little Stewart. Dressed in his new white suit, he stands next to his new mechanical rocking horse. His home was in Burnham, just a few blocks from the steelworks. Stewart's mother mailed this photograph to his grandmother Ellen Swisher. She lived up the valley in Newton Hamilton, Pennsylvania.

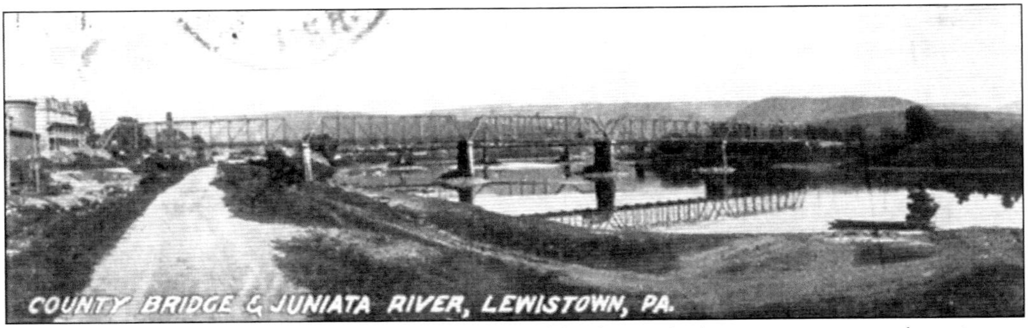

The County of Mifflin replaced an earlier covered bridge with this iron, segmented version as seen in 1905. This was one of the longest of this type of bridge to cross the Juniata River. The old highway, still not much more than a dirt path, ran below. The area on the other side soon saw the building of the American Viscose Plant. Another concrete bridge replaced this one as a World War I memorial.

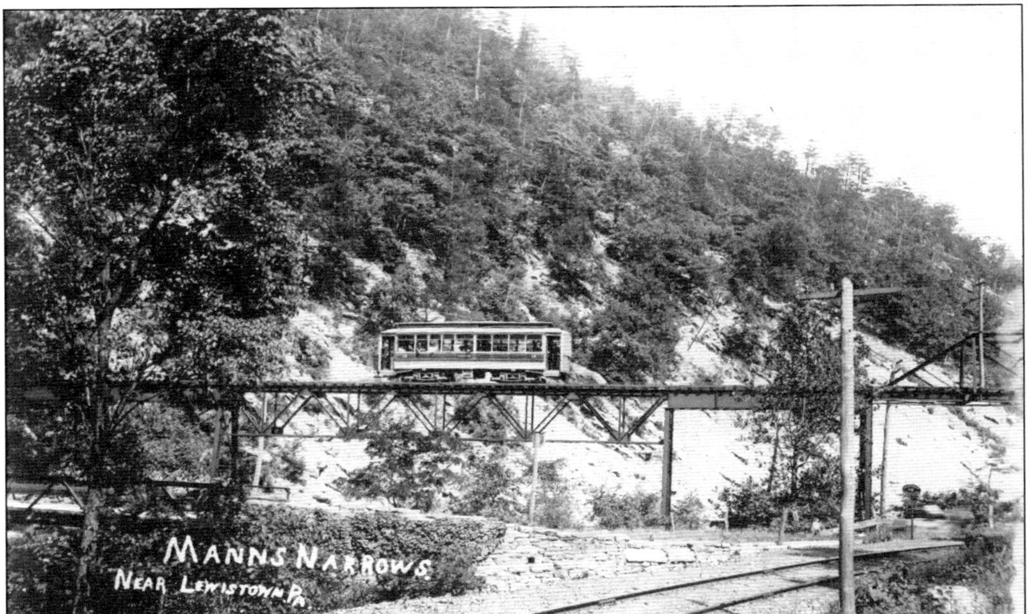

Three competing forms of transportation merge at Mann's Narrows. The Lewistown & Reedsville Electric Railway is perched above the old pike to Bellefonte as it crosses the Milroy Branch of the Pennsylvania Railroad. At the dawn of the 20th century, many private concerns ventured into the realm of providing interurban passenger service. This Brill trolley seated 18 travelers. The nationally famous Mann's Axe Factory was located near this crossing.

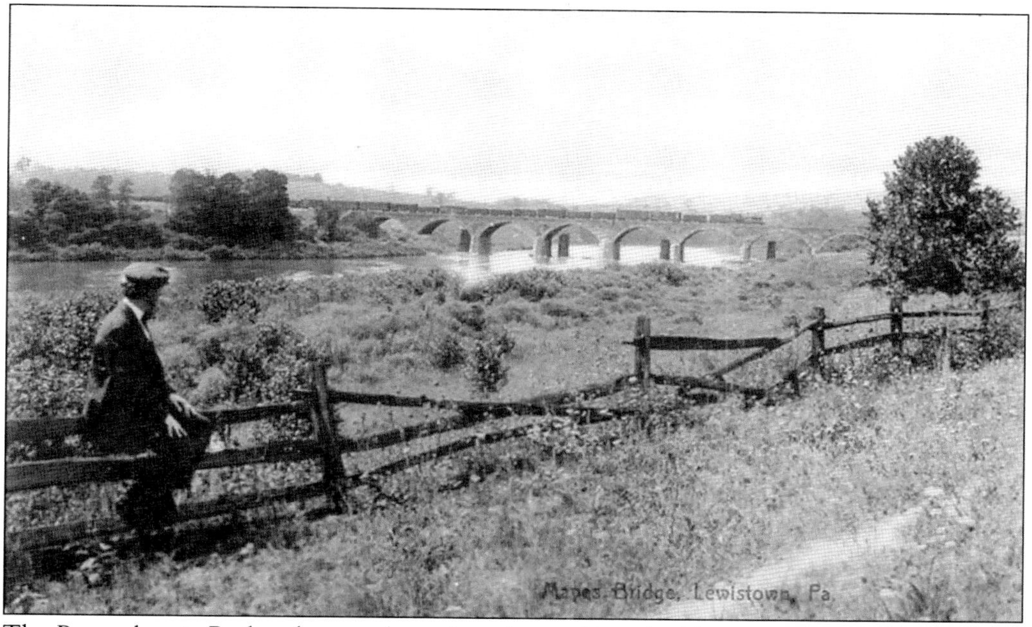

The Pennsylvania Railroad entered another phase of its rebuilding program after the turn of the 20th century. Bridges all along the main line were being widened or replaced. Magnificent cut stone arch viaducts made their appearance from the Susquehanna to the Alleghenies. This classic view at Lewistown looking downriver from a pastoral setting shows the newly completed Mapes Bridge with a freight train in transit.

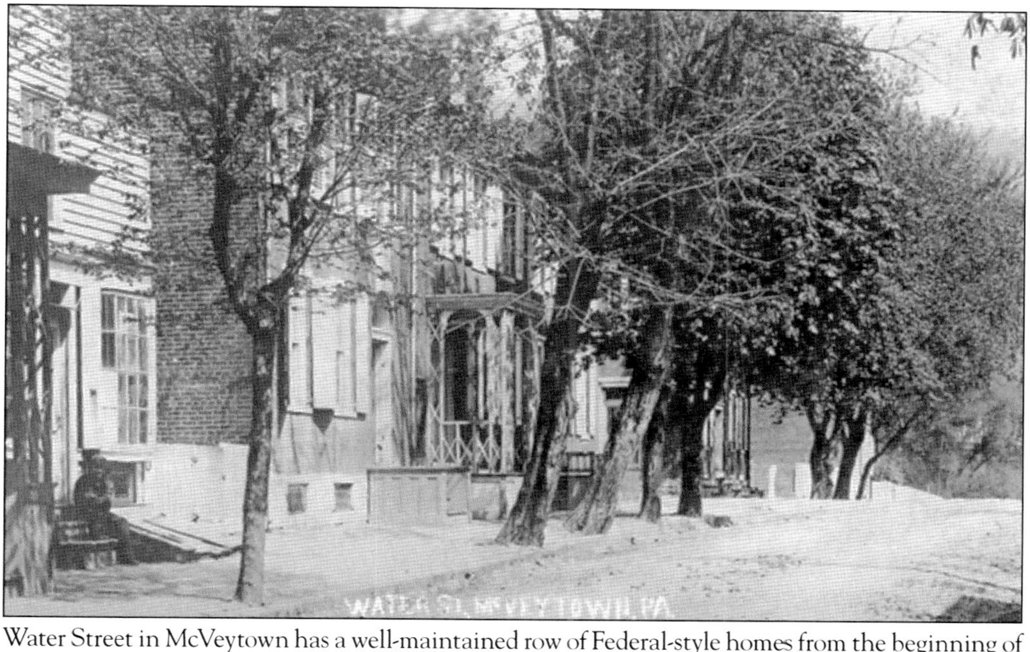
Water Street in McVeytown has a well-maintained row of Federal-style homes from the beginning of the canal era. Facing the canal basin, this street became the residence of businessmen who prospered as a result of the opening of the Juniata canal. Originally settled in 1755 as "Waynesburg," McVeytown was laid out as a town in 1795 and was renamed by John McVey, the actual landowner.

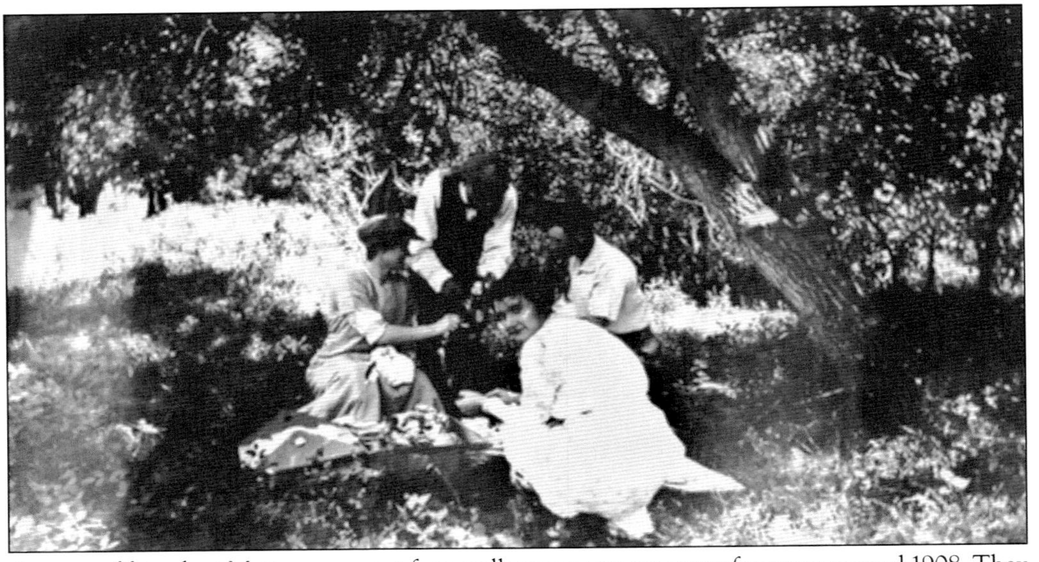

A group of friends at Mattawana went for a walk on a warm summer afternoon around 1908. They crossed Mattawana Island and continued through McVeytown. They chose Furnace Road and continued on for a distance. They had brought pails along with them for berry picking, and certainly were not disappointed on this day. The group found plenty of fruit right along the road.

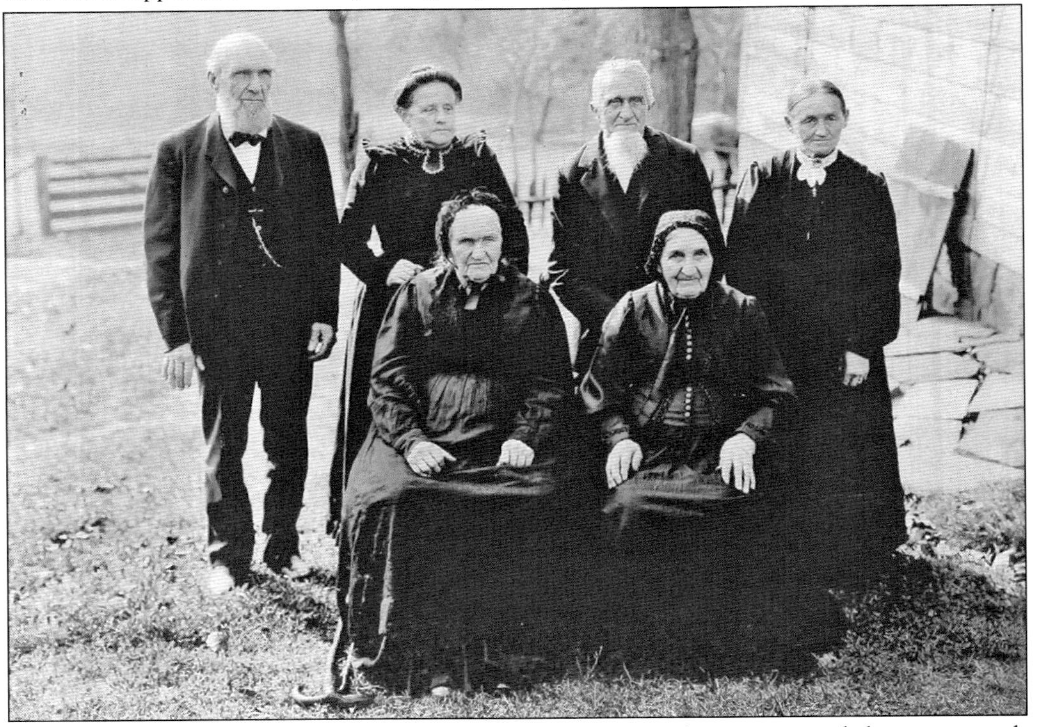

Some elder members of the Esh Family of Juniata County sat for a portrait while visiting with relatives in Mifflin County after the turn of the 20th century. It is noted on the reverse of the photograph that the journey that day was to take a member of the family to see her great-great-granddaughter. In terse pencil it says, "This was a momentous occasion."

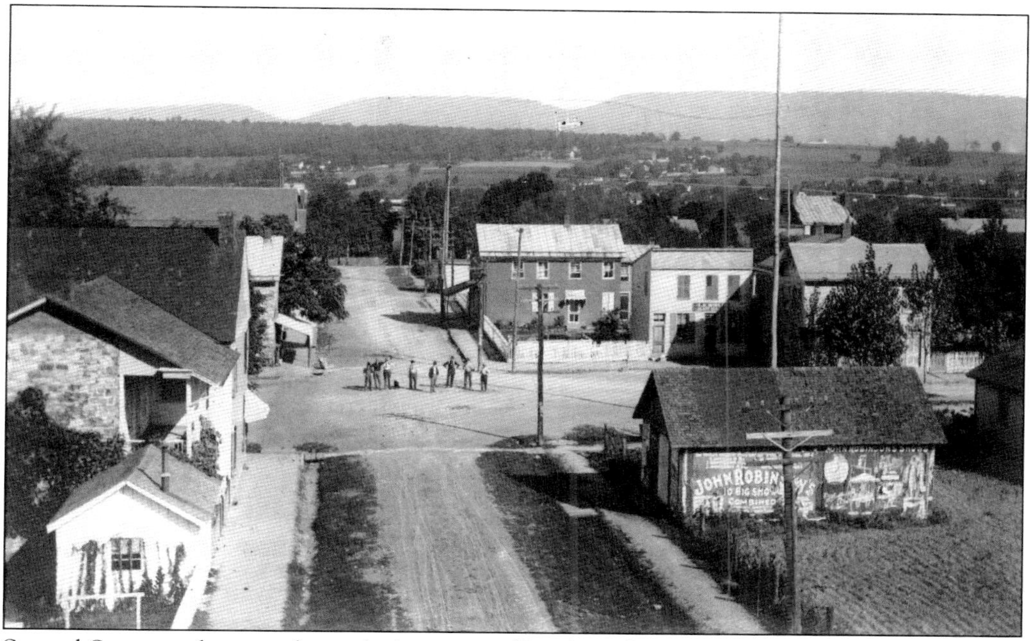

Samuel Stewart, photographer, asked a group of locals and a mutt to meet in the public square at McVeytown around 1908. The only one identified is John Bortell on the far right. Stewart captured the wonderful hills of the Juniata in the background. The town would play host to the Robinson Circus that summer. One of the largest shows in the country, they used innovative billboards to announce their appearance.

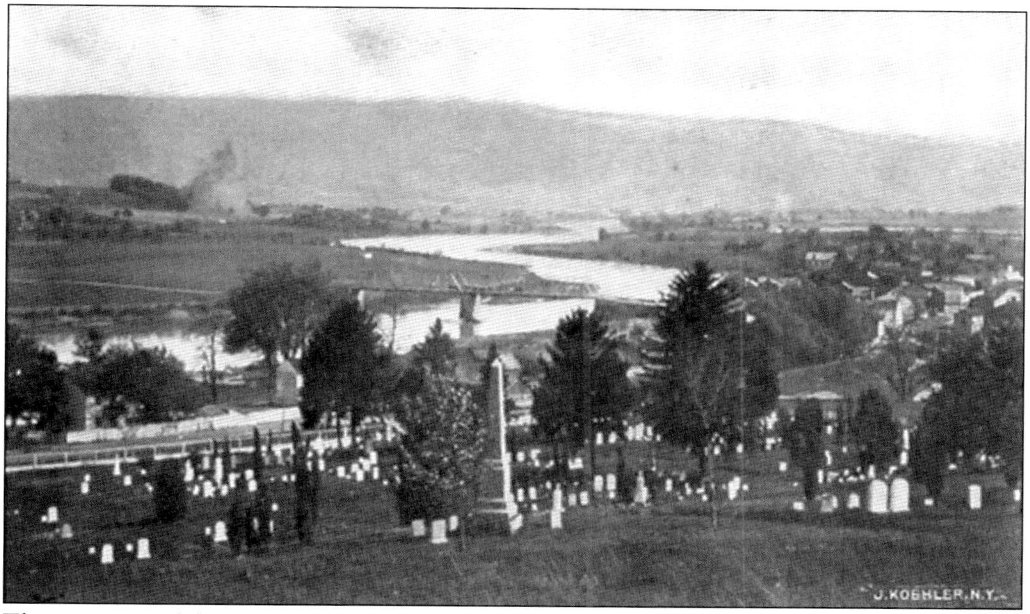

This is a view of the Juniata River as seen from the Mattawana Cemetery at McVeytown. From McVeytown the Juniata actually flows south for a distance because of the ridges of the Tuscarora Mountains. In the center of this view, East St. John Street crosses the river to a 35-acre island in the middle of the Juniata on its way to the town of Mattawana.

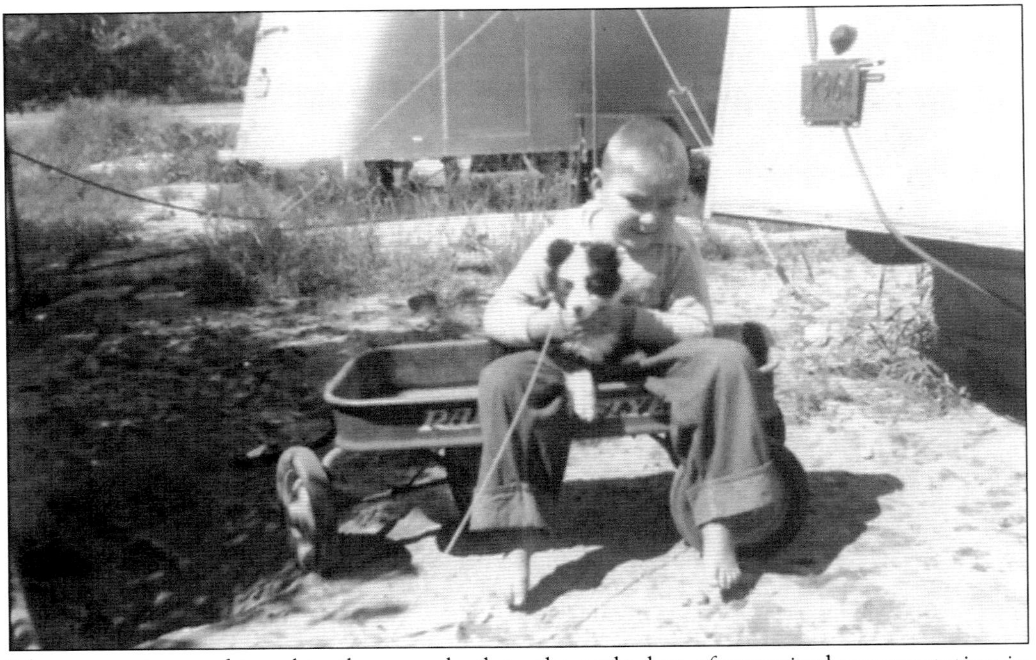

The convenience of travel trailers goes back to the early days of motorized transportation in America. Farmers garnered extra income by allowing the use of the low fields that fronted the Juniata as vacation spots. In some areas, most notably Newton Hamilton, lots could be deeded to the vacationers so they had year-round access to their little home away from home.

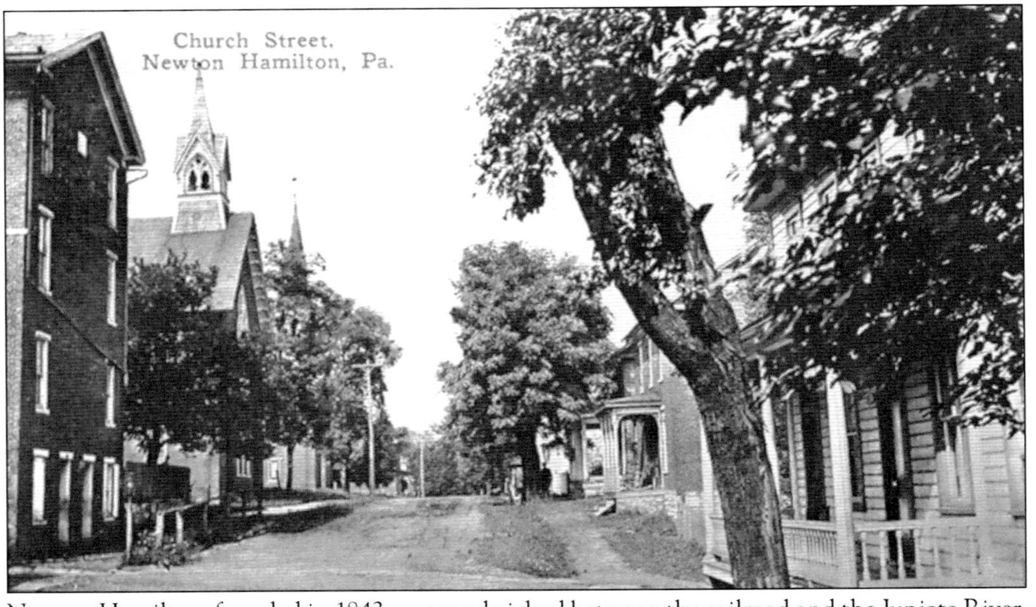

Newton Hamilton, founded in 1843, was sandwiched between the railroad and the Juniata River. A row of meetinghouses and churches was located on Church Street, shown in this photograph from around 1909. Note the horse hitching rails in front of the meetinghouse on the left. The William Penn Highway took a more northern route though this section of Mifflin County, preserving the tranquility of this area of the Juniata.

Outside of a kitchen of one of the many camps established along the Juniata River, four young staff members pause for a photographer during their morning chores. Many local boys and girls had their first paying job tending campgrounds. This gave them a sense of responsibility and a chance to experience nature while performing their duties.

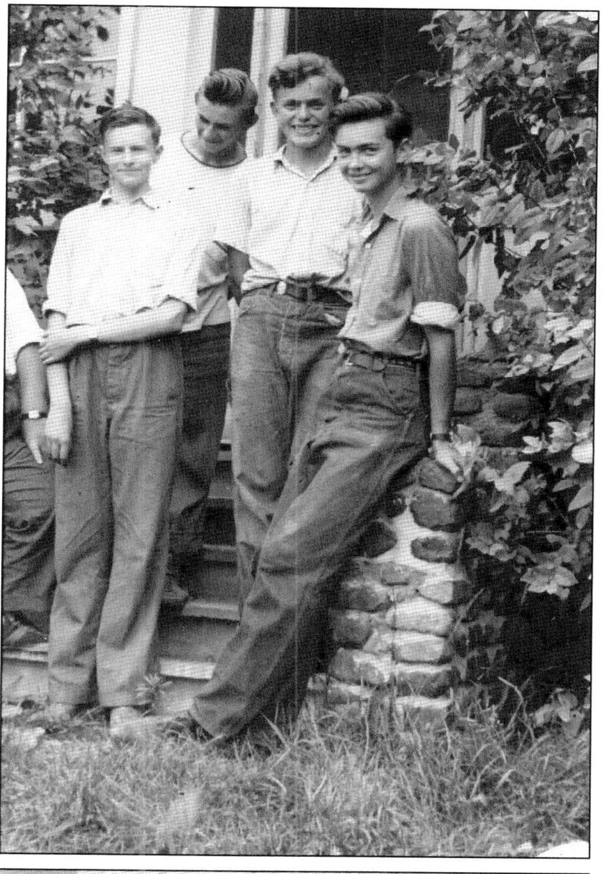

The banks of the Juniata near Newton Hamilton have long been a camping spot enjoyed by many organizations and individuals. The Methodists built a camp here and the Lions Club established a retreat so people with impaired sight could enjoy nature. Shown in this photograph is a well-fitted and comfortable camping village with a cluster of board and batten houses among the Juniata woods.

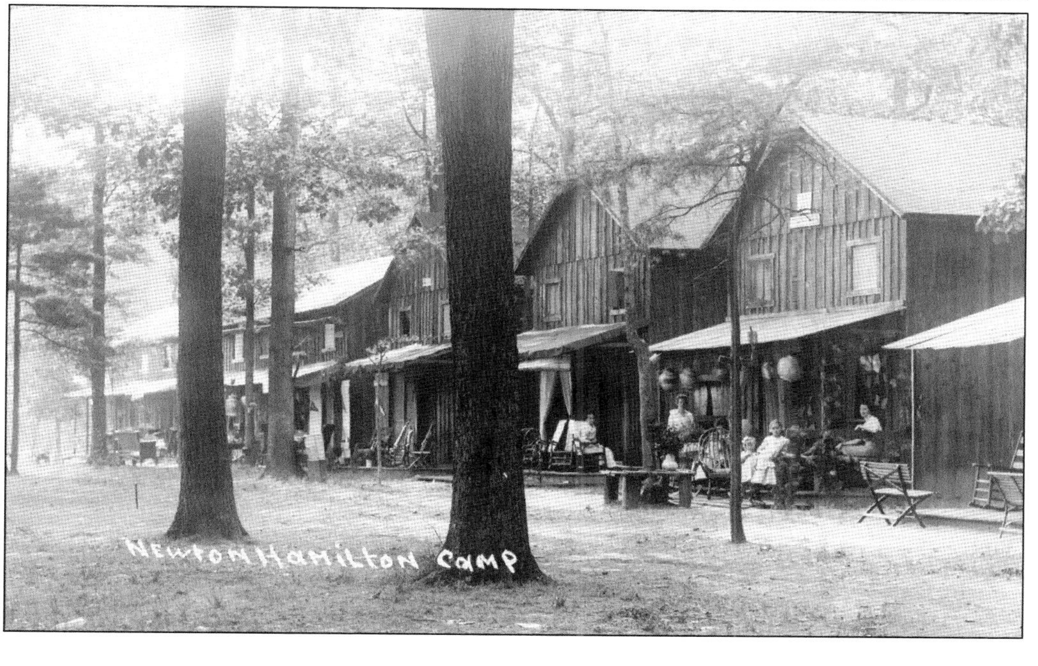

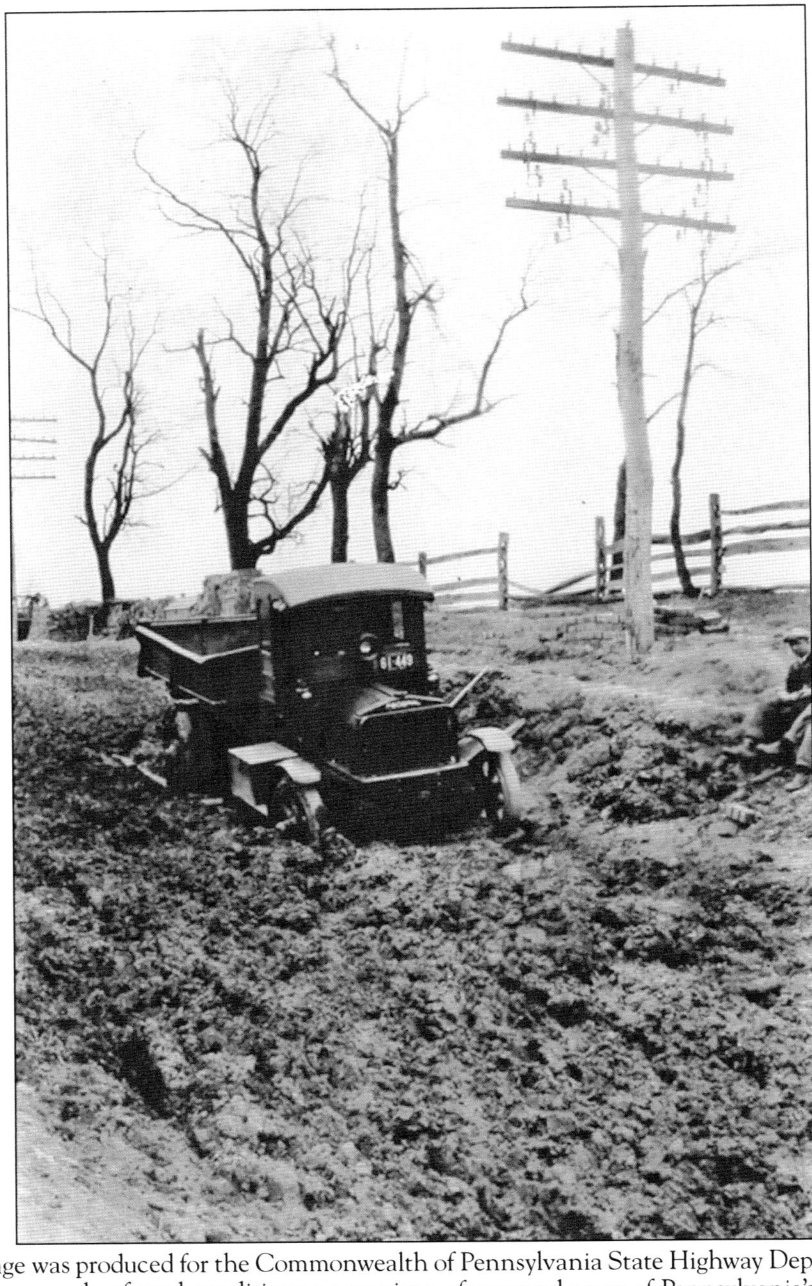

This image was produced for the Commonwealth of Pennsylvania State Highway Department to use as an example of road conditions on portions of unpaved areas of Pennsylvania's highways. It was taken east of Lewistown on US Route 22/322 along the Juniata River in 1920. The official caption was "Condition of sub-grade after spring thaw." William Sproul was elected governor of Pennsylvania in 1919. As a senator in 1911, his monumental Sproul Road Bill was approved. The goal was to link towns with highways that had only been reachable by rail or unimproved paths. As governor, he was able to see his original ideas finalized. The term "sproul roads" was coined in honor of his efforts. Many towns across the Commonwealth have a "Sproul Street" named after him.

Four

HUNTINGDON, THE STANDING STONE

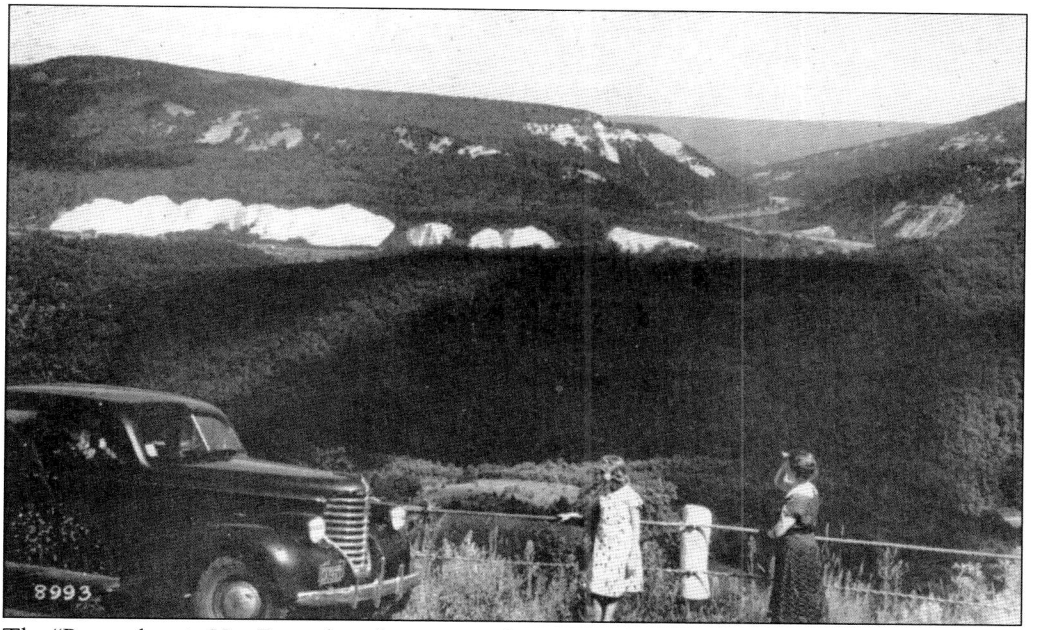

The "Pennsylvania Has Everything" campaign from around 1940 featured this stunning visage of Jack's Narrows as viewed west of Mount Union where US Route 22/322 winds its way along the blue Juniata River. White spots indicate silica rock workings and sand quarries. This photograph is from US Route 76 on Cassville Road south of Mill Creek. The romantic gap is named for Capt. Jack Armstrong, a pioneer trader who, according to legend, was murdered in this district and buried here.

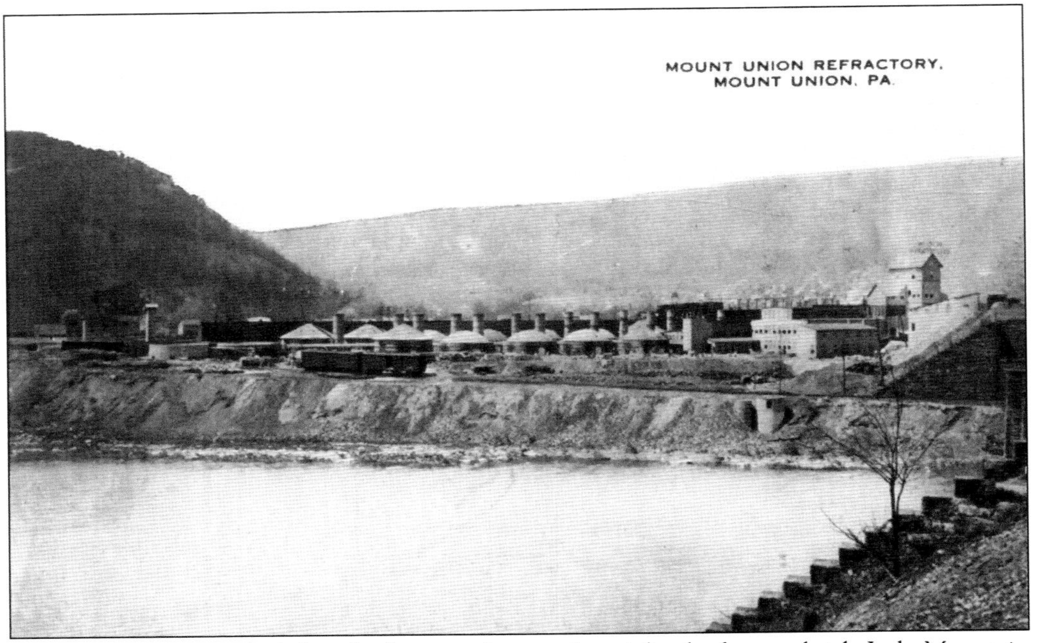

Mount Union was an ideal place for the manufacture of specialized refractory brick. Jacks Mountain is composed of ganister rock. This unusual fine-grained quartzrose sandstone, ground and mixed with fireclay, produces bricks that can sustain extreme temperatures. This silica brick is a necessary component in the blast furnaces of steel manufacturing. Three refractory companies were located here along the Juniata River. Coal carried from the Broad Top Mines by rail fueled the many kilns.

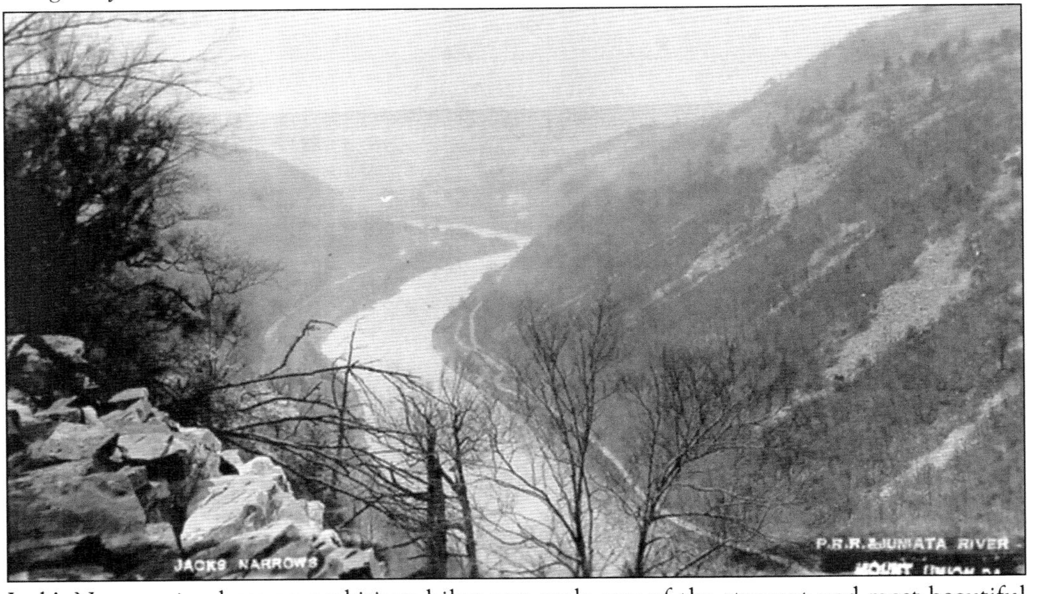

Jack's Narrows is where an ambitious hiker can scale one of the steepest and most beautiful glens in Pennsylvania. This pass, which is more than two miles long, brings the Juniata River through Jacks Mountain. The canal and the railroad found passage here, as did the old turnpike to Pittsburgh and the path of the Native Americans. The narrows took its name from Capt. Jack Armstrong, an early pioneer and Indian trader.

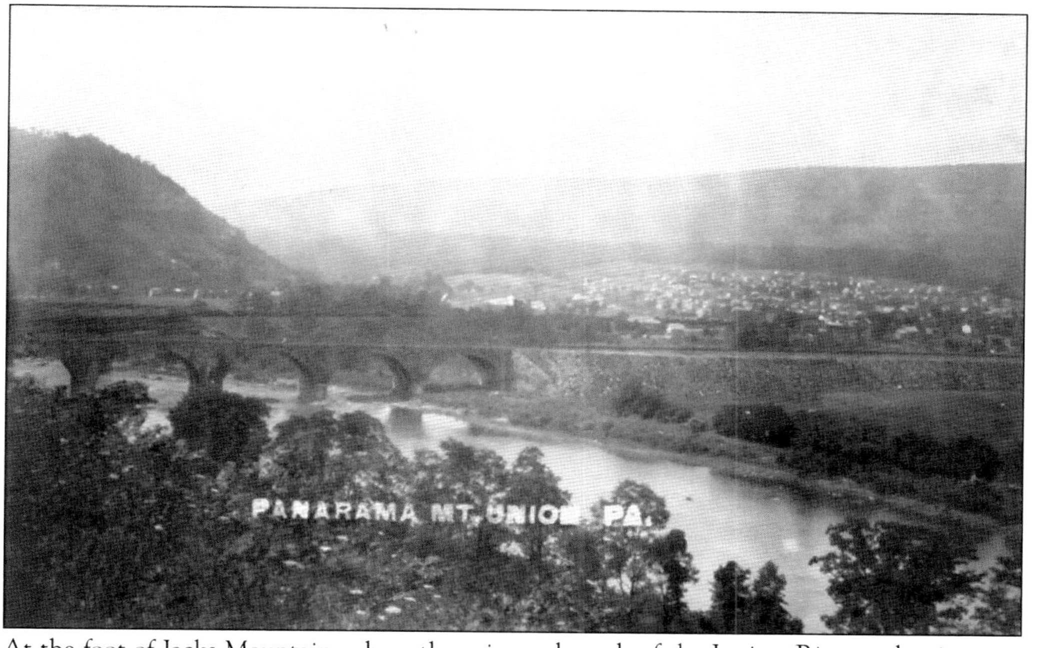

At the foot of Jacks Mountain, where the primary branch of the Juniata River makes its most southern twist, the settlement of Mount Union was laid out in 1849 by a lumbering firm. A crossing named Drake's Ferry was established here as early as 1790. Nonetheless, this geographic point where numerous mountains come together did not warrant significant settlement until rails were in place. The abundant minerals of the nearby hills were brought here for processing.

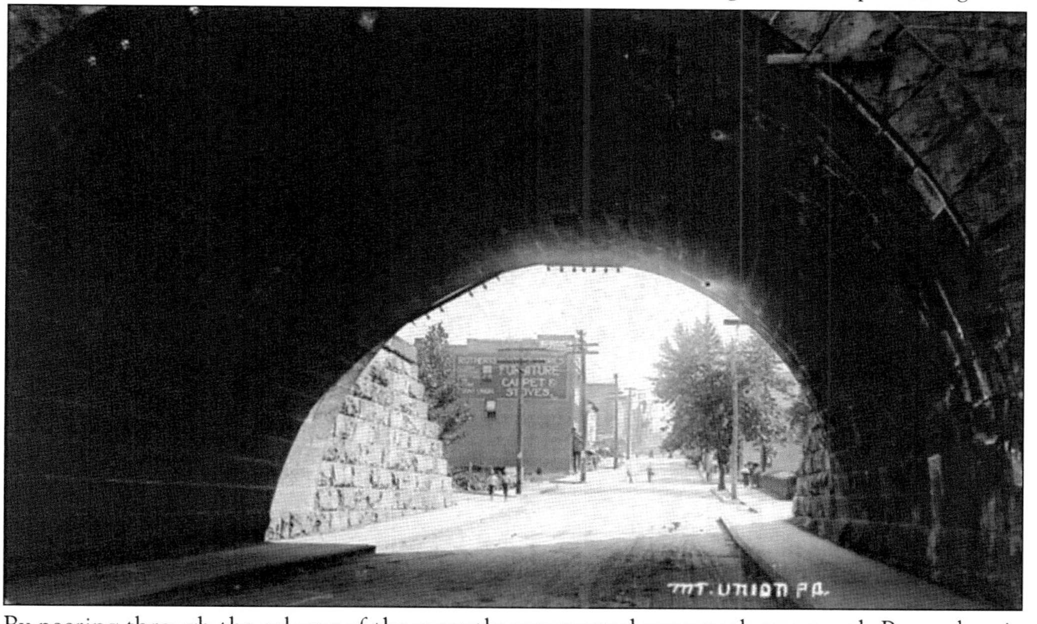

By peering through the subway of the recently constructed mammoth stone arch Pennsylvania Railroad Bridge at Mount Union, shoppers enjoying a summer's day can be seen in the distance. On the left, just past two barefoot boys, is the building occupied by Rothert's Furniture Store. The Rothert chain of six large furniture outlets was popular throughout Central Pennsylvania.

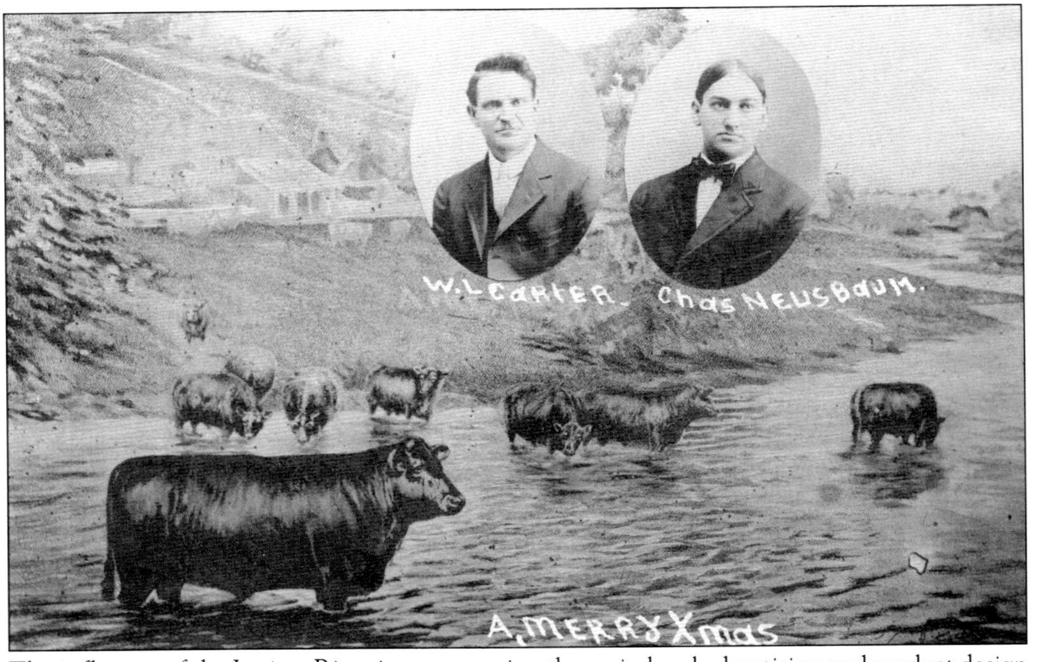

The influence of the Juniata River is a reoccurring theme in local advertising and product design in this part of Pennsylvania. Carter and Neusbaum were dealers in fresh and cured meats, eggs, butter, and chickens. Their market stocked fresh fish and oysters when in season. Located at Division Street in Mount Union, they mailed this striking card with their images in December 1907.

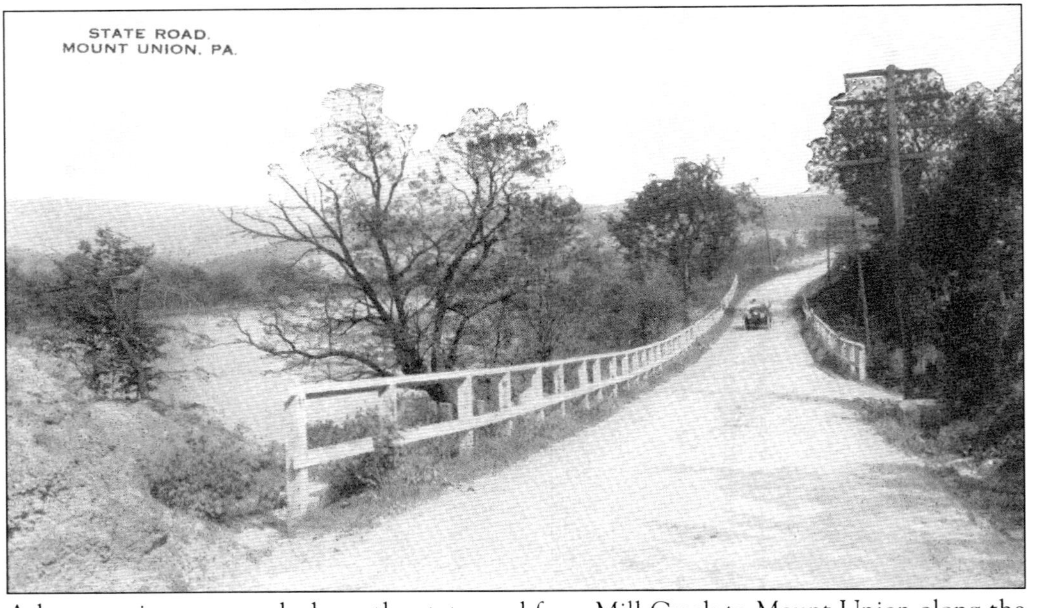

A lone touring car speeds down the state road from Mill Creek to Mount Union along the Juniata River in the 1920s. Here we see the guide rails installed where the road is well above the bank of the river. Painted white, the guide rails appear to be more for show than utility. Lines do not divide the lanes, since motor traffic had not reached a tremendous pace at the time this photograph was taken.

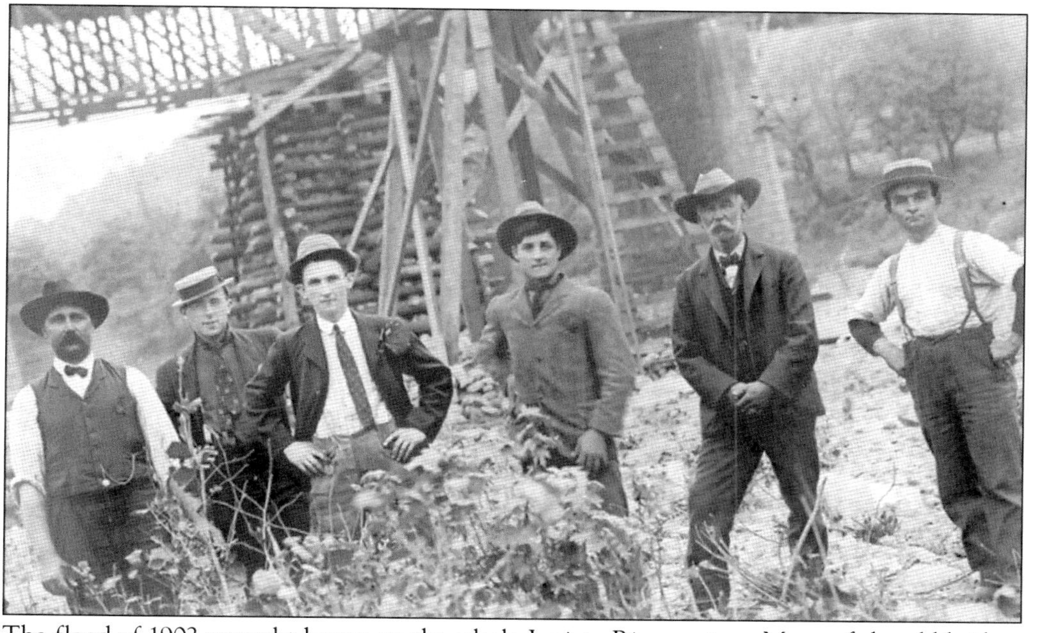

The flood of 1902 wrought havoc on the whole Juniata River system. Many of the old bridges that stood a good number of years were compromised or in need of replacing. At Mount Union, a crew of builders is shown in 1906 with their nearly completed triple span bridge. This same design was being replicated all across the central Juniata region.

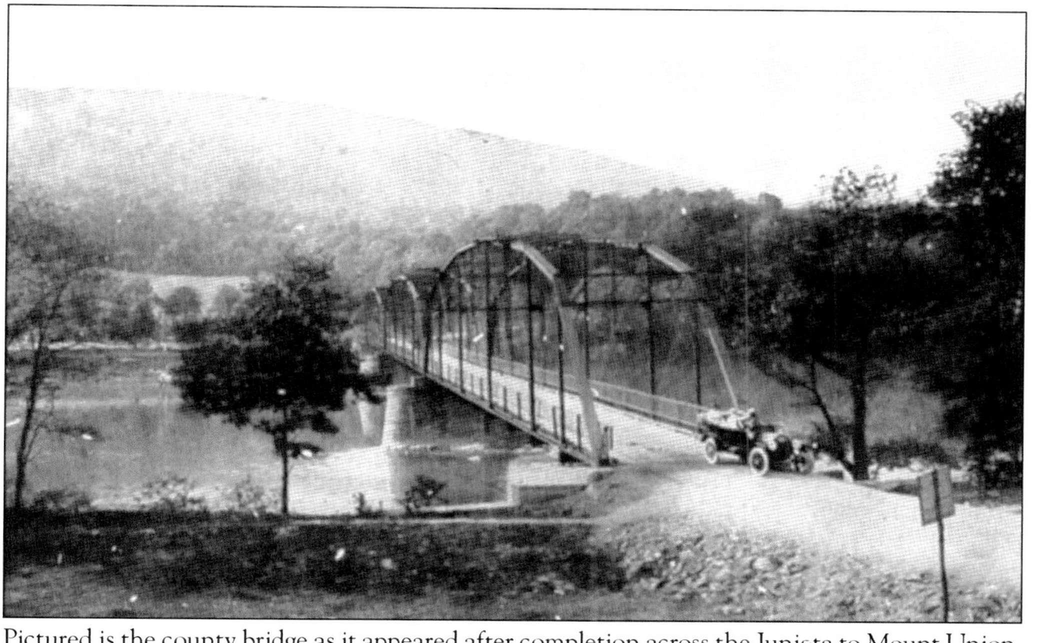

Pictured is the county bridge as it appeared after completion across the Juniata to Mount Union. The roadway meets the bridge with a crushed stone grading. Concrete was not yet the standard. At the start of the 20th century, this multiple trestle-style bridge was replacing the covered bridges and other types of decking all along the Juniata. It is interesting to note that the automobile is on the left side of the road.

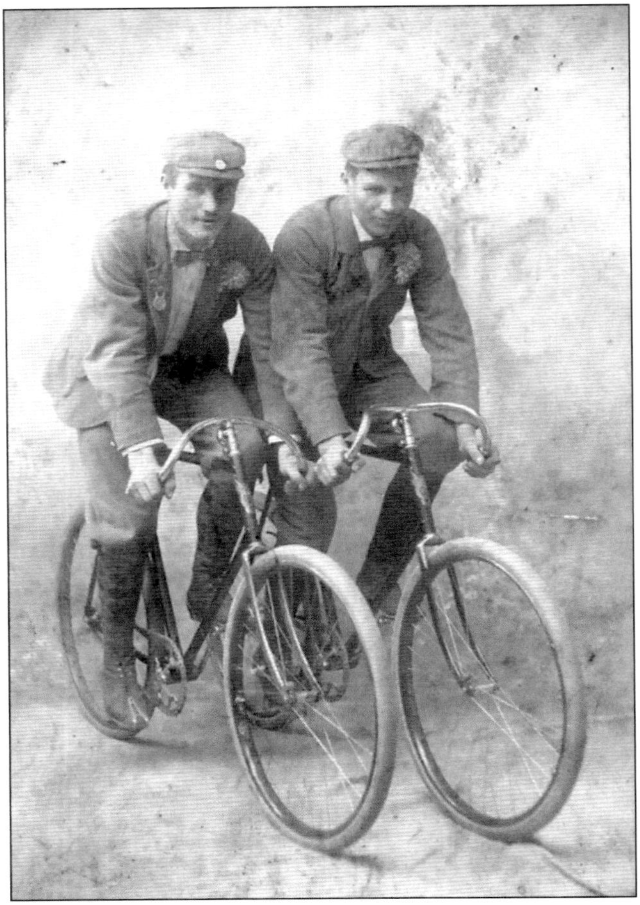

In the late 1800s, bicyclists became common on the Juniata Pike. From Tyrone to Lewistown, cyclists conducted a weekend ride, often meeting up in Huntingdon for a gathering. Their specialized gear included bicycle boots, leggings, and caps. An extra touch was a lapel pin that identified their town of origin. Photography studios encouraged cyclists to visit and often kept a bicycle on hand if the visitor came empty-handed.

A careful look at this stone outcropping reveals stonecutters laboring above Mill Creek. A board has been wedged between two boulders to support the workers as they chip at the rocks. From Mifflin to Blair County, the hills above the Juniata River are flecked with age-old fields of barren rock containing rich deposits of pure minerals.

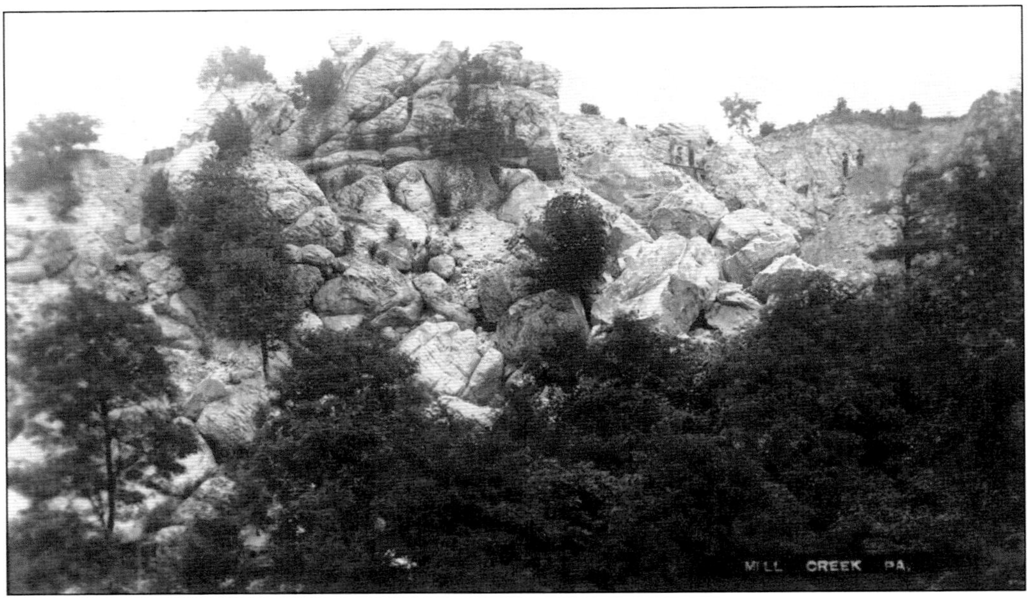

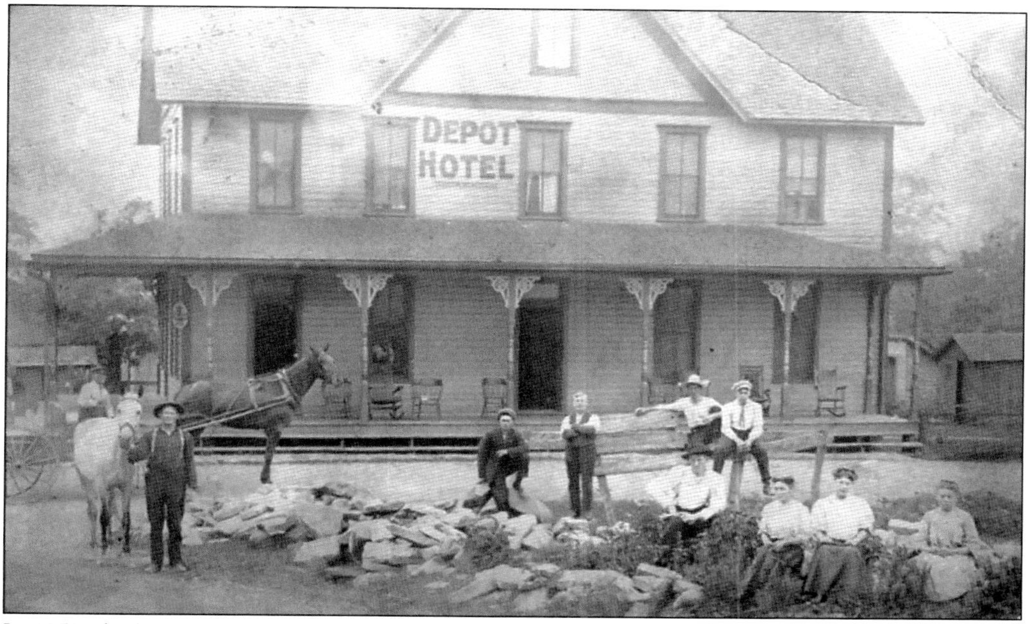

In 1852, the business of quarrying sand commenced at Mapleton. In the early years, the rock was shipped as it came from the ground. The demand for sand used in the manufacture of glass increased, and soon the sand was crushed and washed locally. Before a station was built here, the large hotel at the depot provided all services. Mapleton eventually became known as "Mapleton Depot."

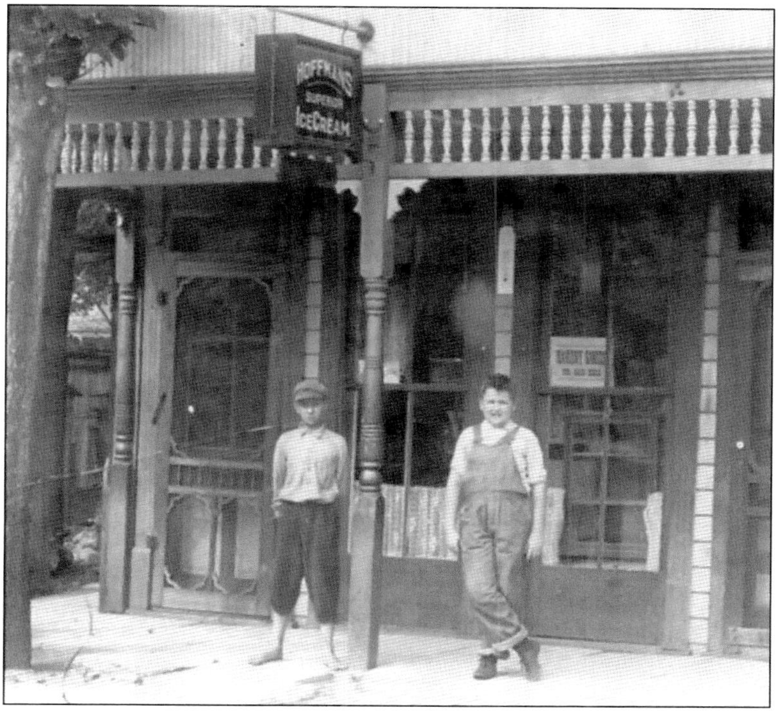

At one time, ice cream was a delight at church socials and summer picnics. Made at home, it was a labor of love. The Hoffman Company of Tyrone found a way to mechanize the process with electric freezer churns and realized a tremendous output. Soon, Mr. Hoffman was delivering baked goods and ice cream to four counties. Shown here is a shop in Mapleton. Paul Henderson (left) and Newt Parker pose for the camera.

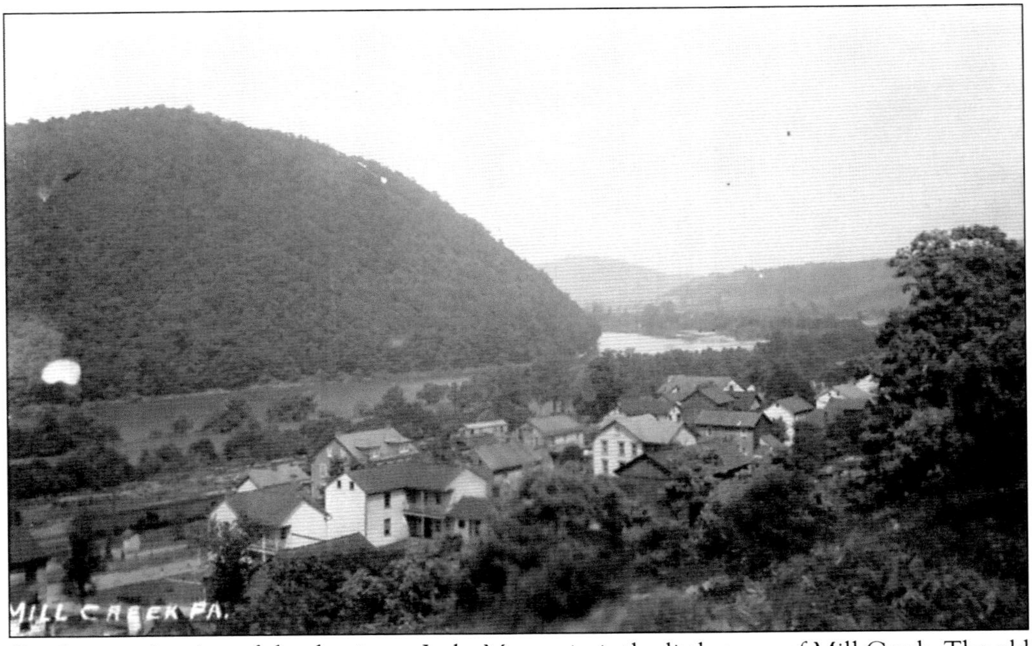

On the river in view of the dominant Jacks Mountain is the little town of Mill Creek. The old Juniata Road crossed through here on Main Street. This hamlet straddles a stream, known also as Mill Creek, where it empties into the Juniata River. Many photographs and wood-cut drawings were done in the Victorian era looking down the Juniata from this location. Founded in 1848, Millcreek found itself in a flurry of activity when the sandy soil yielded the discovery of a form of silica quartzite that has been celebrated in the industry as the purest available. Five sand plants were soon in operation under various names. The telescope lens at the famed Palomar Observatory in California is composed of Juniata quartzite from this location.

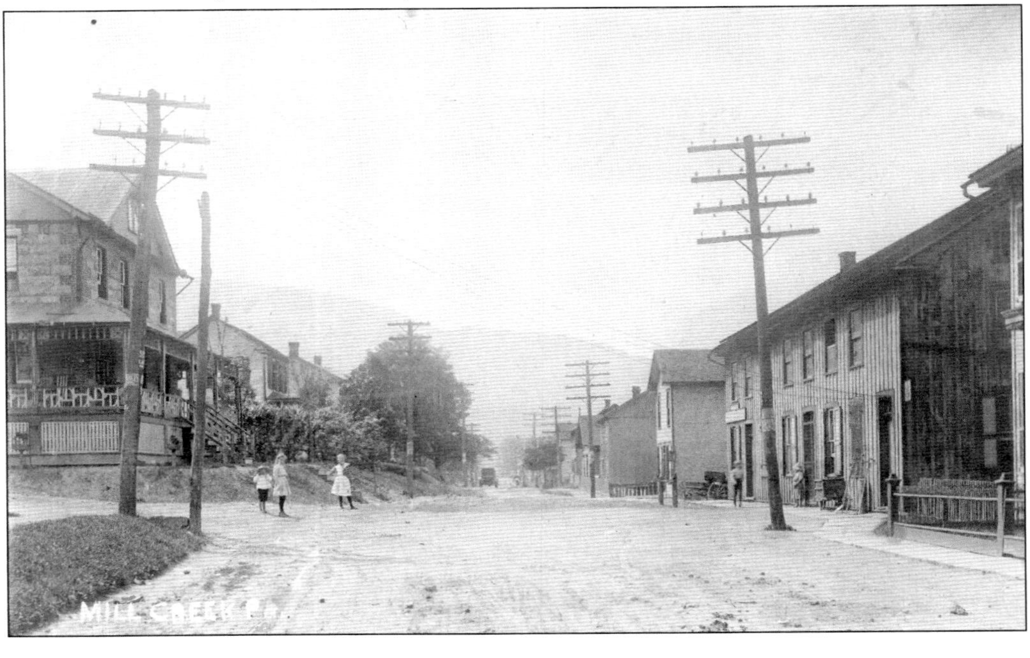

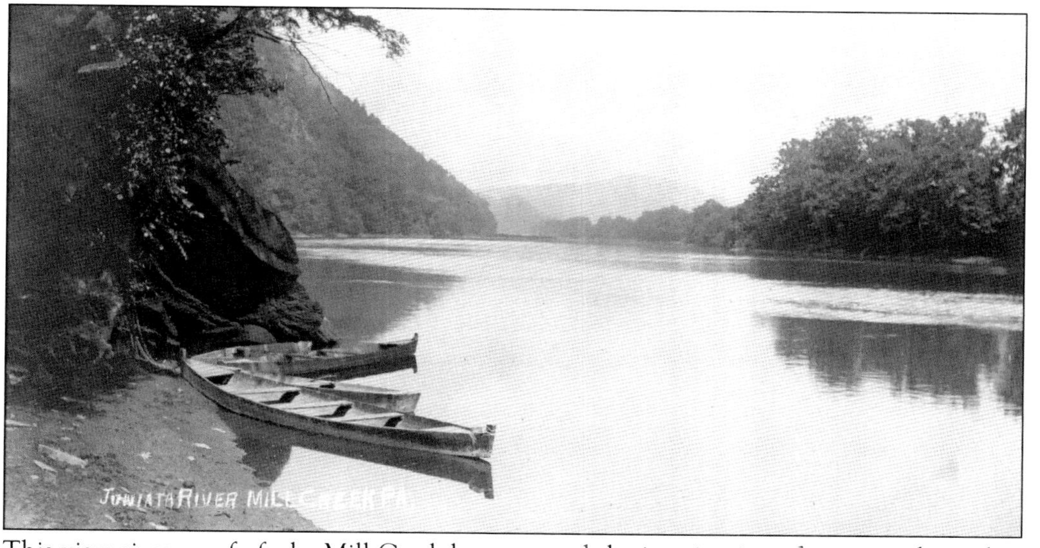

This view gives proof of why Mill Creek has captured the imagination of artists and travelers since the valley was first settled. At this point, the river turns and travels south to Mapleton. This area is popular for fishing. In the springtime the smell of honeysuckle is very pronounced. In the distance, Jacks Mountain is seen.

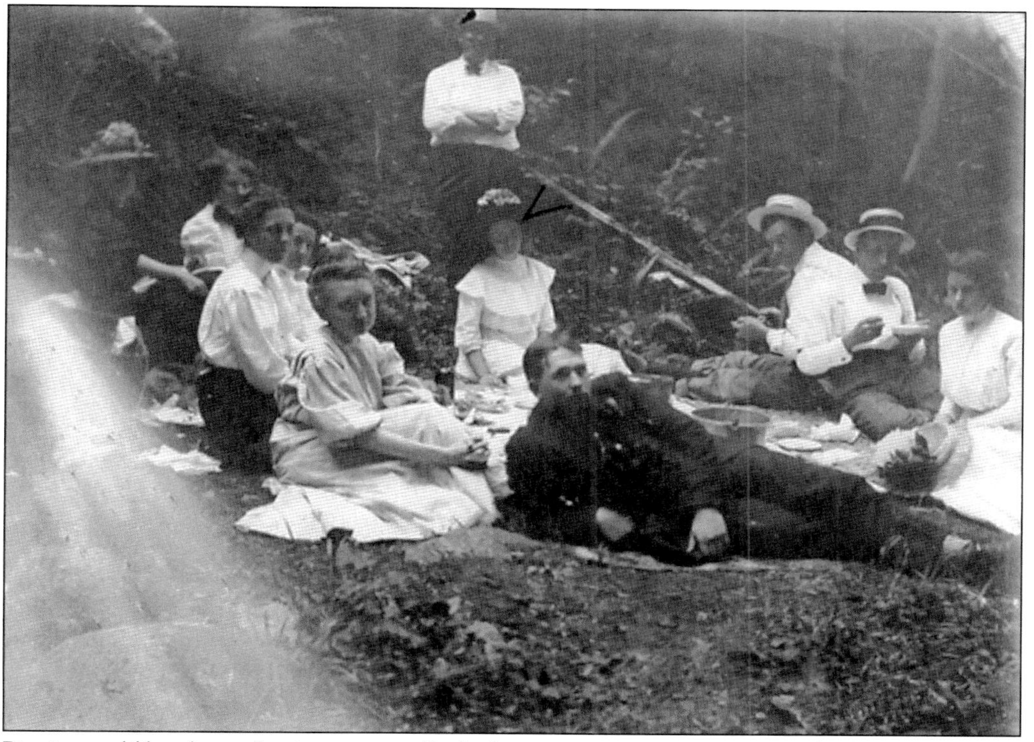

Picnics could be planned or impromptu. Packed onto a carriage or wagon were baskets of cold fried chicken and pickled vegetables. At one time, people were content to bring along a blanket and place it directly on the ground. In later years, picnic tables appeared at spots along the Juniata as a courtesy to travelers. There were plenty of pleasant meadows for spending a lazy afternoon.

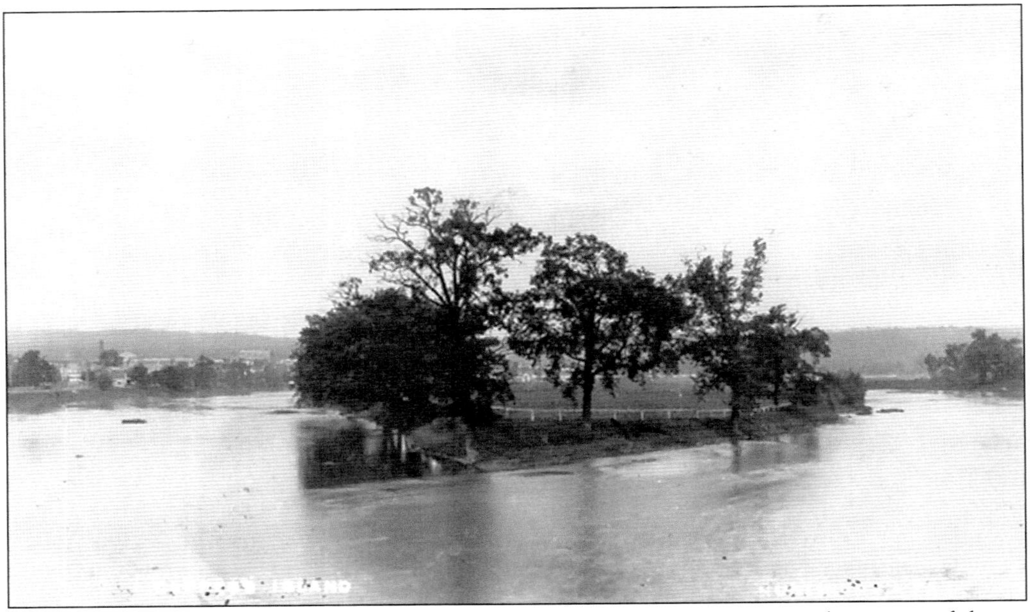

An island occupies the center of the river at Huntingdon Borough, from just above Penn Street at the south to Eighteenth Street at the north end. In the past, Cypress Island has been used for recreational activities and as a pasture for grazing animals, and was said to have been a favored summer resting site for Native Americans on their treks along the valley.

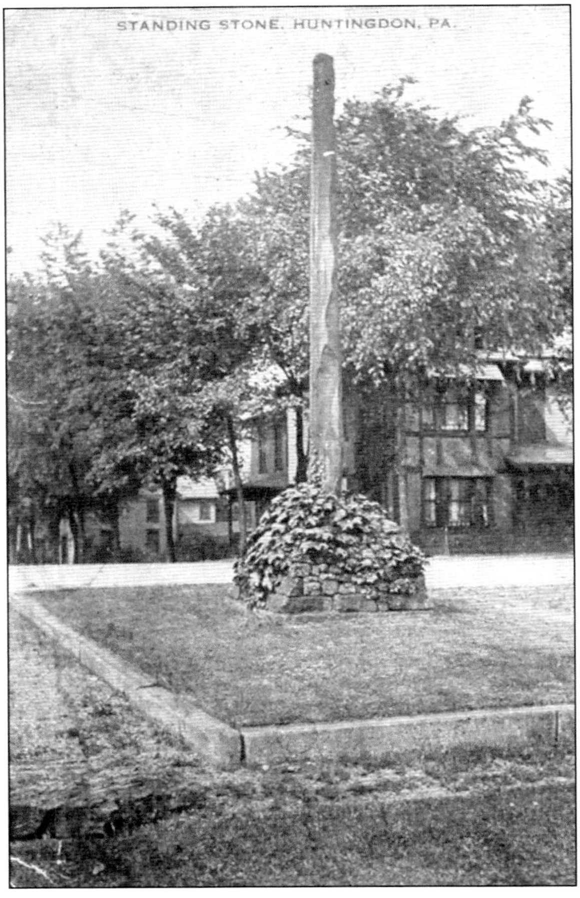

During Huntingdon Borough's centennial celebration in 1896, this monolith was erected as a reminder of the town's ancient origins. The Onohutta-Haga Indians are the earliest known inhabitants of the Juniata Valley. Where Standing Stone Creek enters the Juniata River, a village was home to these mysterious people. The original stone they erected disappeared around the time they ceased to occupy the valley. The name "Onohutta" eventually transformed to the poetic name "Juniata."

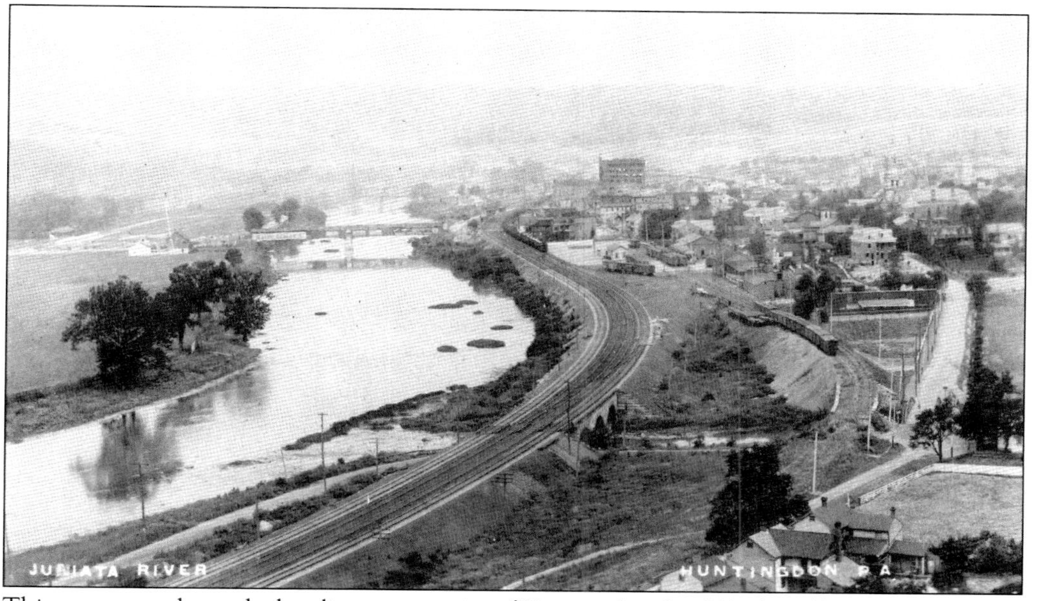

This panorama shows the bustling community of Huntingdon. In 1787, the village of Huntingdon was made the seat of a newly formed county of the same name. This outpost became an important stop on the early turnpike and later the Pennsylvania Canal. Pictured in the center of the photograph is the J.C. Blair Paper Company. The old canal lies abandoned between the new main line of the Pennsylvania Railroad and local service lines.

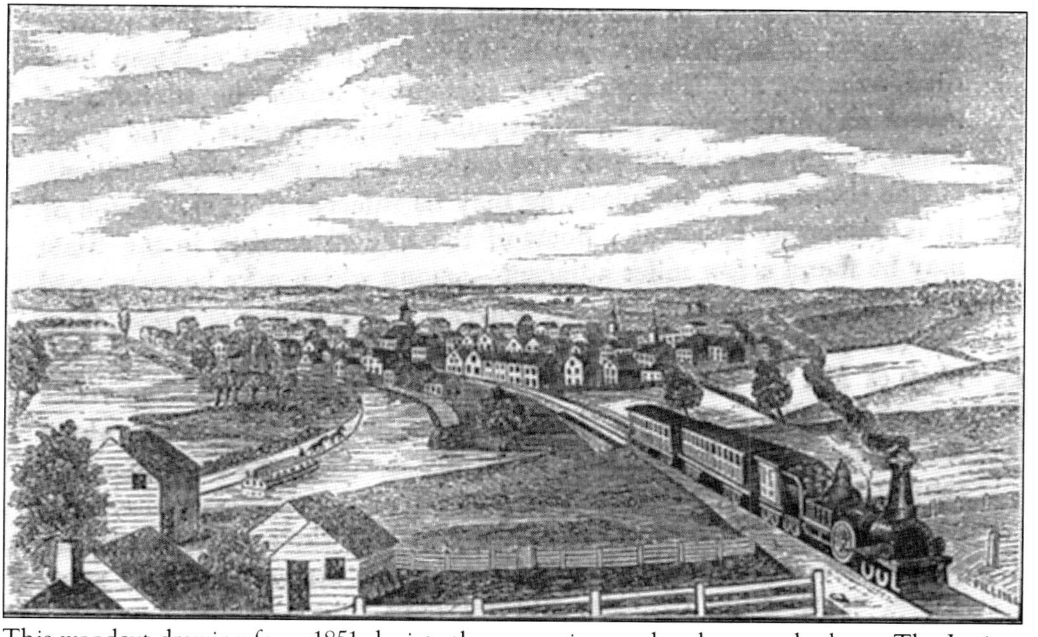

This woodcut drawing from 1851 depicts the same view as the photograph above. The Juniata River, the canal, and the railroad all exist in harmony. The covered bridge at Fourth Street has not yet been built. Once completed in 1857, it stood 73 years until being destroyed by fire in 1930. Huntingdon is the county seat to Pennsylvania's most diverse region with its coal mines, iron furnaces, meadows, and craggy peaks.

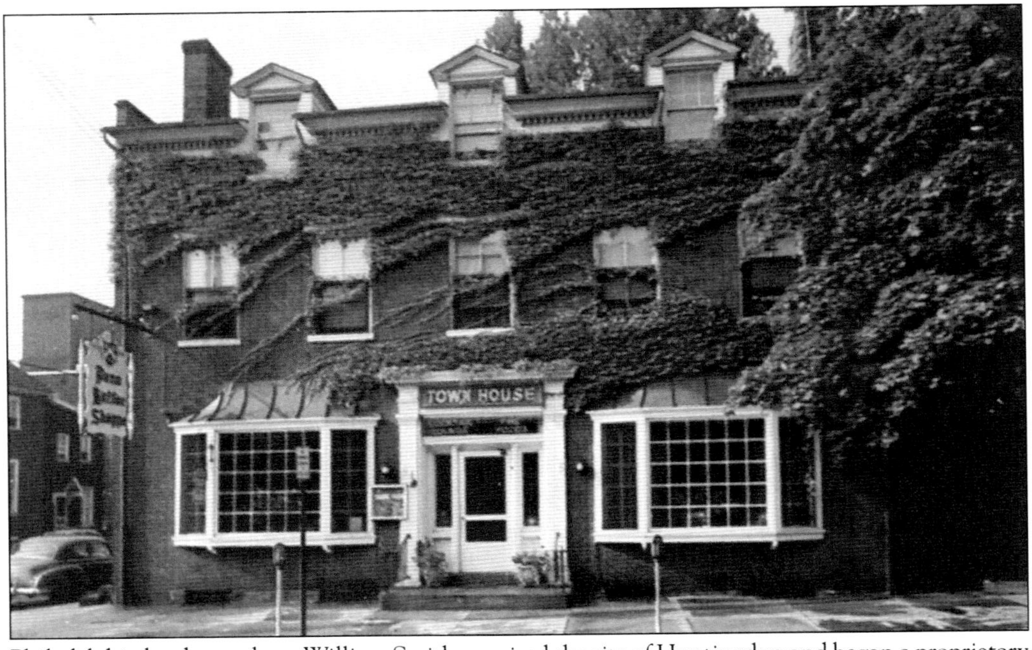

Philadelphia land speculator William Smith acquired the site of Huntingdon and began a proprietary town. Two early trader paths followed the Juniata River's east-west course and the Raystown Branch's north-south pathway. The turnpike brought travelers through the town and for more than 180 years the highway passed by early 1800s homes. This residence at 500 Penn Street was converted to a popular business. In 1948, the highway bypassed Huntingdon Borough to the south.

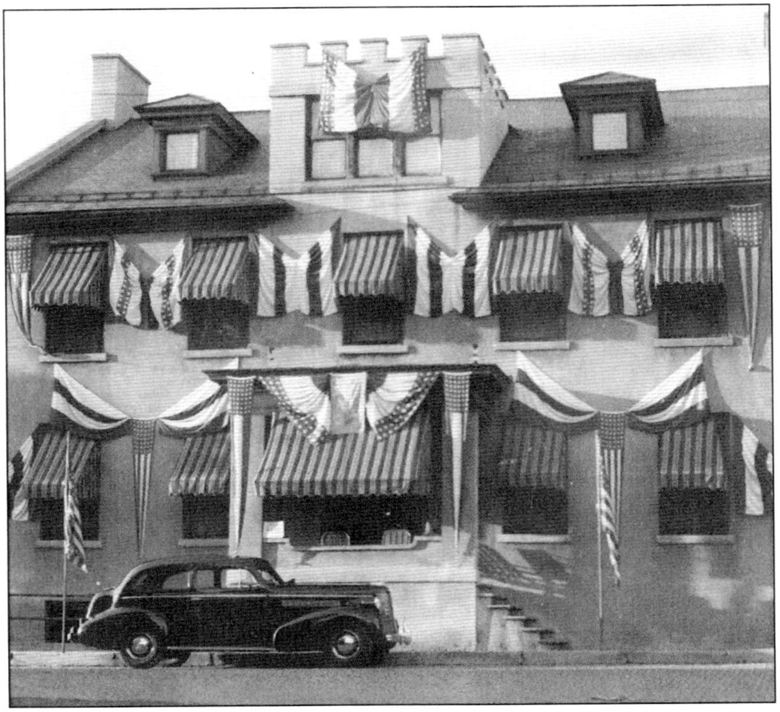

Buildings survived in Huntingdon by converting from homes to other uses. This impressive structure at 241 Mifflin Street is decorated for a holiday around 1940. The five-bay home's center dormer was castellated in the Victorian style. During a subsequent renovation, the stucco was removed to reveal the true, natural, cut stone exterior. Many cut stone houses are found throughout Huntingdon and Bedford Counties.

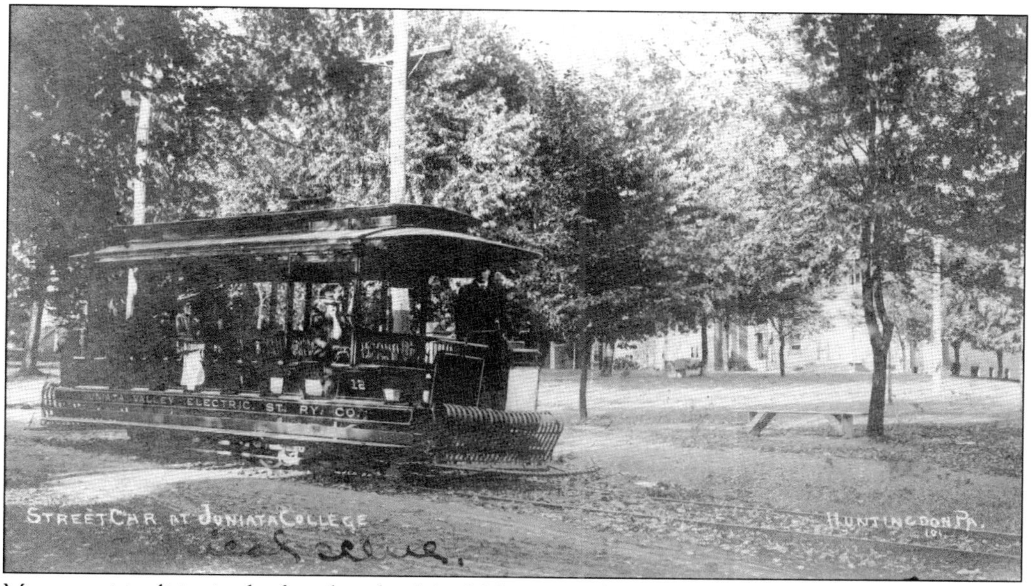

Most municipalities in the first decade of the 20th century had invested in street railway companies. As they became established and profitable, many were joined with other towns to form an interurban transportation company. The Juniata Valley Electric Street Railway Company operated in Huntingdon around 1906. This photograph shows a summer car, which is an open air coach, as it crosses the Juniata College campus.

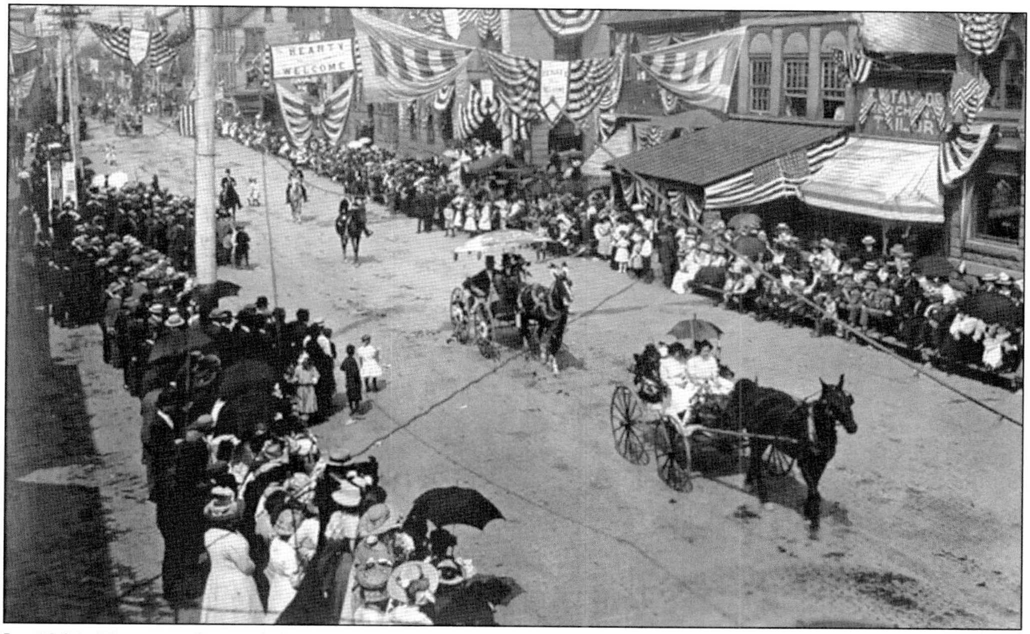

In 1909, Huntingdon celebrated its own version of Old Home Week. With a "hearty welcome," the organizers of a series of parades and civic events greeted former citizens who returned for a hometown reunion. Labor and industry was a major theme in this celebration, with a parade of floats exhibiting the accomplishments and products of local manufactures. The gathering shown here enjoys the flower parade.

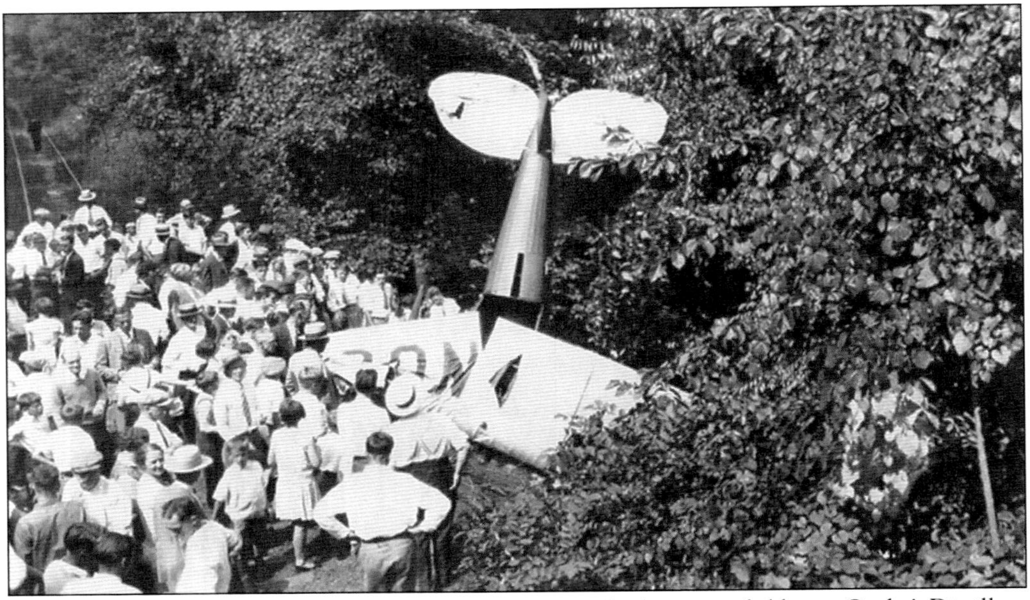

Huntingdon played a role in early aviation. Airstrips were laid out on a field near Grube's Distillery on South Fourth Street. Cross-country flights counted on this strip for landing. People across the county showed up just to watch planes land and take off. Early local flight enthusiasts included Sam Vuille and Mart Heine. Heine survived a crash outside of Huntingdon in 1929. This mishap drew a large crowd of spectators.

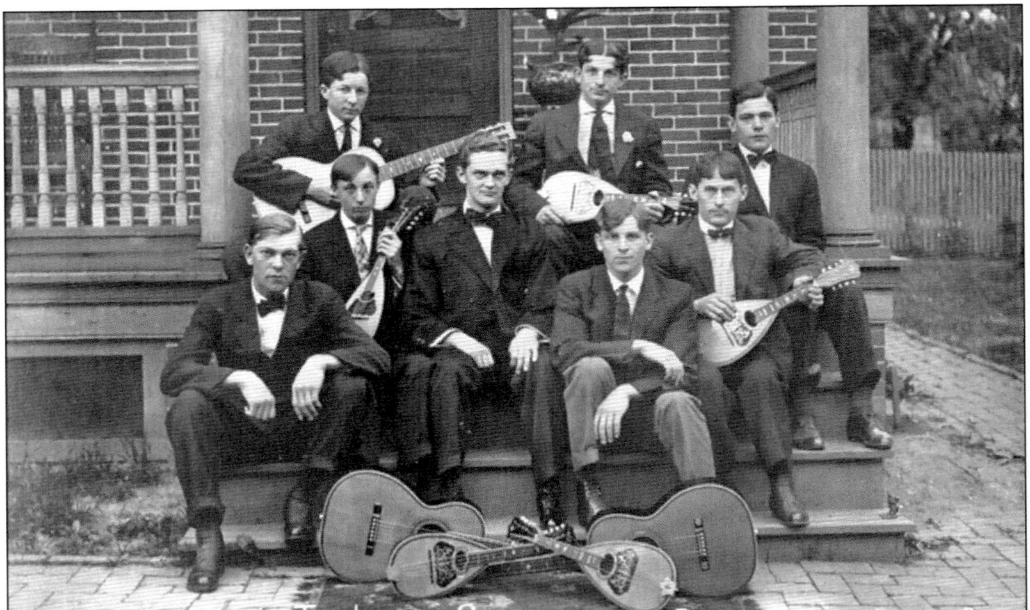

Making popular appearances on campus and downtown, the Lemona Club played simple, popular tunes and light pieces in the refined European tradition. However, it is said that they could wow a crowd by slipping in a little ragtime or early jazz. This new style of string ensemble that combined the guitar with the mandolin was always guaranteed to draw an audience before World War I.

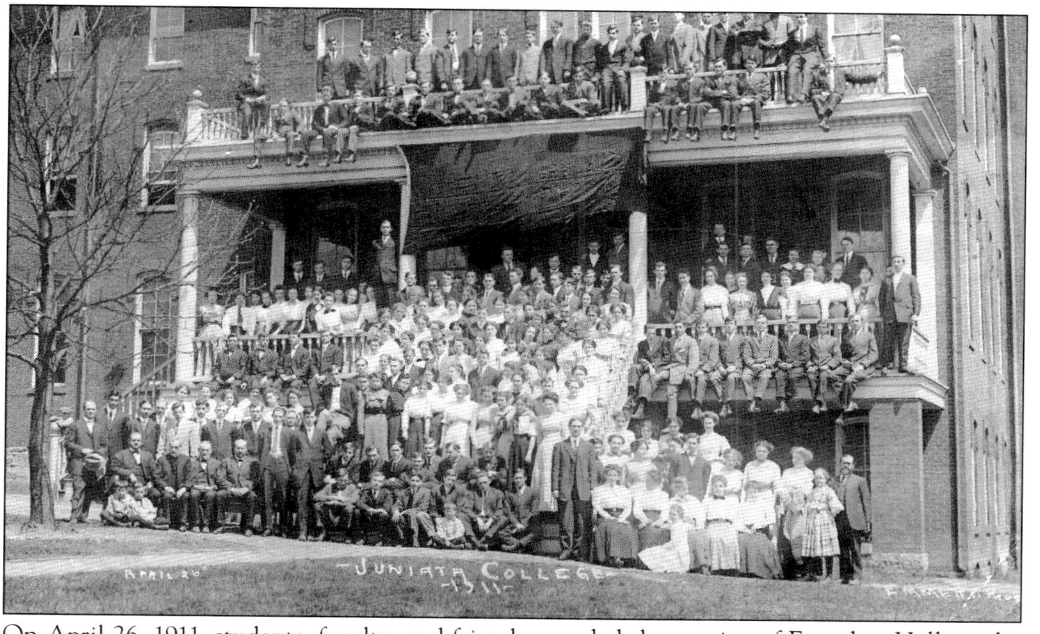

On April 26, 1911, students, faculty, and friends crowded the portico of Founders Hall on the campus of Juniata College to honor the graduates of 1911. Founded in 1876 as Huntingdon Normal School, the name was changed in 1893 to honor the nearby river. This liberal arts institution has been an integral part of the local community and takes advantage of its place in nature. Founders Hall was the first building constructed on the Juniata campus.

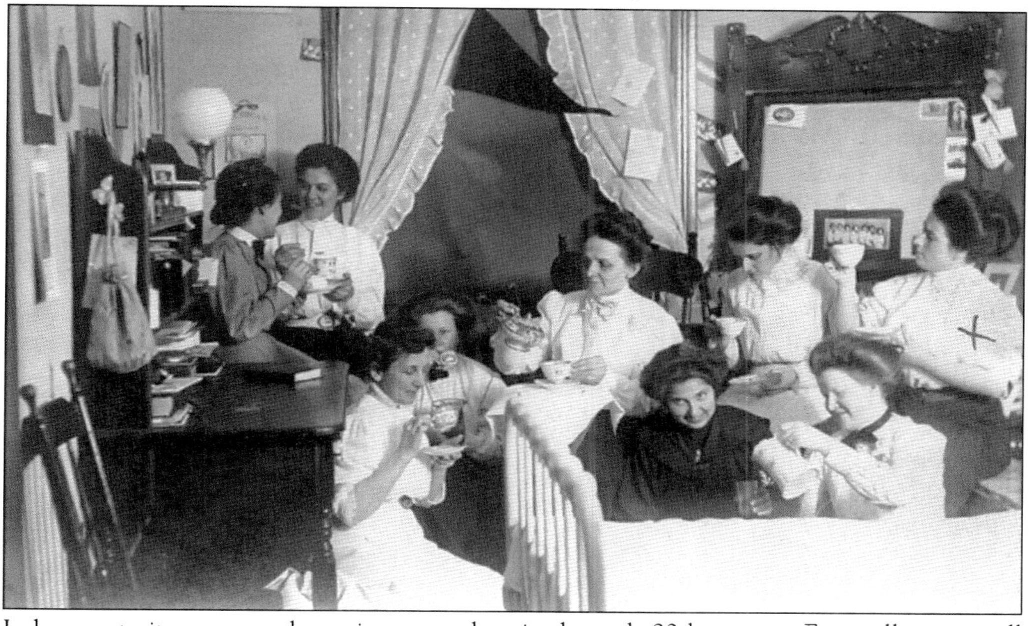

Indoor portraits were not the easiest to produce in the early 20th century. Especially in a small room filled with people. These young ladies in a dorm room accomplished a splendid rare moment when they decided to have tea before going out to a show. An earlier studio portrait of the same ladies can be seen on the bureau to the right.

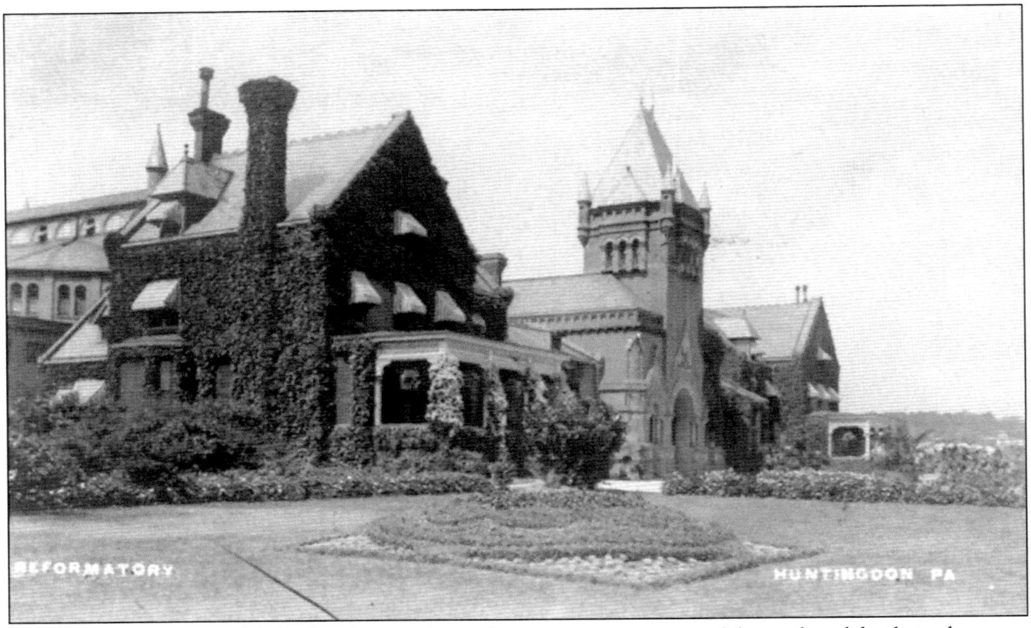

With new reforms established in Pennsylvania's prison system, a need for updated facilities became apparent. In 1889, the State Industrial Reformatory was built at Huntingdon. Prisoners had the opportunity to contribute to society through productive employment while incarcerated. The institution included a 663-acre farm and a forestry camp along with shops for shoe repair and the manufacture of items that were to be sent to market. The prisoners received a nominal wage for their services.

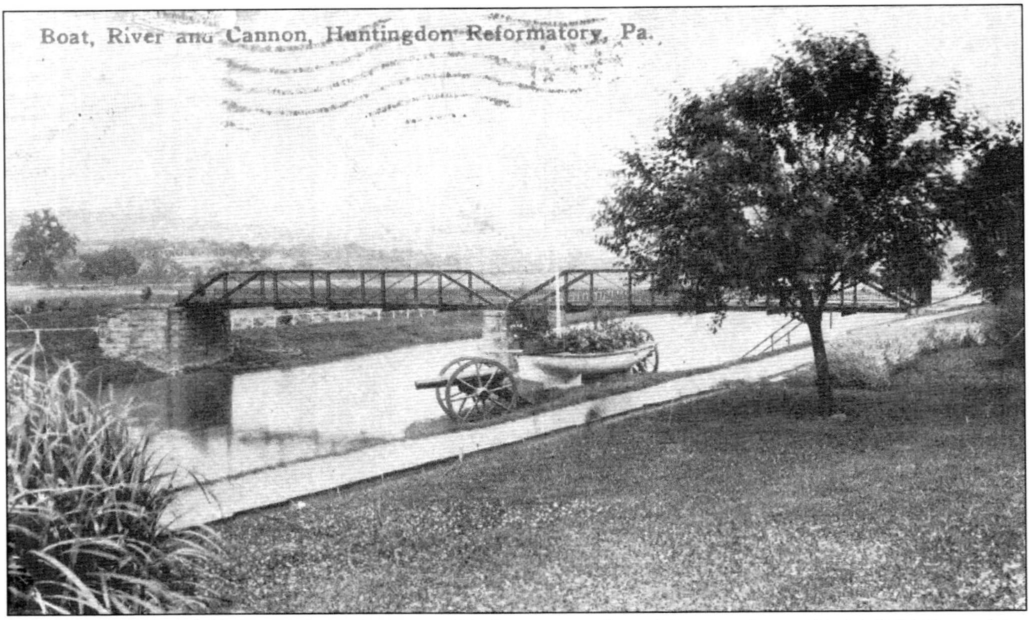

A river walk passed along the State Industrial Reformatory above Huntingdon at Smithfield Township. Bridge Street crossed over to Cypress Island from the Alexandria Pike; it is the island's only link to the mainland. Civil War–era cannons flank a retired boat that is brimming with perennials..

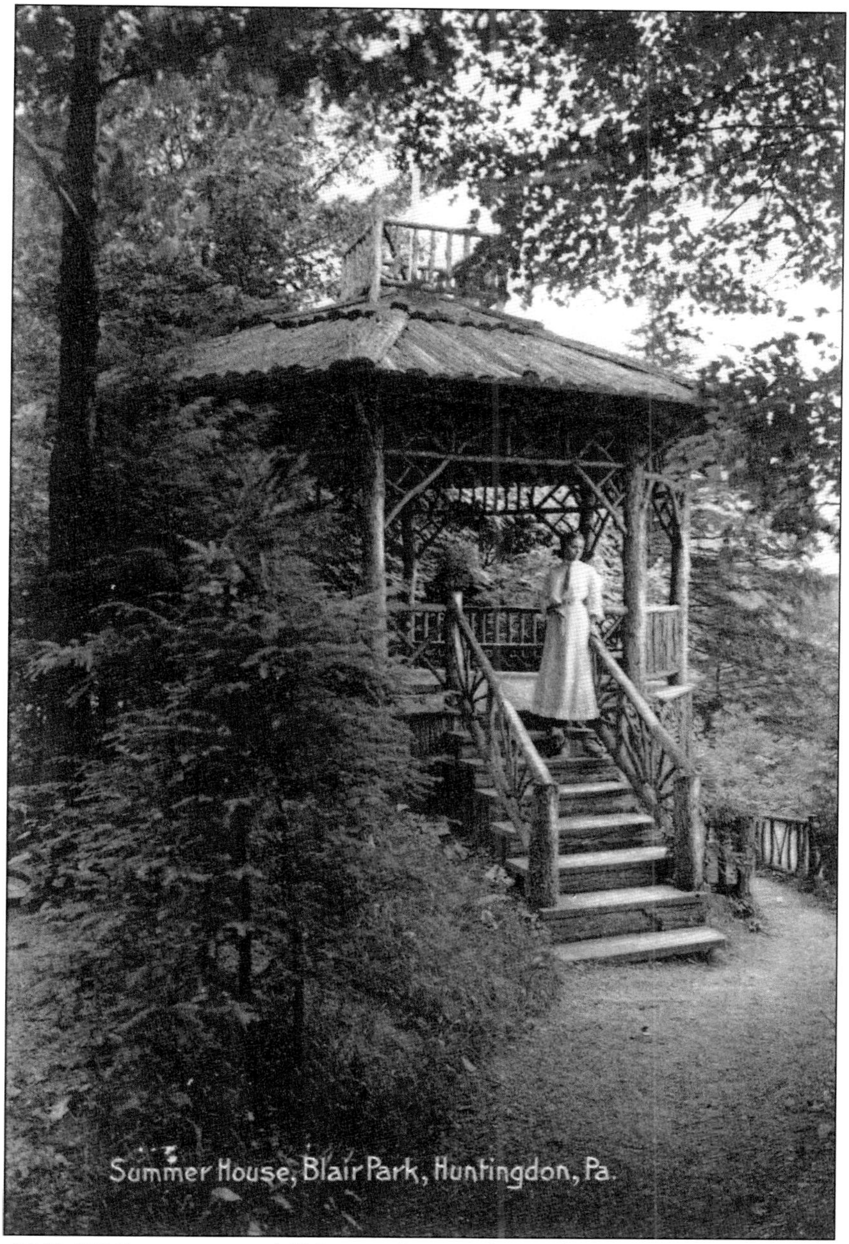

J.C. Blair (1847–1896) was a successful Huntingdon merchant who revolutionized the business world with his introduction of the paper writing tablet. The idea came to him when he was assigning verses for his Sunday school class to memorize. Sheets of paper bound together and attached at the top seemed better to him than the loose paper that was the only choice. With this in mind, he founded Huntingdon's largest industry under his name. Starting out in an unused church building, Blair eventually built one of the tallest buildings in Pennsylvania as the business grew. To encourage employees to enjoy their leisure time, Blair laid out Blair Park along Standing Stone Creek. In the park were natural walkways and bridges. After his untimely death, his widow, Kate Fisher Blair, became a benefactor by having a hospital built for the community.

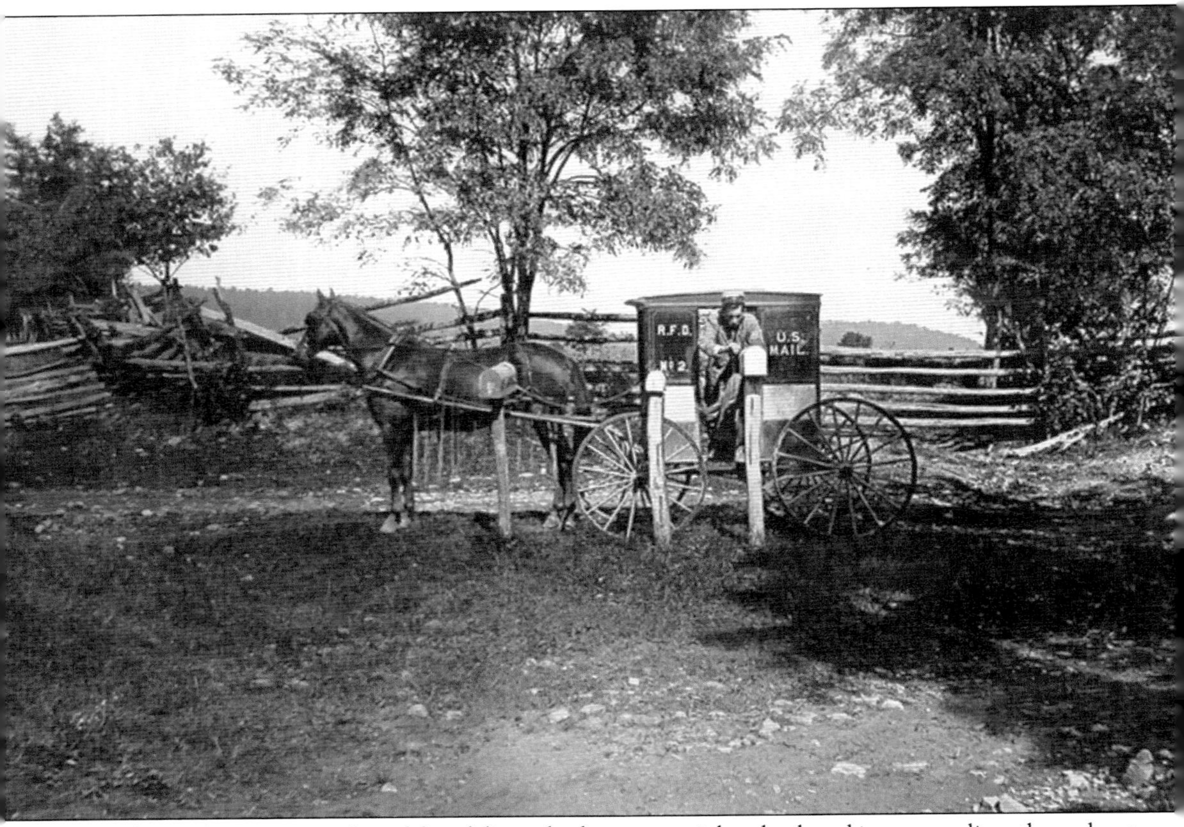

The implementation of rural free delivery had a great social and cultural impact on lives throughout the region. With mail and newspapers brought directly to the house, farmers saved much time by not having to go to town as often. They also felt less isolated from the community. Beginning around 1897, the need for the postal service to travel quickly and safely fueled the demand for road improvement in rural areas.

Five

THE RAYSTOWN BRANCH

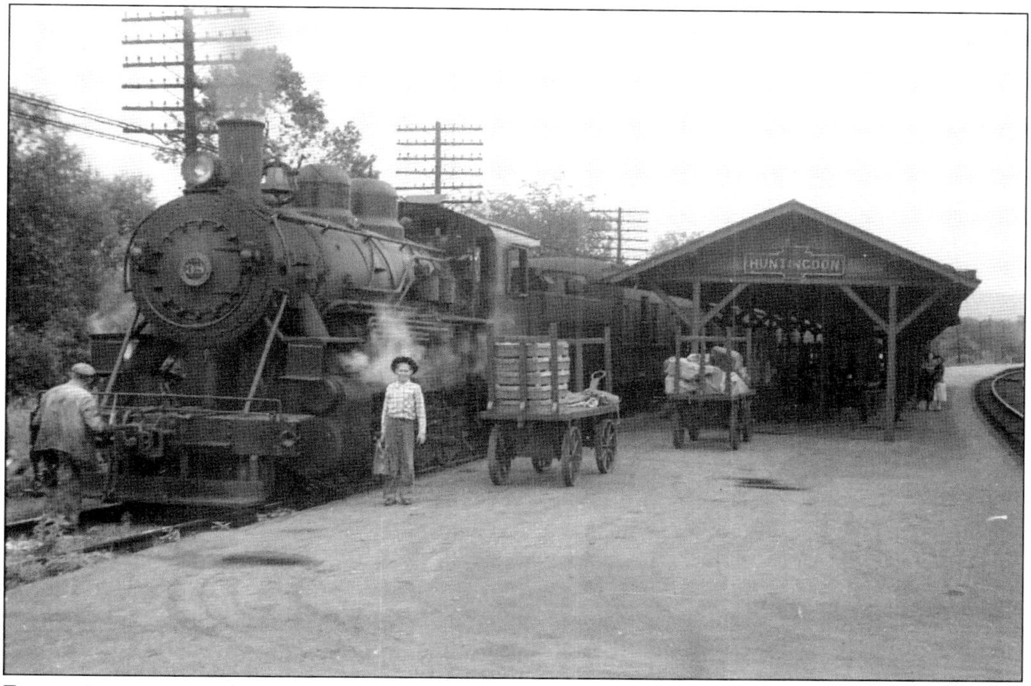

Engine No. 38 is tended at Huntingdon Station after completing a run on the Huntingdon and Broad Top Mountain Railroad (H&BTM). This line from Saxton to Huntingdon was organized in 1853 with the purpose of providing a rail link from Huntingdon to Bedford. This coal route also carried passengers and freight. The H&BTM ceased operation in 1954. The No. 38 is the only surviving locomotive. It was built by Baldwin Locomotive Works in 1928.

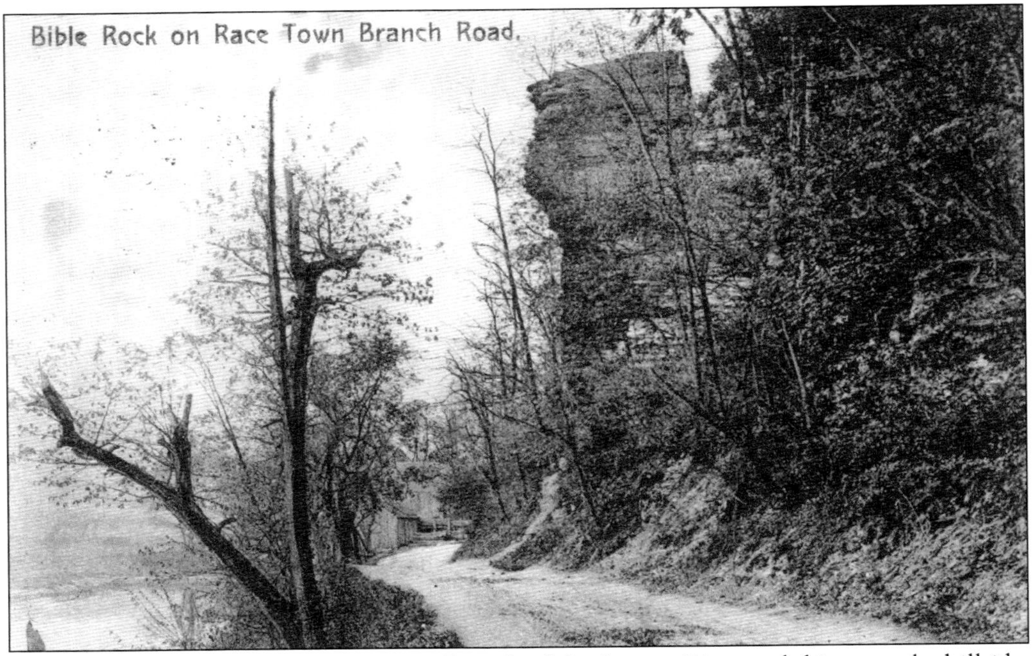

An old road snakes along the Raystown Branch of the Juniata River and skirts a rocky hillside. Born along the Allegheny Front in Bedford County, the Raystown Branch is the longest tributary of the Juniata River and flows at an irregular pattern throughout Bedford and Huntingdon Counties. Quirky rock formations, such as Bible Rock, are found while traveling this region. This is how the road appeared in 1908.

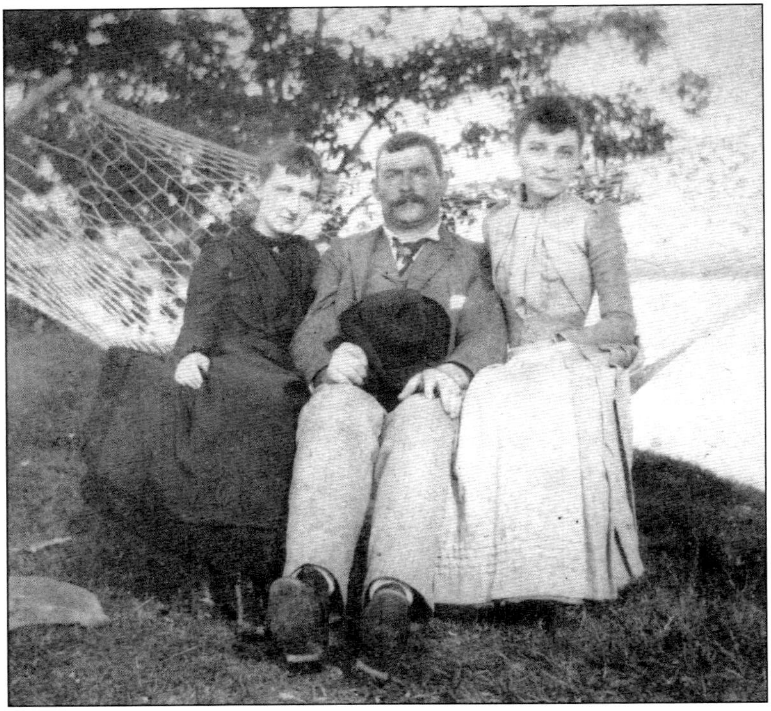

Throughout the Juniata region, much of the river system is cut off from the personal property of the general public. Culverts and roads compete with the railroad for riverside access. Farmland and parks share the shore. The Juniata can be taken for granted as people go about their business. However, there are some lucky individuals who find fate kind. This photograph taken in July 1891 shows a family relaxing in its backyard on the Raystown Branch.

Usually only seen from a distance, few travelers of the lower Juniata Valley got a chance to view this curiosity up close. There were 449 known fire watchtowers constructed on the hills of Pennsylvania between the 1880s and 1950. This Tuscarora Mountain tower, put in place in 1921 in Fulton County, stood guard over the Juniata watershed until its removal in 1978.

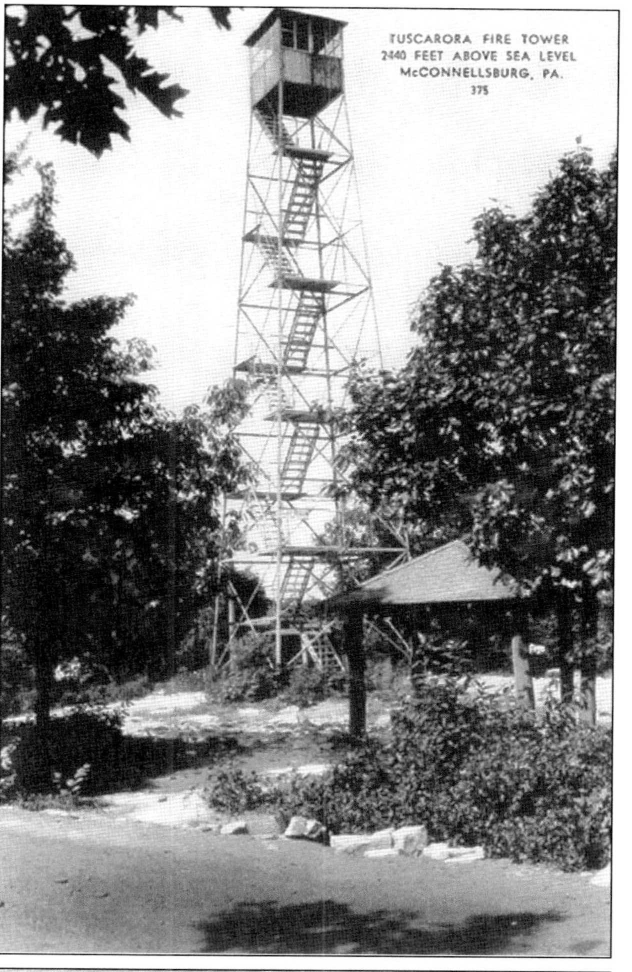

With a Sunday free of chores, a group of relief workers hitched a ride in the 1930s. Their destination was Raystown. Pennsylvania was high on the list of states that took advantage of the Works Progress Administration and Civilian Conservation Corps programs that put those unemployed to work and taught new skills to the workforce during the Great Depression. This resulted in better roads as well as improved parks and recreational facilities.

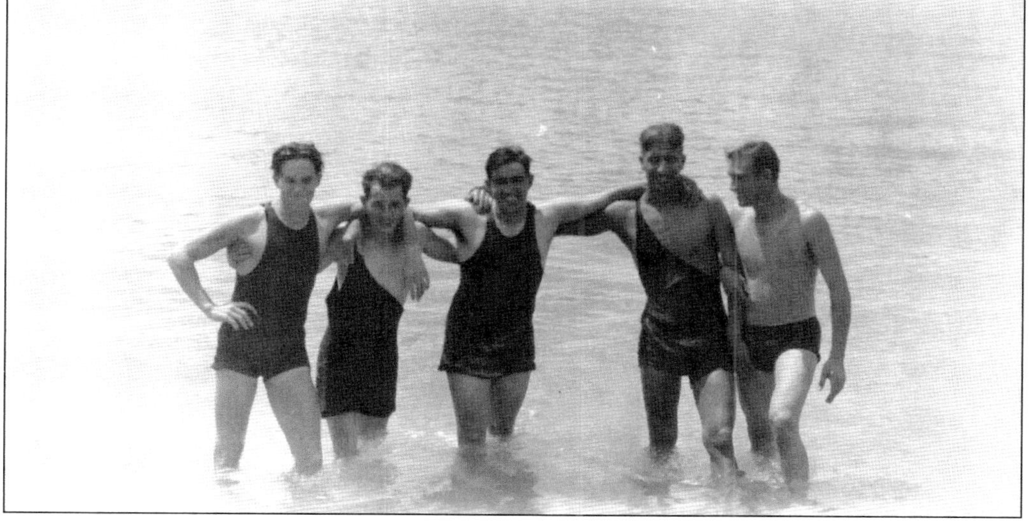

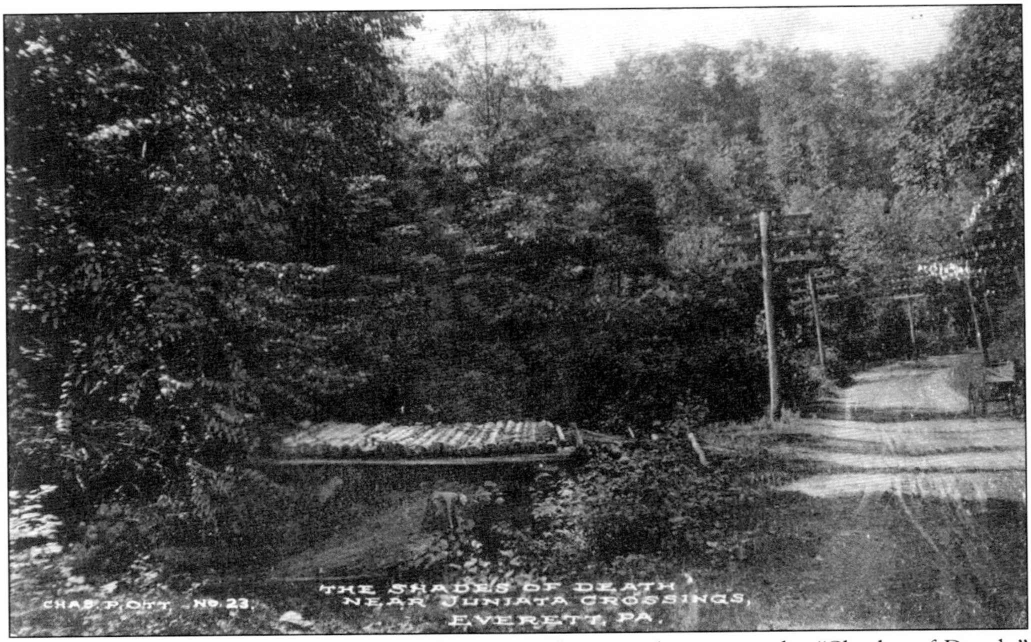

A corduroy bridge crosses the Juniata River at a location known as the "Shades of Death." Constructed with logs fastened in place, the bridge dismantles with ease when it is no longer of use. The drawback is a bumpy ride. Under the bridge, a fisherman collects crawfish to be used as bait. At the Shades of Death, the dappled sunlight throws eerie shadows on the roadway as dusk nears.

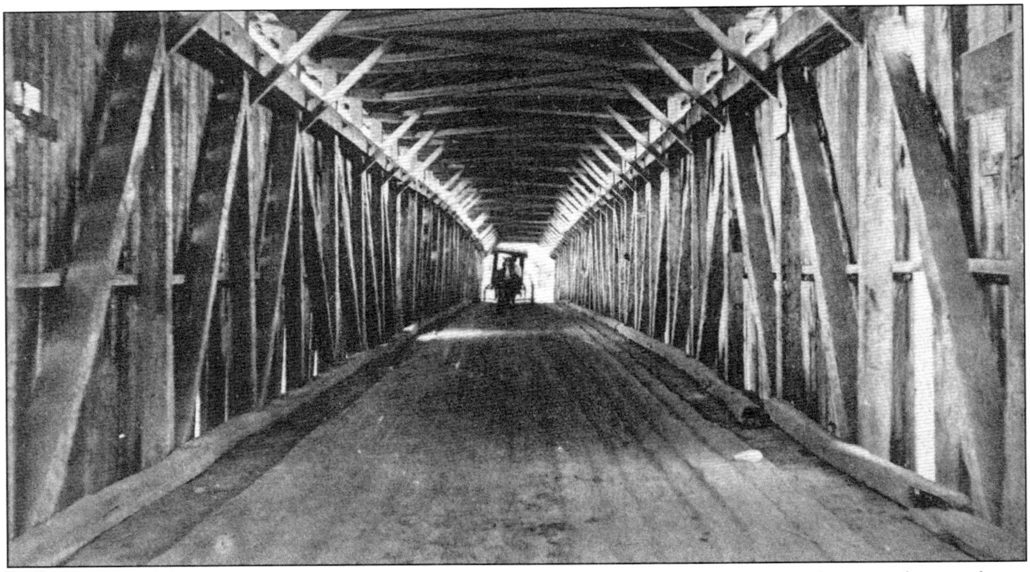

There was a time when the Keystone State had more than 1,500 covered bridges. Today, perhaps 200 still exist. It is the practical design of these picturesque structures that have permitted their survival. By protecting the timbers from the elements, a wooden bride that might have survived 20 years can outlast a century. A seldom seen interior view of the Everett Bridge shows an approaching single horse and carriage.

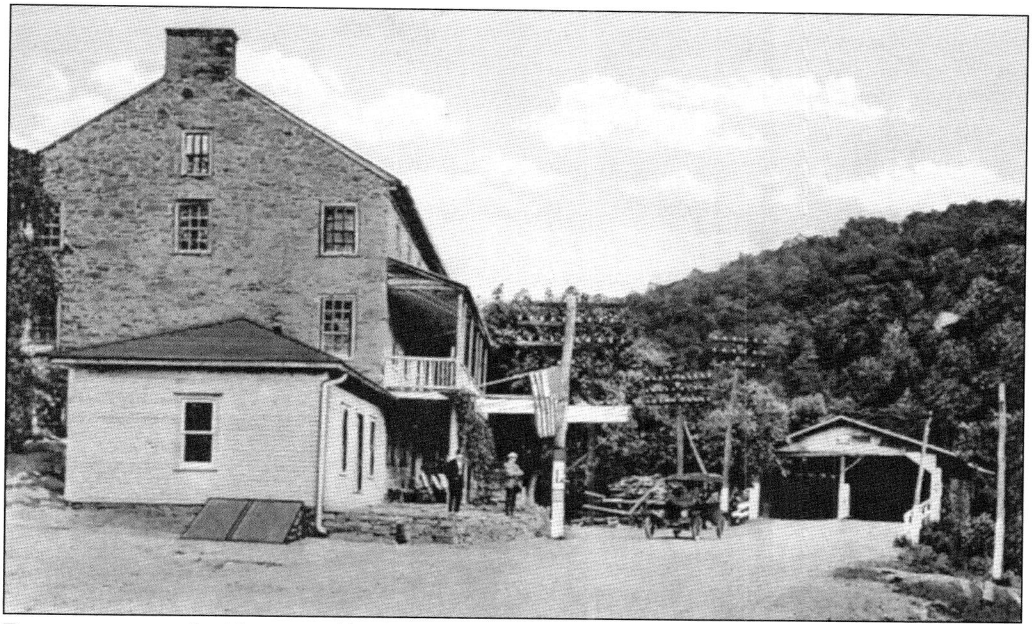

For many years, a double covered bridge crossed the river at Juniata Crossing. The old Forbes Road, one of the first long-distance roadways in the country, used this route. Forbes Road connected eastern settlements with the Ohio Country during the French and Indian War of the 1750s. In 1913, the Lincoln Highway, later US Route 30, assumed this route. Note the "L" for Lincoln on the telephone pole. This old inn, pictured around 1818, still stands today.

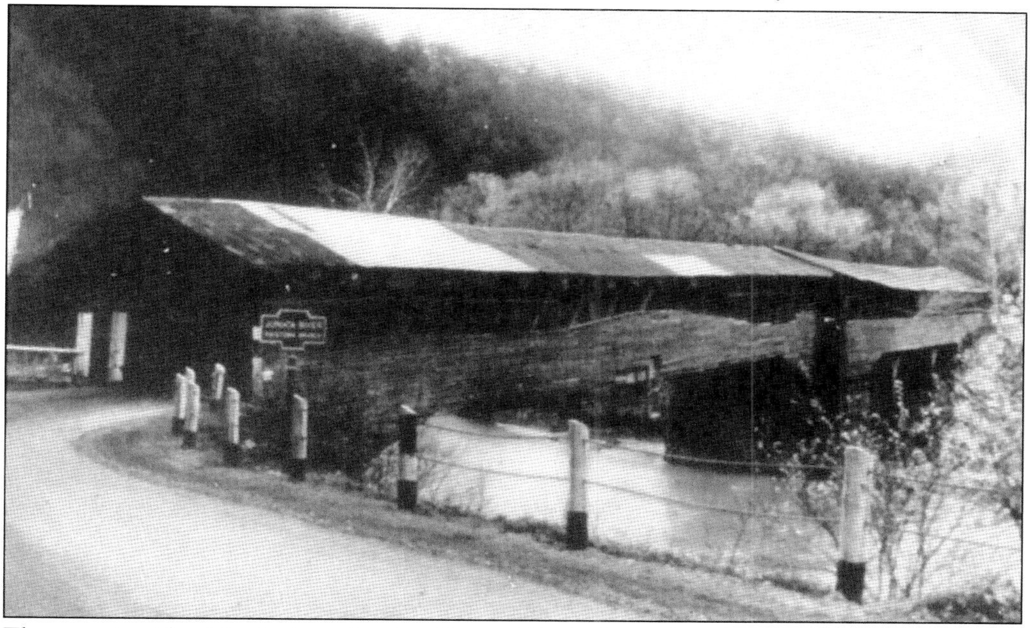

The opposite side of the Juniata Crossing Covered Bridge has a sharp hook in the road. The bridge was converted to a single-lane bridge by the time this photograph was taken. The original design before the alteration was referred to as a double barrel Burr arch. Folks in Pennsylvania referred to these as "shotgun" bridges. This bridge was lost to the great St. Patrick's Day flood of 1936.

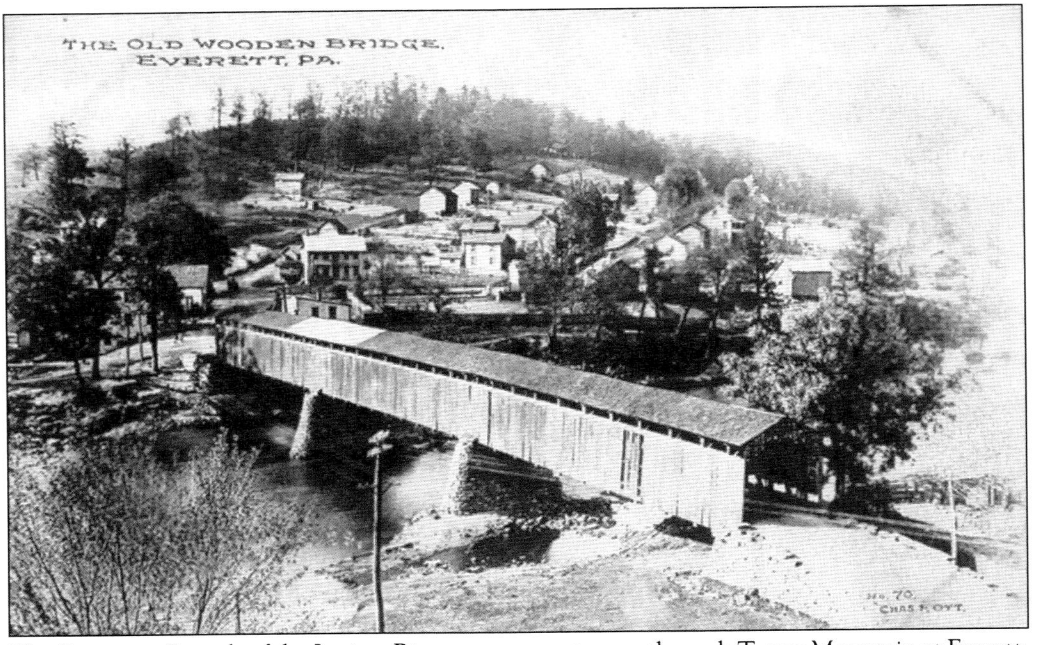

The Raystown Branch of the Juniata River carves a water gap through Tussey Mountain at Everett, eight miles east of Bedford. This proud little town was once called "Bloody Run." Everett has a strong industrial history and enjoyed a profitable economy from the highways that crossed here. It did, however, lose its covered bridge in the 1936 flood. Today, 12 of these traditional structures survive in Bedford County.

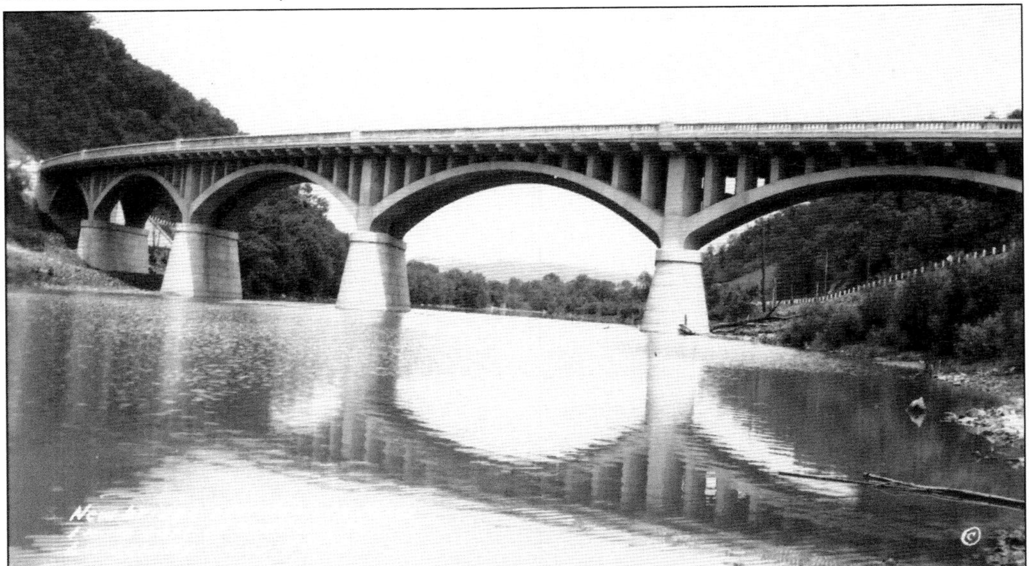

With increased automobile usage and the ravages of floods, the old wooden truss bridges on the main highways of Pennsylvania slowly started to be retired in the 1900s. Many were more than 50 years old. The 1930s ushered in a new age when road crews took on relief workers during the Great Depression. Roadways across the state were rebuilt with the automobile in mind. Narrow, one-way bridges gave way to modern concrete structures.

Getting to a vacation spot in the 1920s and early 1930s required a good map and some planning. Tires blew out, radiators overheated, and roads washed out. It was all part of the adventure. This driver found that his two boats fitted perfectly between the fenders. Of course, everybody had to climb over them to get into the car!

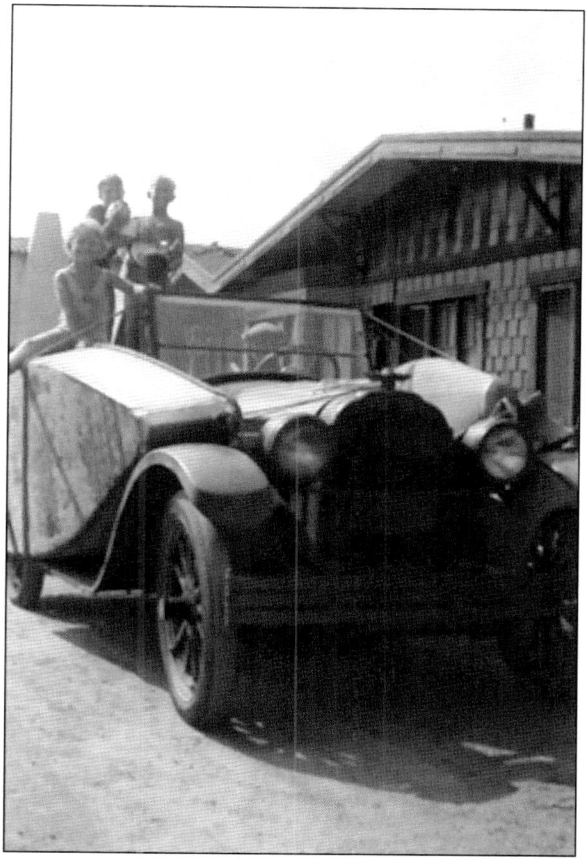

Another mode of transportation, usually seen only a few months of the year, was the sleigh. Stored in the rear of the barn under canvas, at the sight of snow clouds it was pushed forward so it could be hitched for a ride. The sleigh had an advantage. It could travel over fields and directly onto the water if the ice had thickened enough. One this size was usually kept by the local doctor.

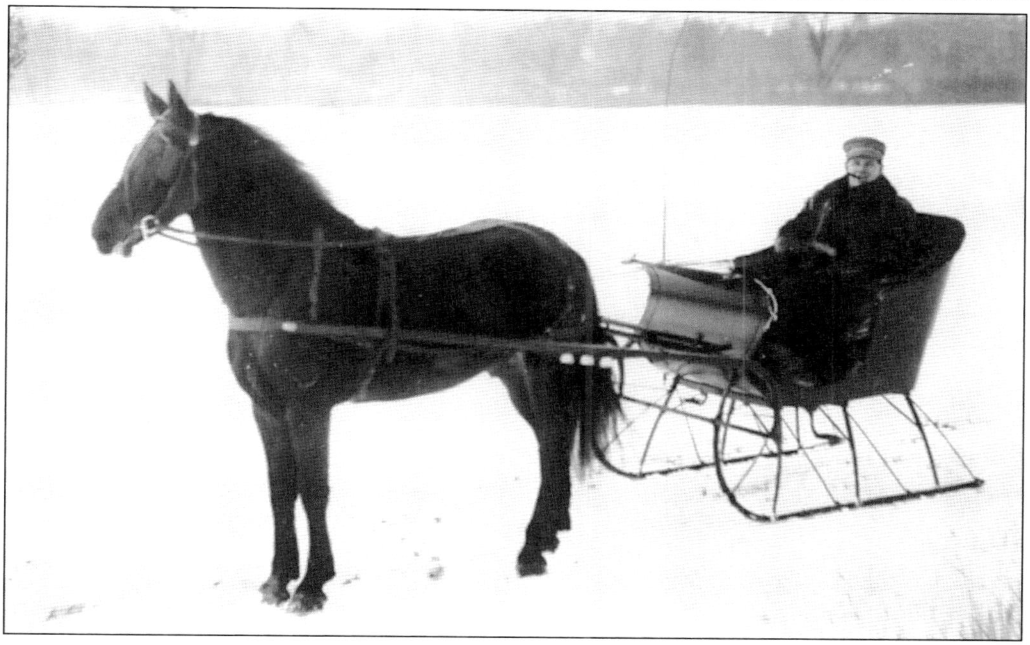

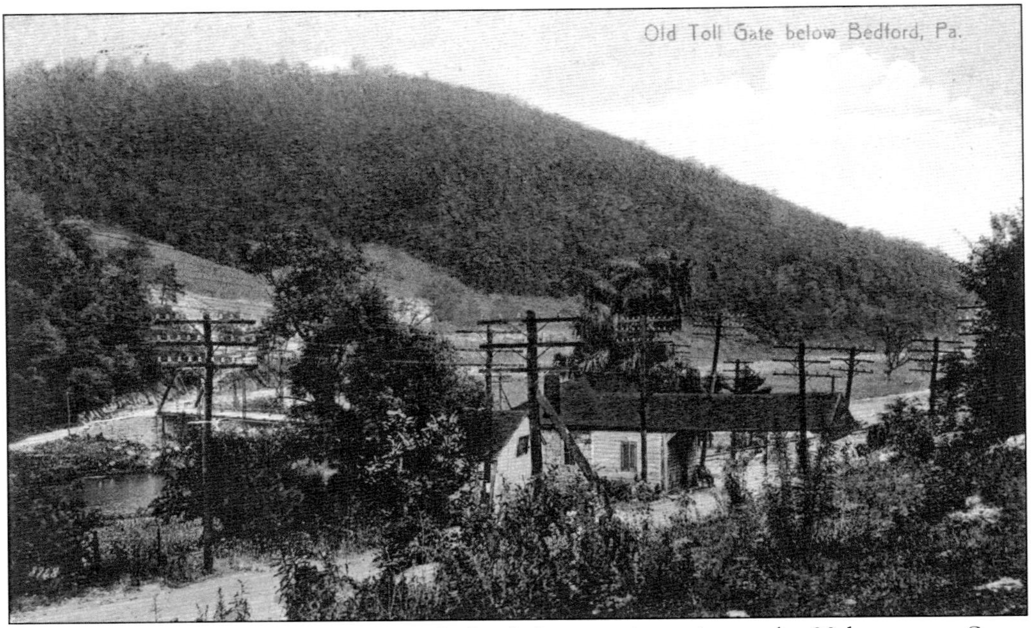

Highways in Pennsylvania were privately funded enterprises prior to the 20th century. Some were built by selling subscriptions or stock. The maintenance of the roadway was continued by charging a toll. Sometimes the road crossed private lands and the owner charged for access. This tollbooth with the elongated roof stood along the Juniata River below Bedford. A new iron bridge crosses directly to the rear.

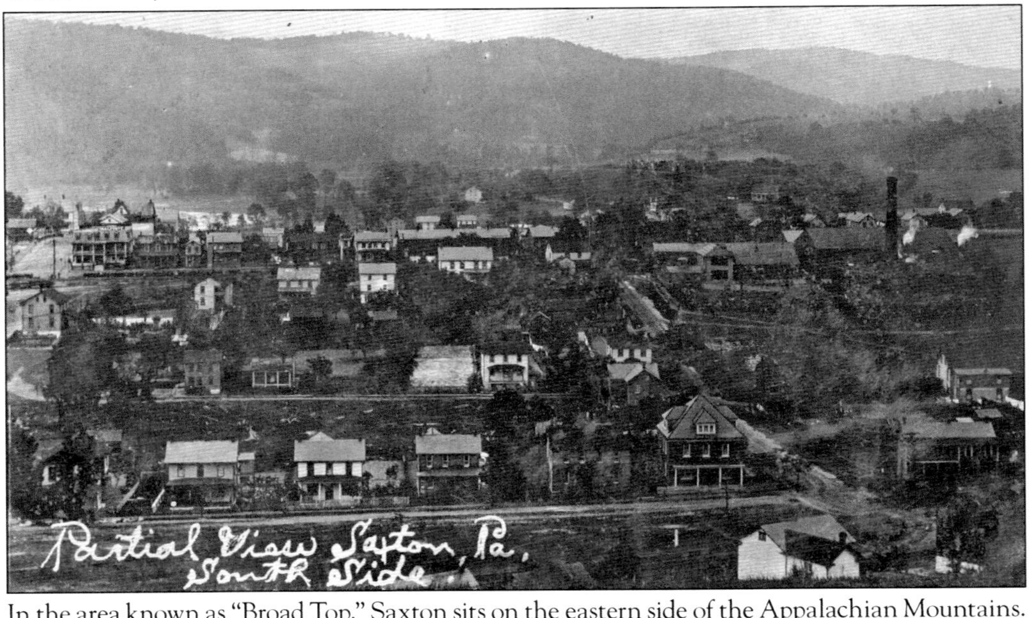

In the area known as "Broad Top," Saxton sits on the eastern side of the Appalachian Mountains. Just north of the town, Raystown Lake starts to form, giving Saxton the distinction of being the gateway to this beautiful, man-made waterway. Officially founded in 1855, Saxton was a thriving community until the Huntingdon and Broad Top Mountain Railroad shut down in the 1950s. The rail shops and coal yards were a profitable establishment.

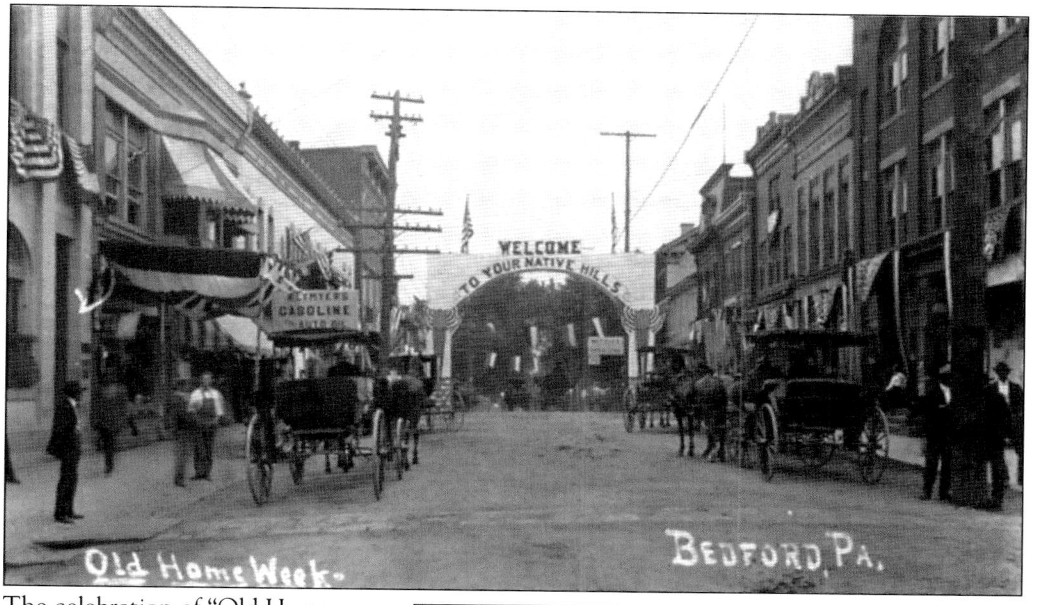

The celebration of "Old Home Week" was a common event at one time in American towns and cities. This well-anticipated gathering was used to draw former citizens back to their town of origin and to promote and celebrate not only community but to show off the recently developed improvements and innovations in the town. Interestingly enough, two signs tout gasoline in this 1907 view; however, there is not a motorcar to be seen.

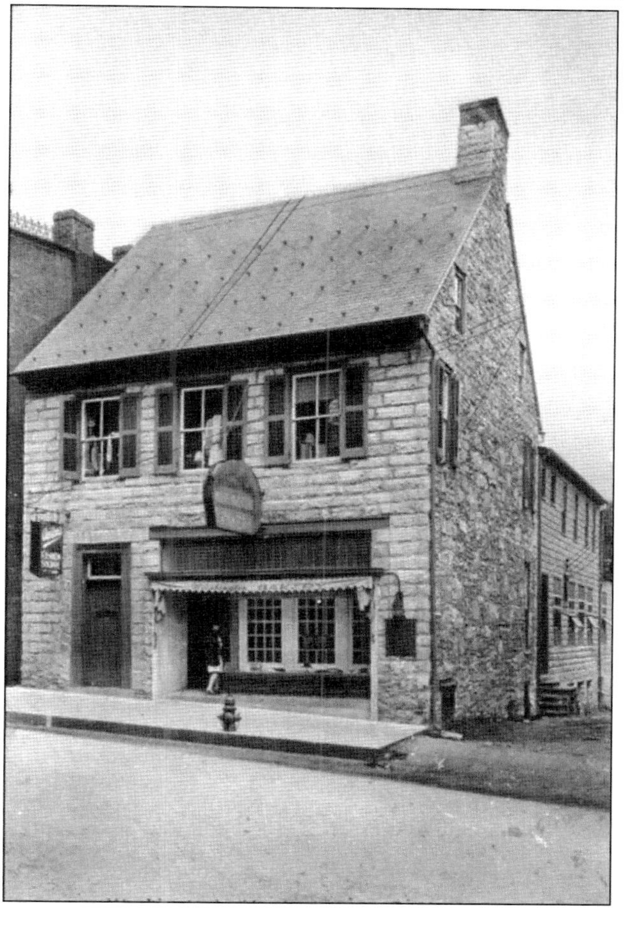

This limestone structure, built in 1756, was known as Espy House and was the largest house in Old Bedford. On October 19, 1794, Pres. George Washington headquartered on the second floor while a Federal army of 7,850 men encamped in a nearby field during the Whiskey Rebellion. This was the only time an active president directly commanded troops. Once home to Washington Bakery, the building houses a candy store today.

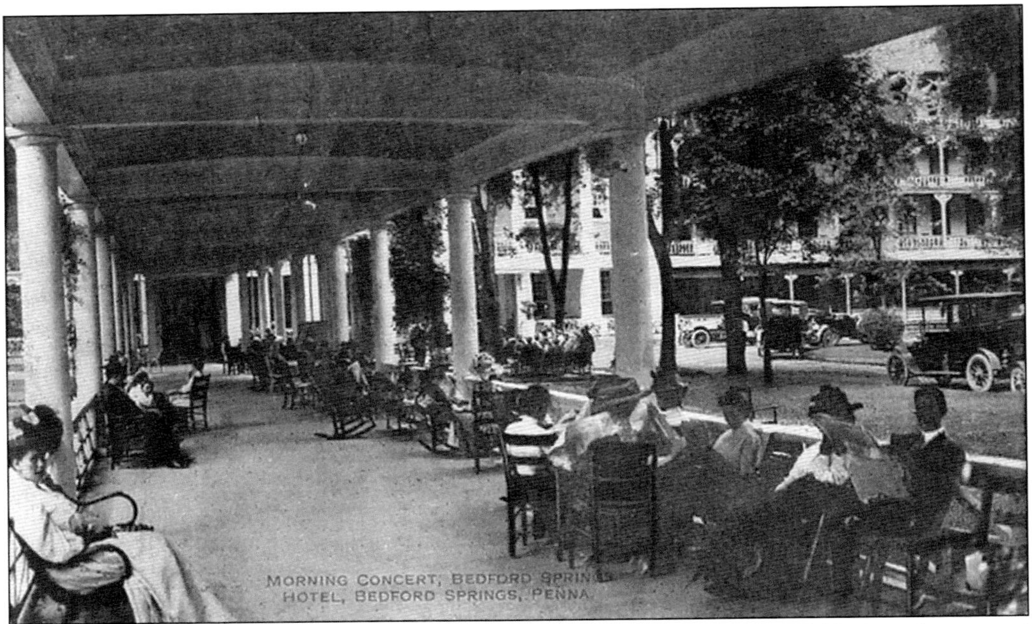

Bedford, originally known as Raystown, became a popular destination after 1804 when the reputed curative powers of the many local springs became news. Bedford Springs and other resorts opened here, attracting many famous people of the times. Seven presidents paid a visit. Pres. James Buchanan used Bedford Springs as his summer White House and received the first transatlantic cable message from Queen Victoria in his room in 1857.

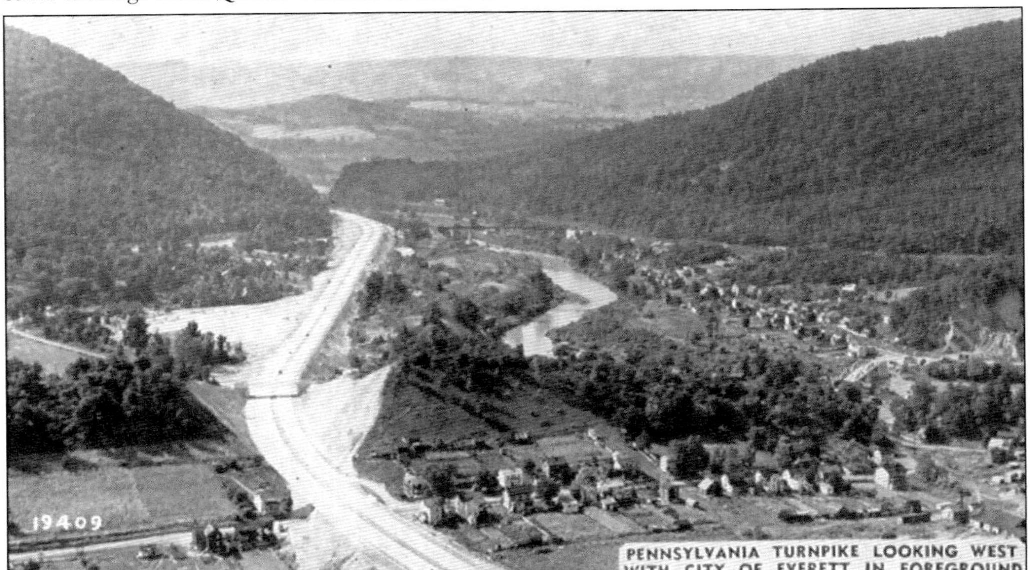

In October 1940, the country's first superhighway ran right through the lower Juniata region. This innovative, relatively straight stretch of concrete ran 160 miles from Harrisburg to Irwin. The Pennsylvania Turnpike was planned with national defense in mind. On the reverse, it is mentioned that a 10-wheeled antiaircraft gun could easily maneuver this roadway. An immediate sensation, this highway changed the way America thought about travel.

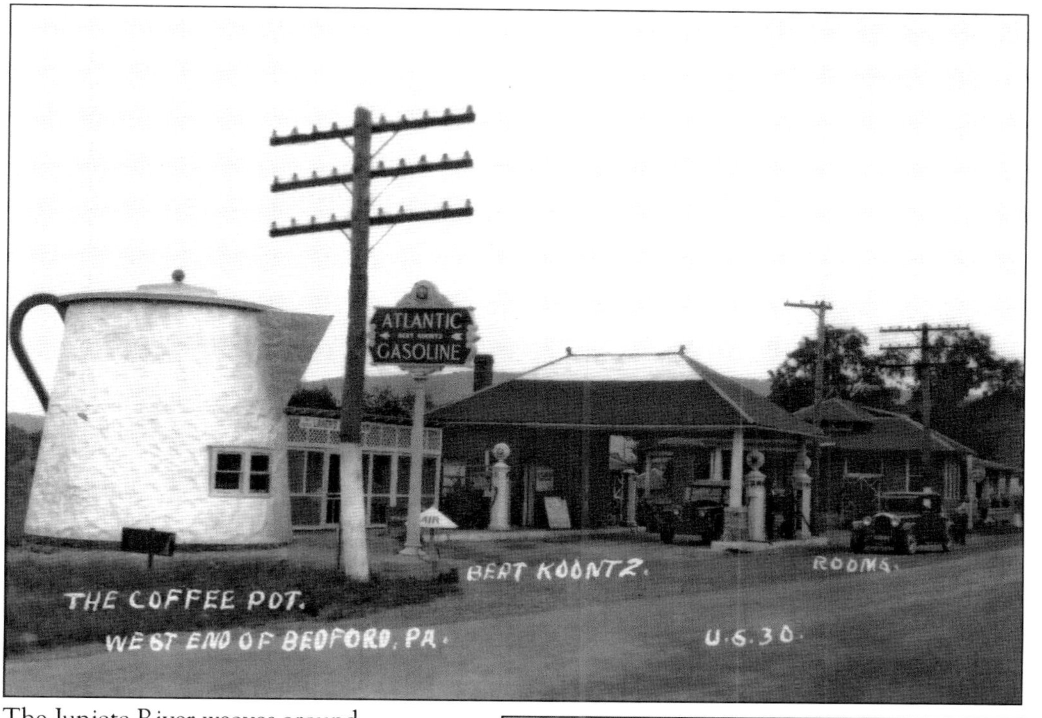

The Juniata River weaves around Bedford, where US Route 30 and the Pennsylvania Turnpike meet in south central Pennsylvania. Being a component of the first road across America, this stretch dates to 1913. Known as the Lincoln Highway, roadside attractions became popular stops for photograph opportunities. A ship stranded on a mountainside, buildings shaped like animals, and sights such as this whimsical coffee pot greeted travelers and made a long trip enjoyable.

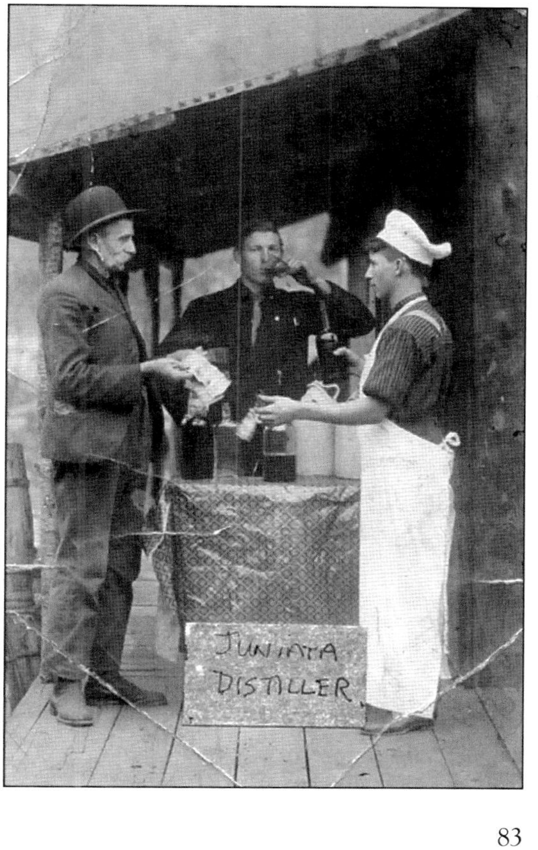

A prominent social issue of the early 20th century was temperance. The sharing of alcoholic beverages was looked upon by many as an evil. While wives and mothers attended meetings and debated the proper path of conduct, husbands and brothers went to their hunting camps for fishing and the enjoyment of nature. In this photograph, some hunters spoof their predicament while on retreat.

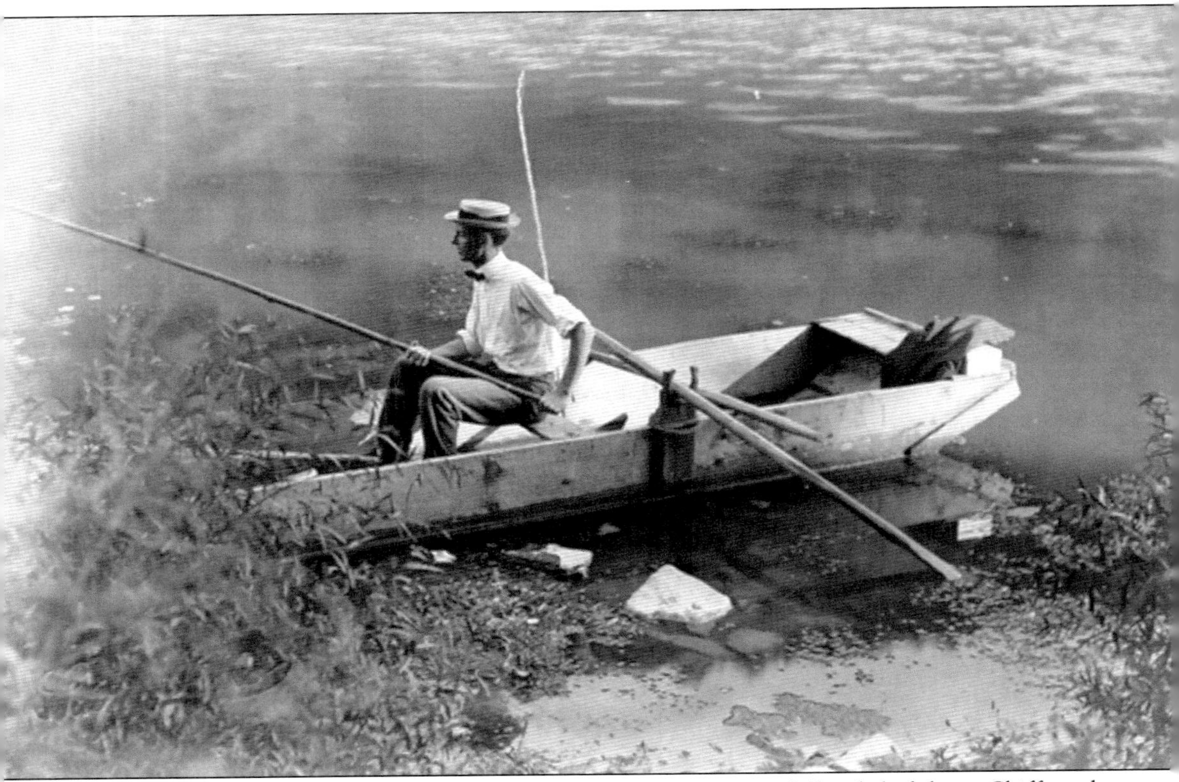

On the Raystown Branch of the Juniata River, a man sits peacefully while fishing. Skiffs such as this were a common sight on all branches of the Juniata. This typical, small, flat-bottomed open boat with a pointed bow has the traditional flat stern. These were built as an inexpensive and easy to use boat. Originally designed to be powered by rowing, the form evolved to be efficiently powered by outboard motors.

Six

FRANKSTOWN, THE BEAVER DAM BRANCH

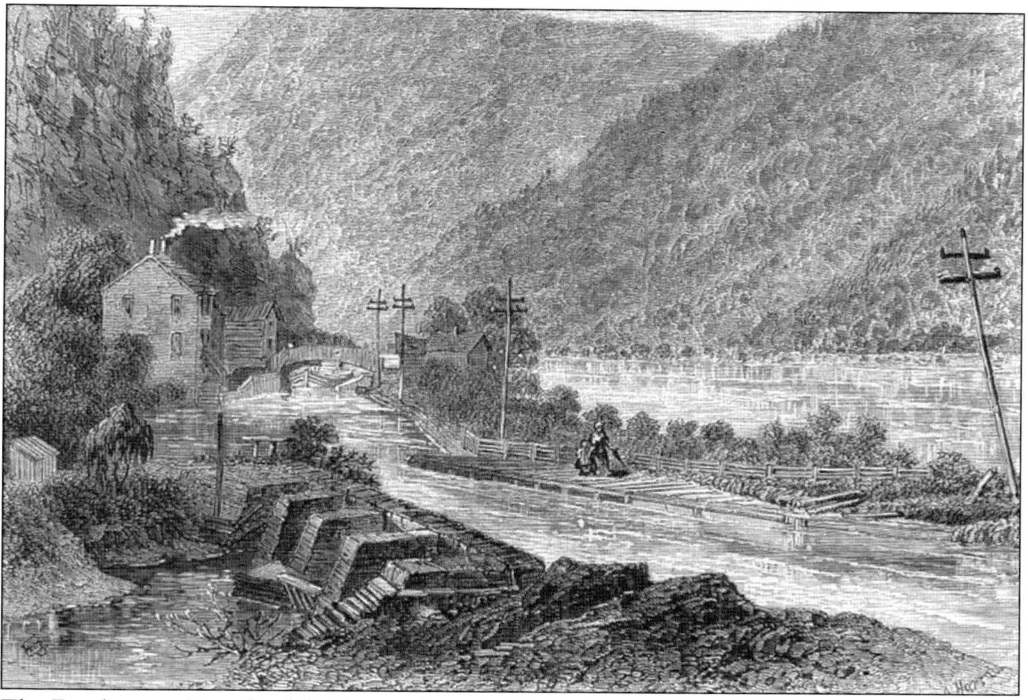

The Frankstown Branch of the Juniata River is joined by the Little Juniata near Petersburg. The river at Huntingdon is the Frankstown Branch. Below Huntingdon, at Ardenheim, the Raystown Branch meets the Frankstown Branch and forms the Juniata River. In this 1850s woodcut view, a woman and child await an approaching packet boat on the Juniata canal below Huntingdon. The Frankstown is also commonly referred to as the Beaver Dam Branch.

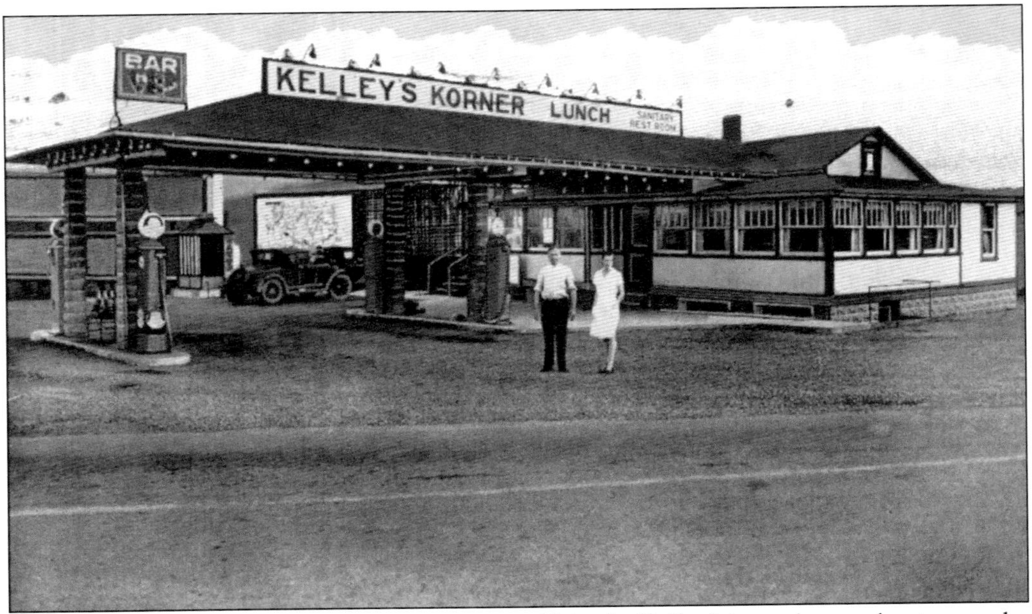

Despite the misspelling of their name, George and Martha Kelly did not change the sign on the roof of their popular lunch establishment. The Kelly family purchased this property in 1929 and added the extended roof, which was fashionable at the time. Their barbecue sandwiches and glass display cases of big game were an attraction on the William Penn Highway. Still in operation after 80 years, Kelly's Korner has seen many owners over the years.

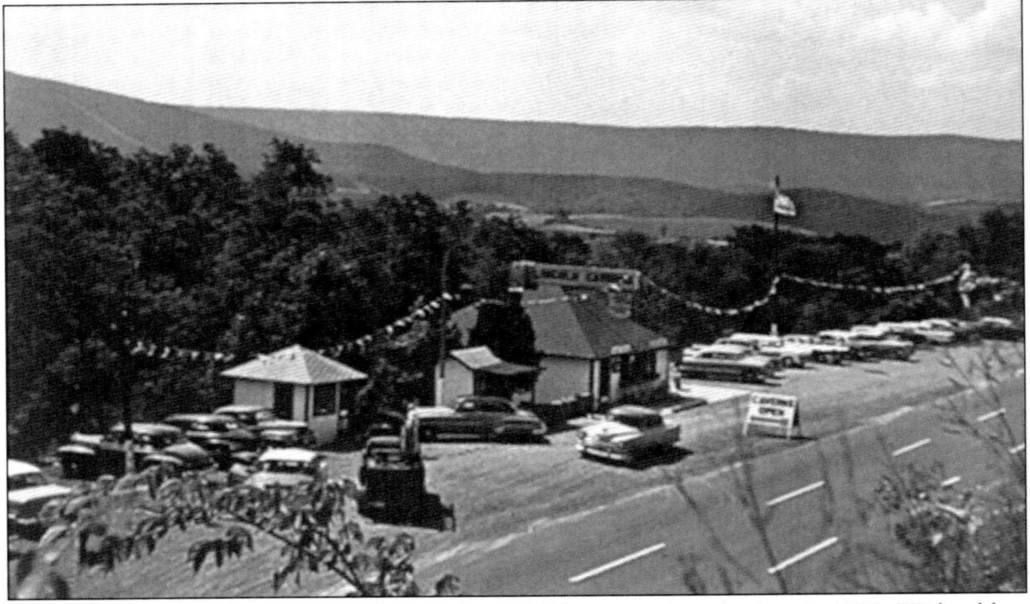

The accidental discovery of one of Pennsylvania's "show caves" took place in 1930. With a blast of dynamite, road crews modernizing the William Penn Highway found themselves peering into a spectacular cavern. Once called "William Penn Cave," it became Lincoln Caverns in 1937 after its purchase by the Dunlavy family. The site contains a large variety of spectacular formations and continues to be a popular attraction to this day.

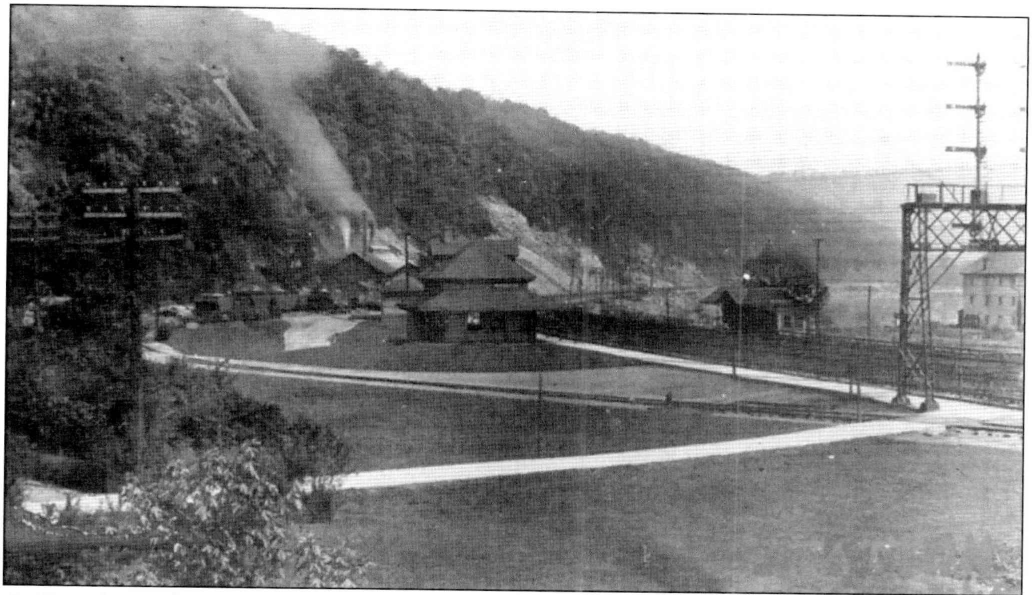

At Petersburg, the canal and the railway, which had been companions for more than 100 miles, parted ways. The canal followed the Frankstown Branch west while the railroad followed the rugged path cut for it by the Little Juniata River. Petersburg station was the terminus of a branch coal rail line that ran to Williamsburg with a connection to Hollidaysburg. The strategic Tussey Mountain ridge forms a backdrop for Petersburg.

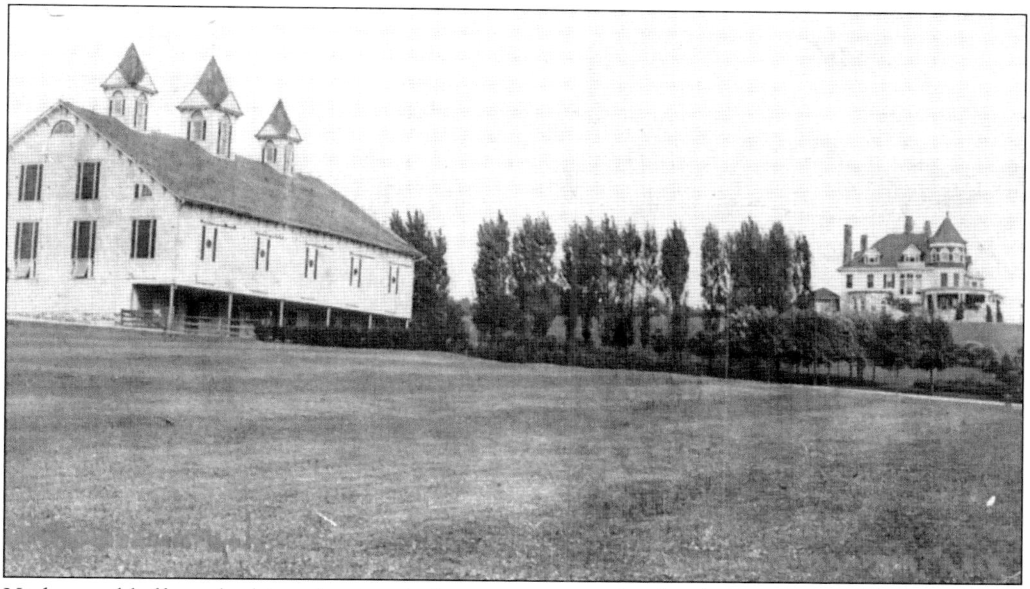

High on a bluff overlooking the river is the most spectacular farmhouse one would see traveling the Juniata. Woolverton Farm, the residence of the Rohrbaugh family, dominates the landscape from its perch at Juniata Valley Pike and Coddington Lane. The manicured lawns and nice trees give this farm one of the most pleasant appearances in the central region of the state.

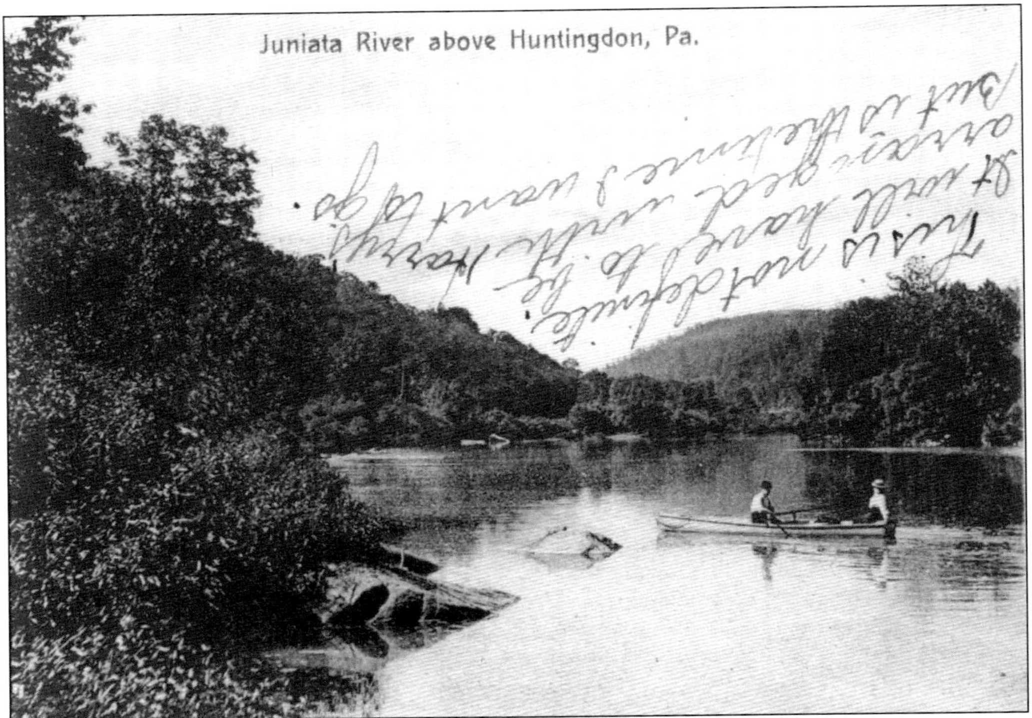

On a sunny day, the Juniata River near Huntingdon is a pleasant place to be for a relaxing afternoon. Seen here in a small boat, a man and a woman drift idly. The Water Street Gap is in the distance. From the river, the area seems timeless. The trees block houses and the occasional automobile. Rocks from the high hillside on the left side of the river have fallen into the Juniata.

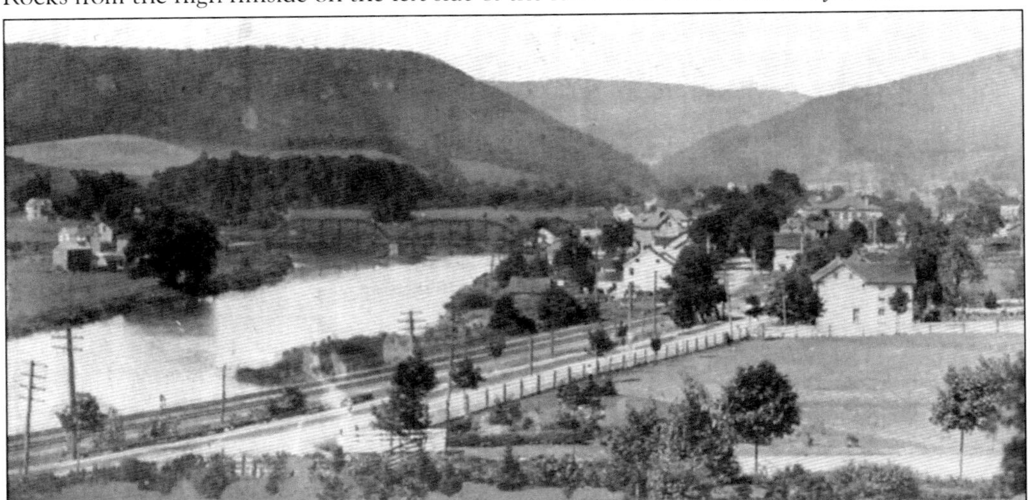

The view from the bank of the Rohrbaugh house looking down at the Juniata River shows the beautiful village of Alexandria and the Water Street Gap in the distance. "Hartslog" was the original name of the village, which dates to 1744. John Hart, a colonial trader, fed his horses from a hollowed log while conducting his business. Later settlers used this log as a surveyors point when laying out their village. Today, Alexandria is home to many distinct buildings.

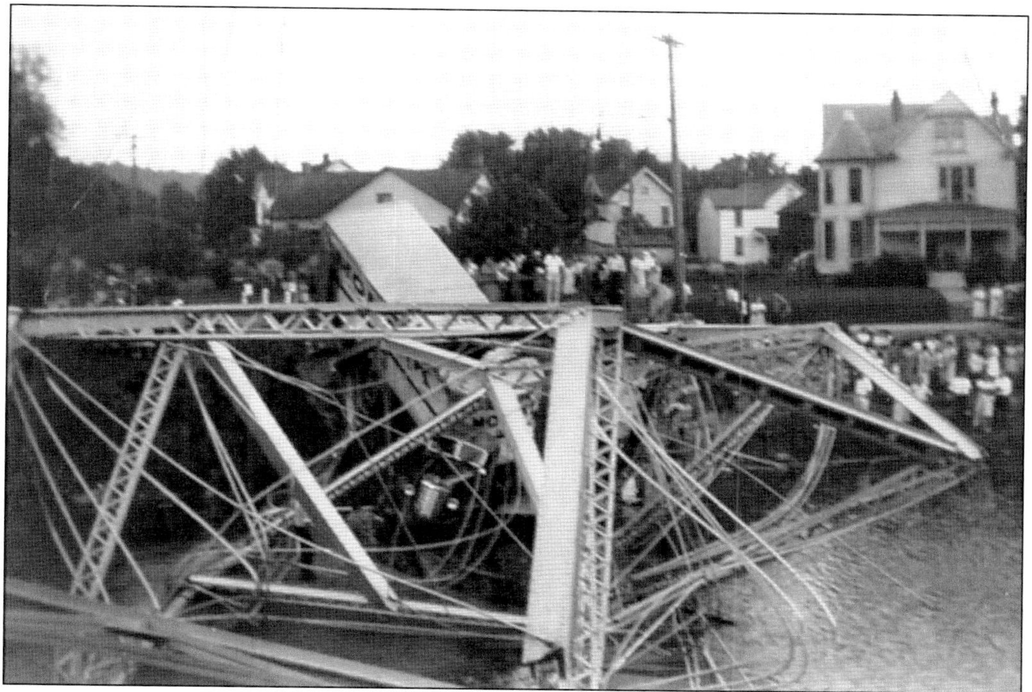

A tractor trailer carrying cigarettes missed the south end of the Alexandria bridge in July 1939. The cab plunged into the Juniata River and knocked the end of the bridge from its pier. Although the driver survived the harrowing crash, a family of tourists from New York crossing the bridge in a sedan did not. Marvel cigarettes from the damaged cartons were enjoyed for months in Alexandria.

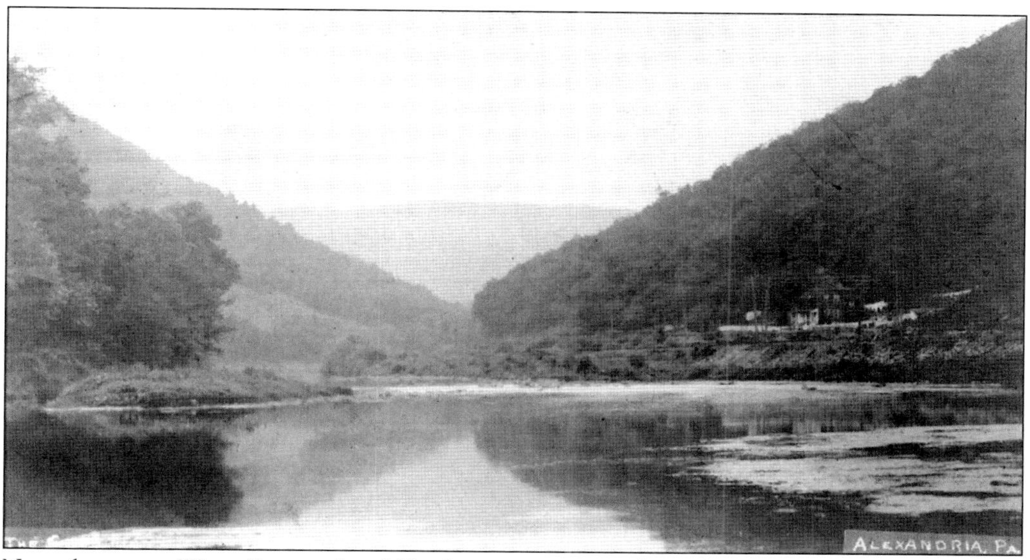

Near the gap at Water Street, the old highway appears on the right. Below that, the railroad to Williamsburg runs along the river. At this point, the river seems to spread out. The rocks in the water become infrequent. Many years earlier a dam stretched across the stream and guaranteed the canal and its locks would have a good water supply for boats maneuvering the gap.

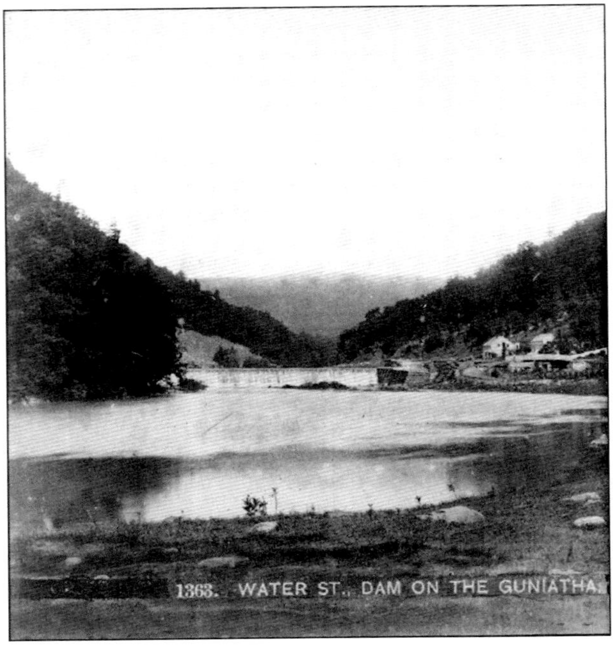

The dam at Water Street is shown as it appeared in the 1870s. Water Street was settled after 1800; however, there were citizens living in the vicinity 70 years earlier. The town was named for a spring that bubbled to the surface in the narrow gap that forced travelers to navigate water. Tussey Mountain and Short Mountain meet and form this distinctive land formation.

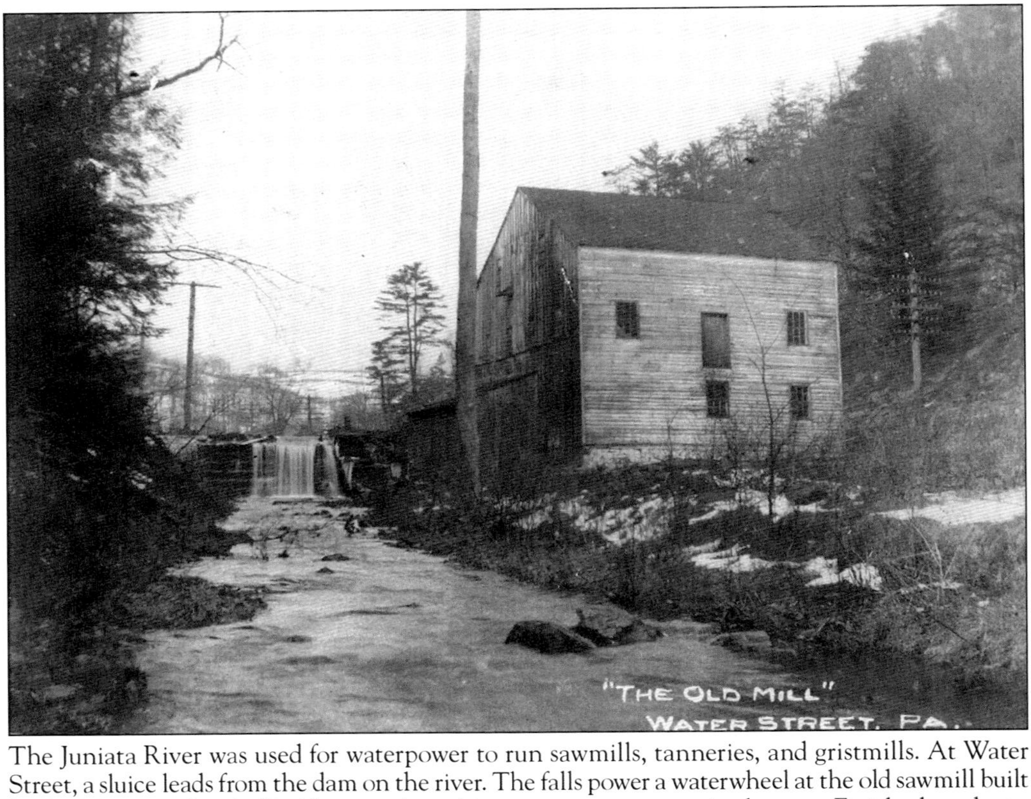

The Juniata River was used for waterpower to run sawmills, tanneries, and gristmills. At Water Street, a sluice leads from the dam on the river. The falls power a waterwheel at the old sawmill built by the Mytinger family. Buildings such as this were once common in the area. Finished products, such as flour and wood, were floated down the river on arks before the days of the canal.

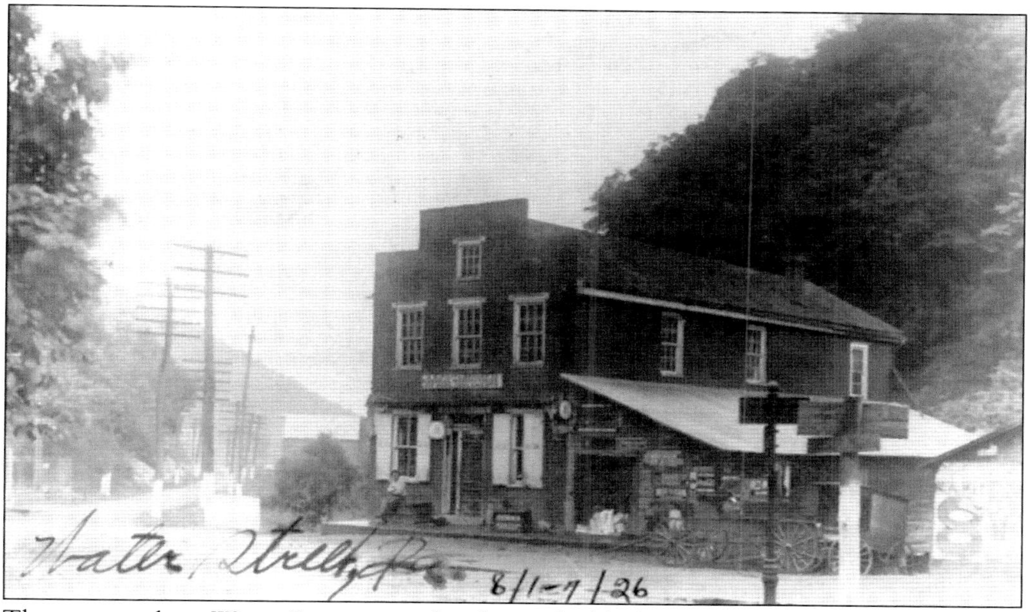

The crossroads at Water Street proved to be profitable for a business. In this photograph, A. Waite rests on a crate in front of his general merchandise store in 1926. Waite provided groceries and provisions. He also was a dealer in ACME farm implements. At the left is the William Penn Highway heading toward Huntingdon. Waite faces the highway toward Tyrone. The road on the right passes an inn and winds through Canoe Valley.

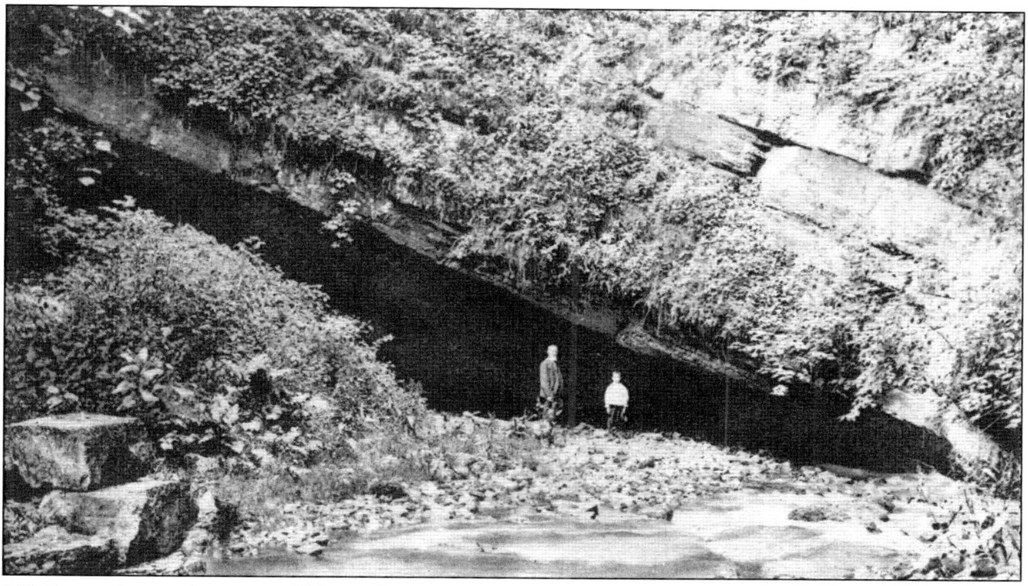

While staying at the inn at Water Street, guests were encouraged to visit Sinking Valley, just off the road to Tyrone. A natural stone arch was an attraction along with unusual limestone caves. One cave, Tytoona, once known as "Indian River Cavern," has a peculiar opening. Here, a spring burrows under Tussey Mountain and then reappears at Water Street.

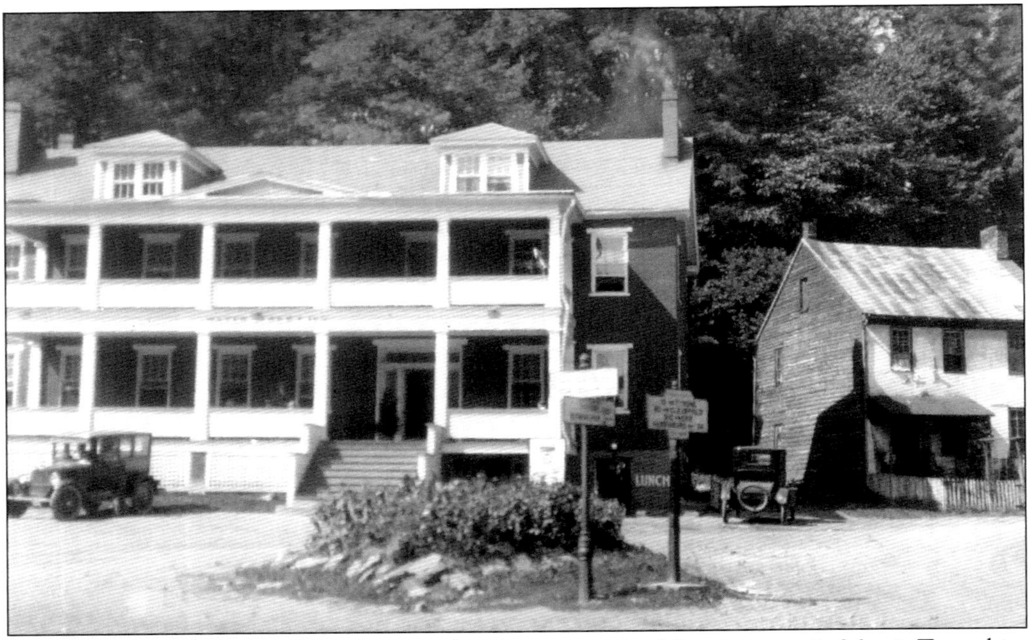

For generations, the Water Street Inn stood at the crossroads of the water gap in Morris Township. It was built in 1842 as a stage tavern and hotel, and the canal provided steady customers. With the closure of the canal and the location of the rails in another valley, activity slowed. In 1922, business became brisk with automobile traffic. After World War II, this type of establishment fell out of favor. The building stood until the 1990s.

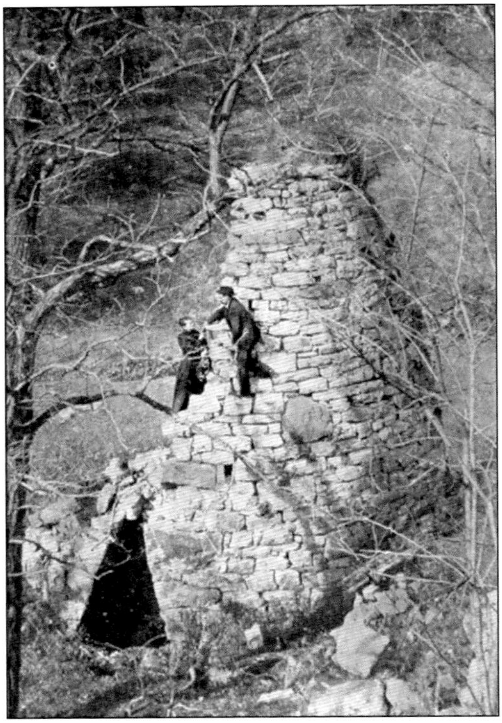

Near the Juniata River on Township Run, Canoe Furnace was in operation from 1838 to about 1850. In later years, a train stop and village called "Point View" was located here. Blair County had 19 of the estimated 500 iron furnaces in Pennsylvania. Canoe Furnace was of a round variety. The remains of the furnace were in good standing in 1905 when this view was produced. Four other furnaces were operated along the Frankstown Branch.

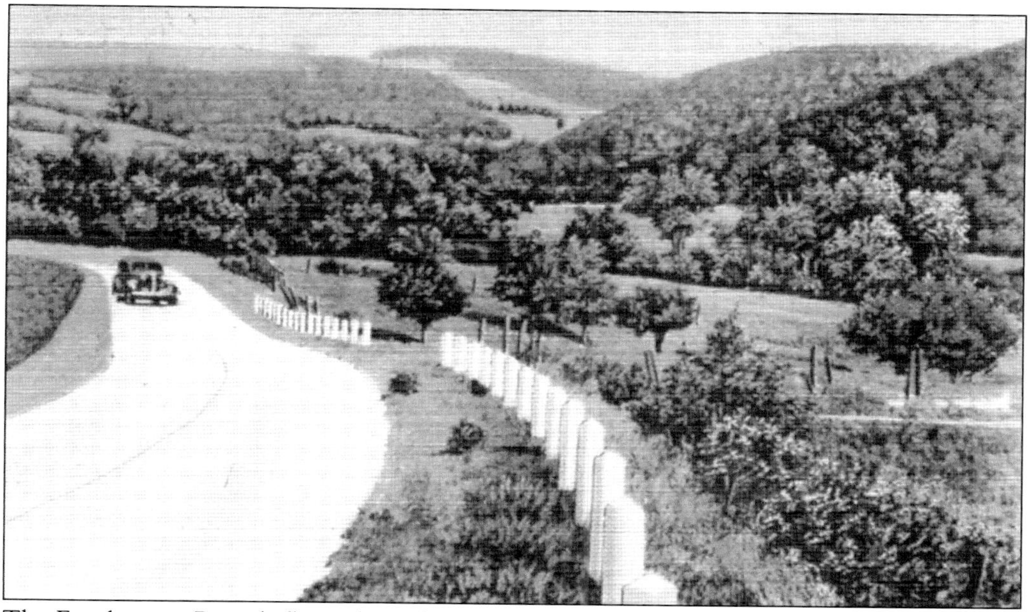

The Frankstown Branch flows through Canoe Valley west of Water Street. This view shows how it appeared in the 1930s. The vast openness of Canoe Creek State Park is exemplified with a panoramic view when the crest of Canoe Creek Road is reached. In 1979, a 938-acre park was dedicated here, and the public got its first chance to see the 155-acre lake that provides excellent year-round fishing.

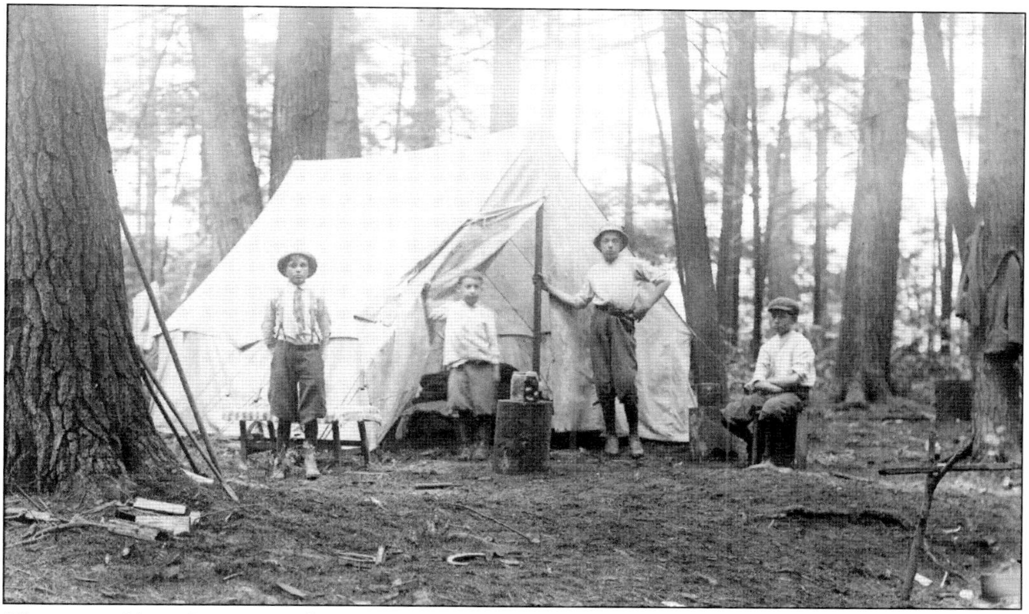

"Camping Blair County Style" is written on the reverse of this photograph. The message also points out the uniform on a tree. Although these may not be Boy Scouts, these boys are meticulous about setting up their campsite and may follow the tenets of the Boy Scout movement that began in the United States in 1910. Note the large mason jars used for storing provisions.

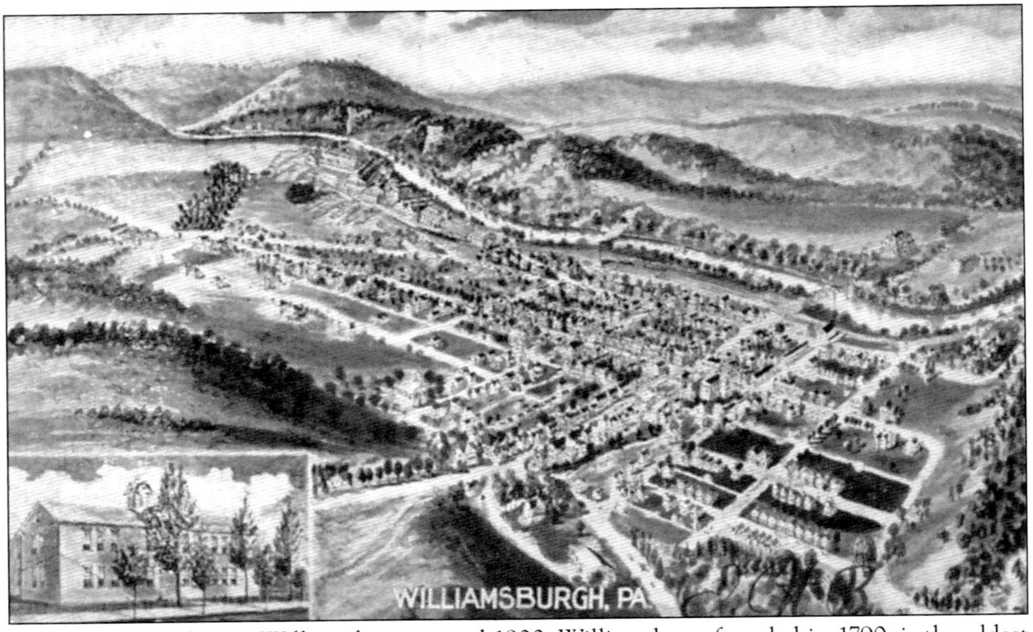

This panorama depicts Williamsburg around 1900. Williamsburg, founded in 1790, is the oldest borough in Blair County. This locale was once Shawnee and Lenape hunting grounds where a big spring flowed. In the 1830s, Williamsburg was an active canal stop. In 1873, the Hollidaysburg and Petersburg Branch of the Pennsylvania Railroad replaced the canal activity. Today, the Lower Trail, a 17-mile rail trail, attracts hikers and provides access to the Juniata River for fishing and kayaking.

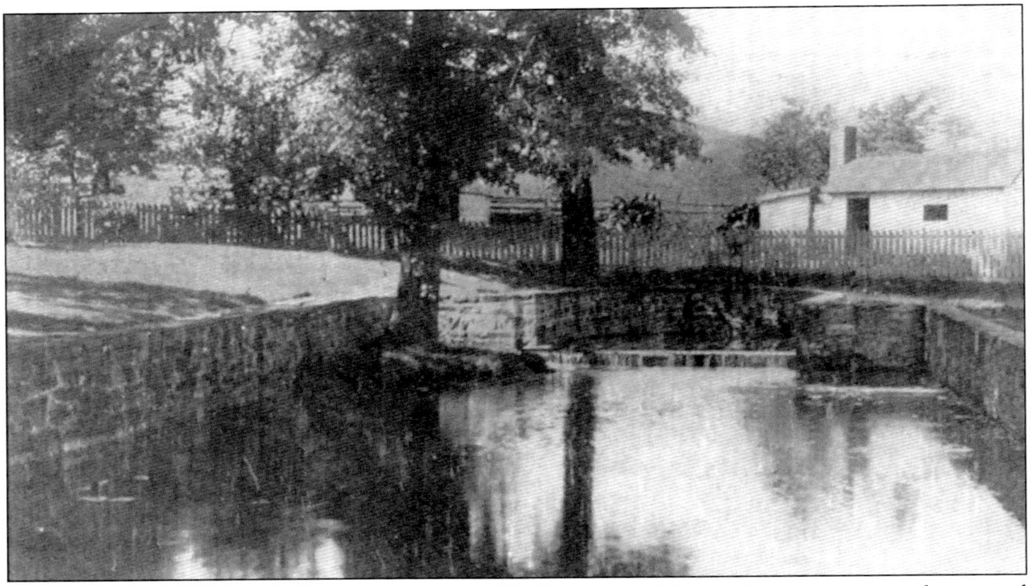

Water has played a major role in the history of Williamsburg. Native Americans were fascinated with the Big Spring. The Pennsylvania Canal brought beneficial commerce to this growing community. Industrialist Charles Schwab loved the Big Spring and proposed building a steel mill here. However, the process required a larger river than the Frankstown Branch. Schwab settled on locating a paper mill in Williamsburg and building a housing development here.

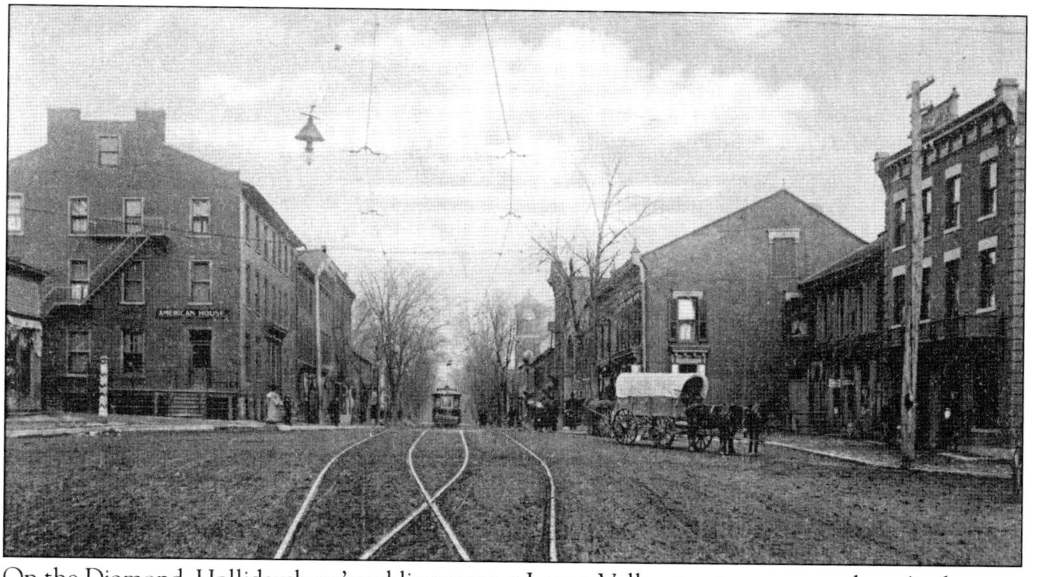

On the Diamond, Hollidaysburg's public square, a Logan Valley street car approaches. At the start of the 20th century, a number of large 1830s Greek Revival–style buildings stood here. These represented the prosperity of the canal era. This is where the Pennsylvania Canal terminated before making an ascent over the Allegheny Ridge by way of the Portage Railroad. Laid out in 1796, Hollidaysburg became the county seat of Blair County in 1846.

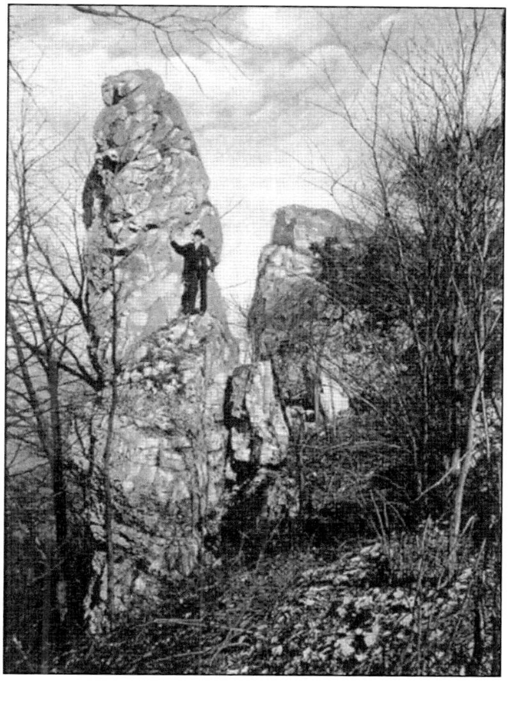

The borough of Hollidaysburg faces an unusual wall of rock on a nearby ridge. A series of weather-worn stone extensions jut above the landscape. These "chimney rocks" have been an attraction for generations. In recent years, a landscaped park has been developed behind the rocks. This park offers a spectacular view of Hollidaysburg and the Allegheny Front. A stairway gives access to the top of this stone.

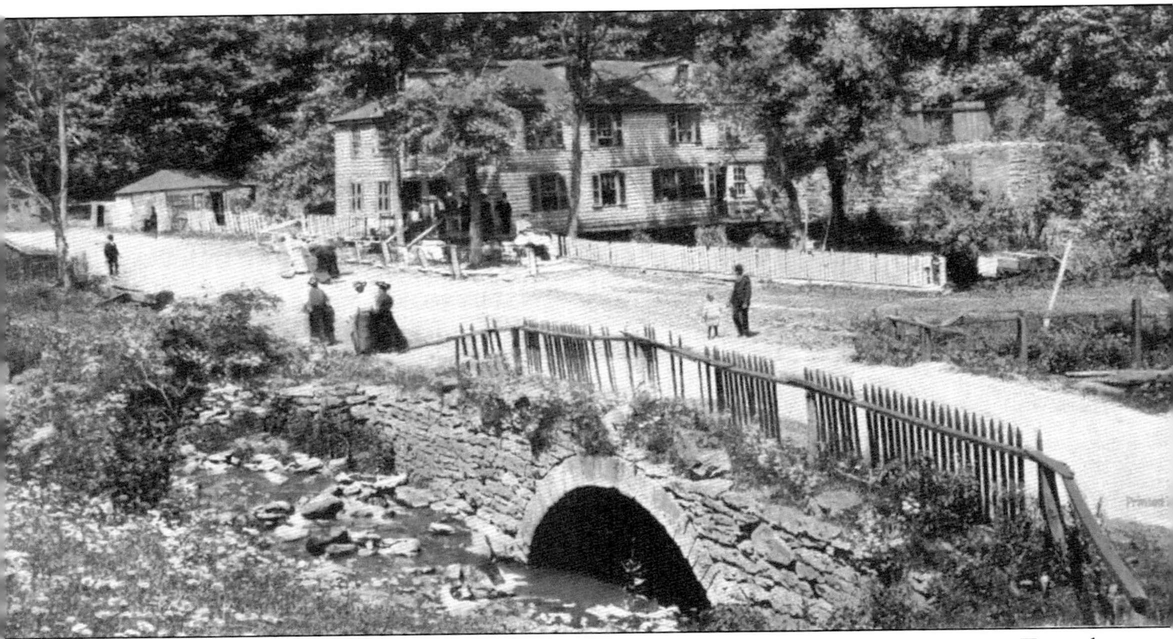

At the terminus of the Juniata Canal System was the Fountain Inn. Built in Juniata Township, Blair County, this inn dated from the days of the Huntingdon, Cambria, and Indiana Turnpike. Situated at Blair's Gap, the inn was a short distance from the loop of the Mule Shoe Curve at the foot of the number eight incline of the old Portage railroad. The lifting of canal boats over the Allegheny Summit took place here.

Seven

The Little Juniata, Allegheny's Gateway

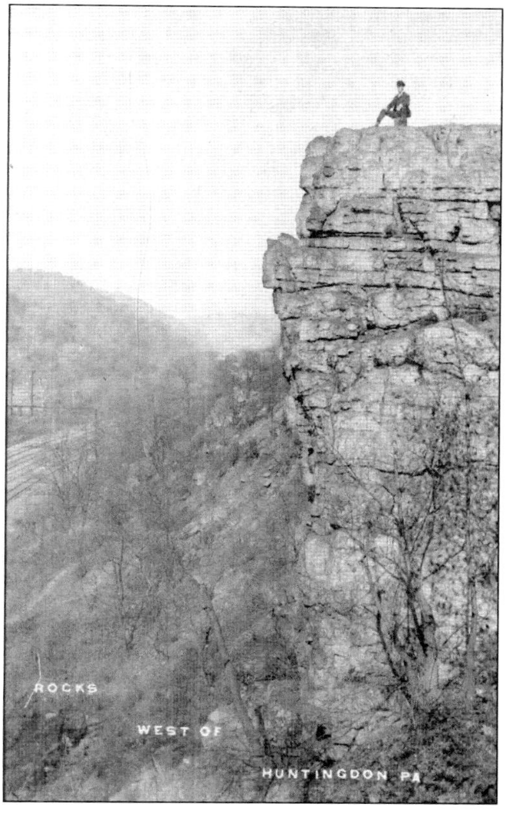

Although the construction of the Pennsylvania Railroad across the state in the 1840s was labor intensive, nothing compared to the terrain west of Huntingdon. The railroad parted ways with the Juniata River and headed toward the Allegheny Front to the northwest. Through a tunnel under Tussey Mountain, it joined the Little Juniata River. The stretch through the remainder of Huntingdon County would be described in travelogues as "some of the most wondrous country one could hope to encounter!"

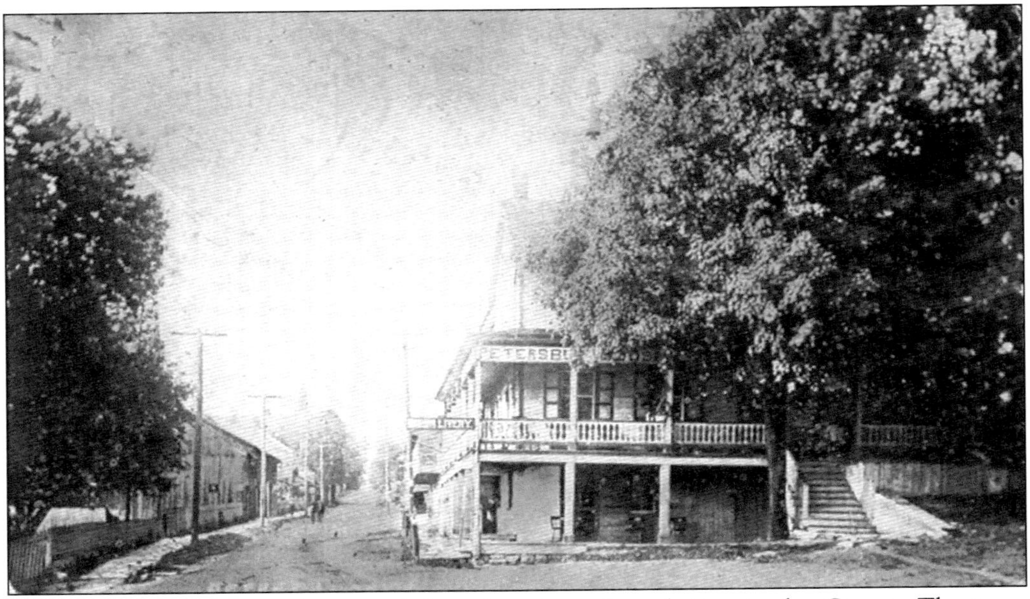

King Street is the main road that trails from Petersburg through Huntingdon County. This town flourished during the age of the canal and was an especially active interchange on the railroad. Petersburg House, shown here, was an important landmark for more than 100 years. A fire destroyed the hotel in the 1920s. The daylight basements are typical of Petersburg architecture. Steep hillside buildings had their main entrances on the second level.

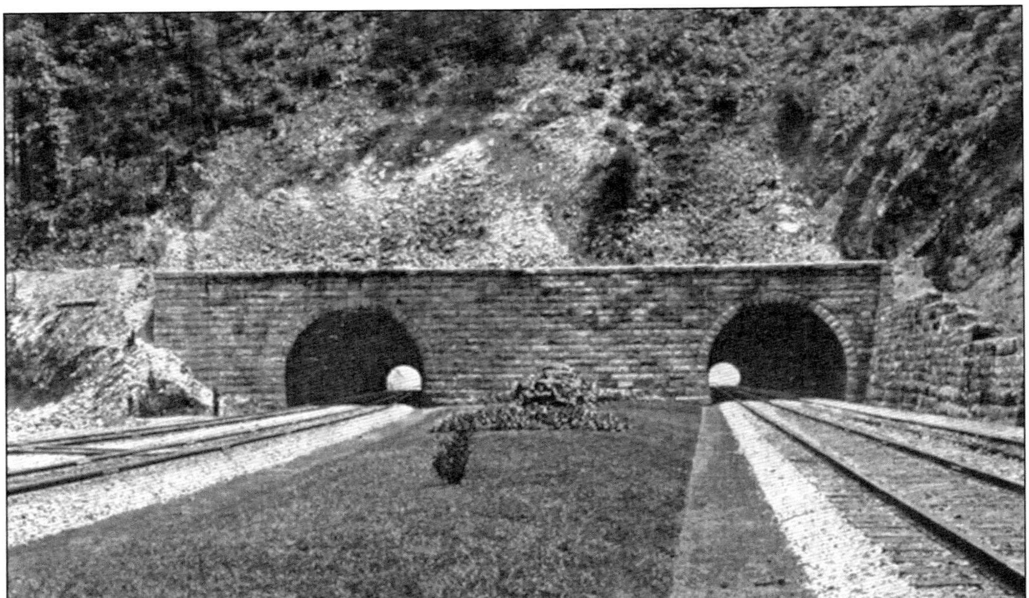

The railroad met a formidable barrier when it reached Tussey Mountain. A tunnel was required. Scotch-Irish laborers did much of the work by hand in 1849. Fifty years later, with the expansion of the railroad infrastructure, the single tunnel was enlarged and a second tunnel was dug. It took one year to complete this task. The tunnels were placed under guard during World War II.

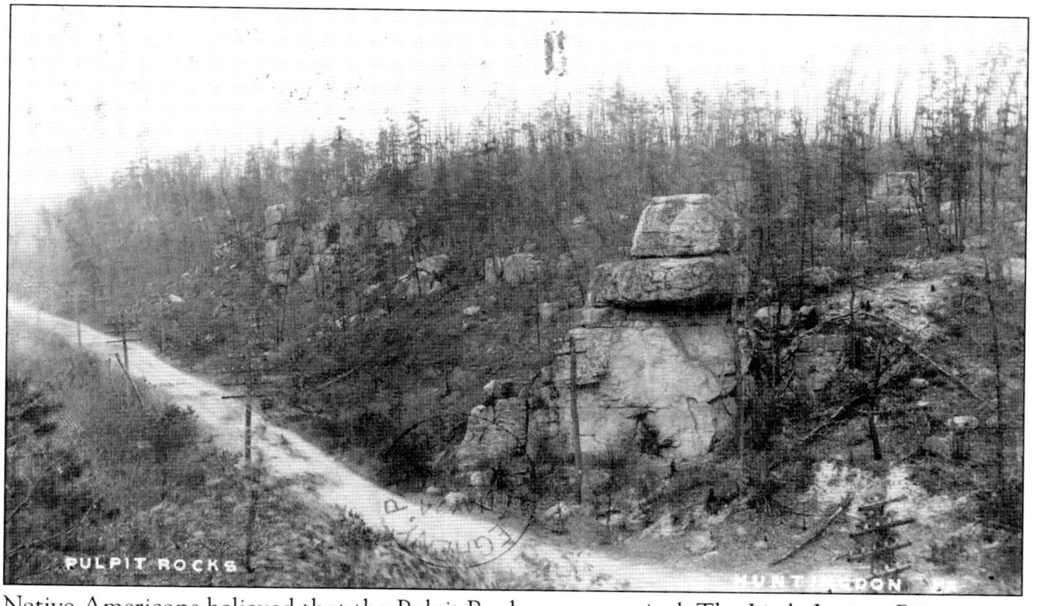

Native Americans believed that the Pulpit Rocks were mystical. The Little Juniata River cuts a picturesque four-mile gorge between Huntingdon and Petersburg. Here, on Warriors Ridge above Petersburg, are the Pulpit Rocks, horizontal bands of sandstone layered on top of limestone. These unusual formations dot the landscape along the old ridge pike. In 1836, this site was chosen as the starting point of the first Pennsylvania Geological Survey.

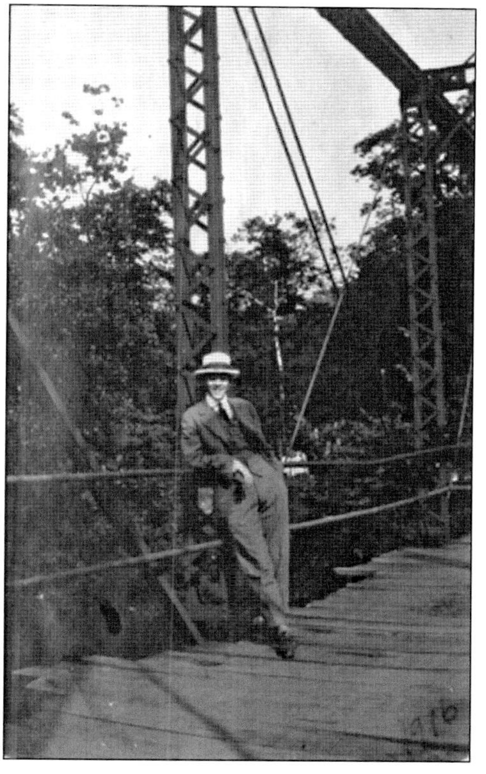

One of the Wilson Boys from Tyrone pauses on an iron bridge crossing the Juniata River at Barree, not too far from where the Little Juniata River joins the Frankstown Branch. Barree was home to an iron furnace that evolved into an important ironworks on the Juniata beginning in 1794. For a time, the Barree Forge was managed by David R. Porter, who was governor of Pennsylvania from 1839 to 1845.

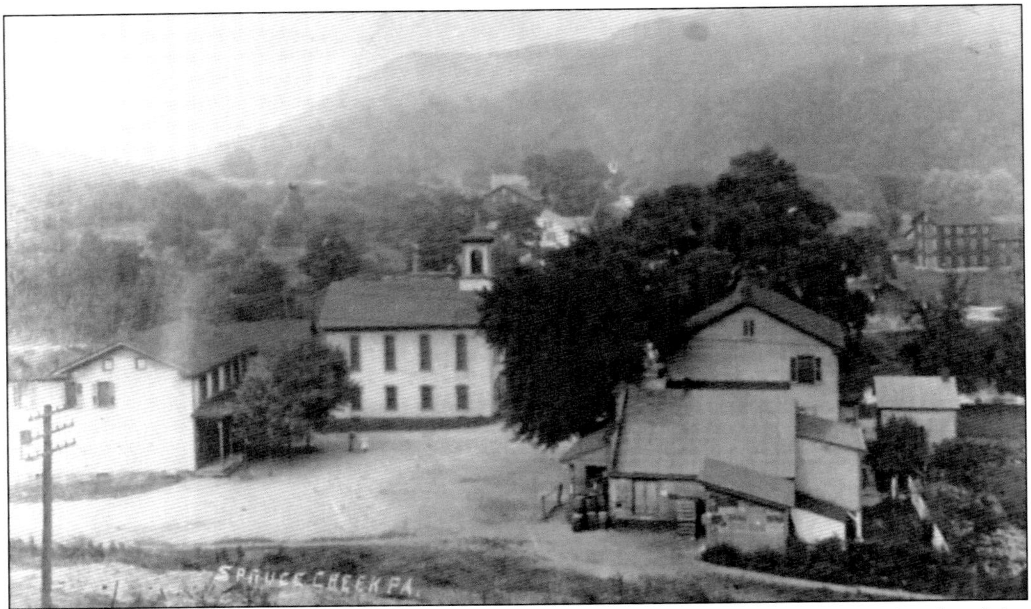

Spruce Creek is a very picturesque village. It originally was two towns, one on each side of the Little Juniata River. Graysport and Stockdale lost their titles when the railroad renamed the village after the creek that enters the Juniata River here. Inhabited since about 1775, Spruce Creek had a great deal of small industries and was considered the wealthiest town of its size in the commonwealth for a period.

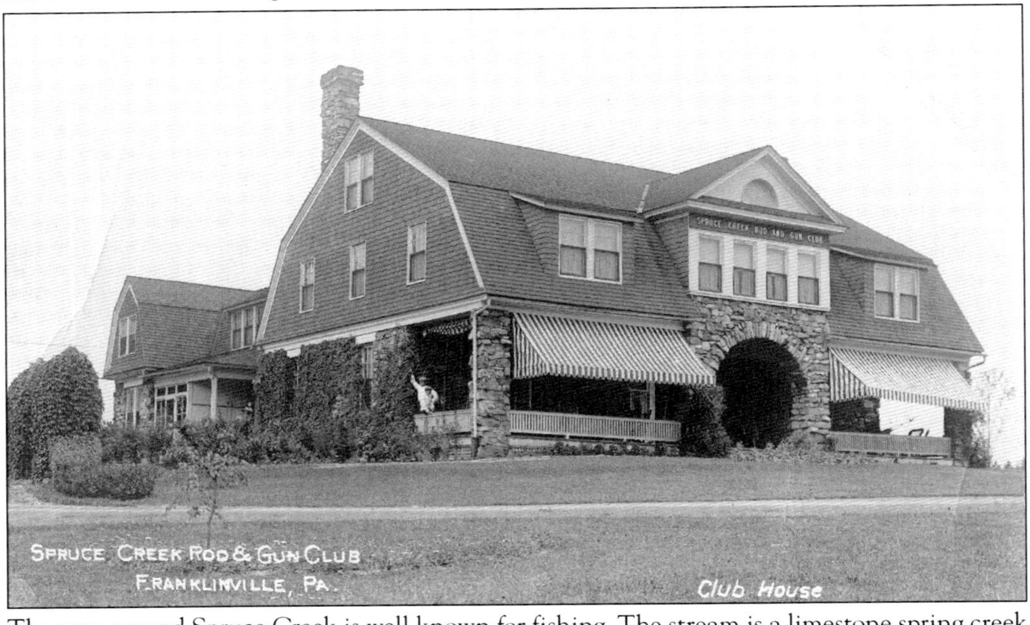

The area around Spruce Creek is well known for fishing. The stream is a limestone spring creek that runs cold for miles until it empties into the Little Juniata Creek. Spruce Creek is maintained by landowners as a premier catch and release fishery. It is not uncommon to see 20-inch-long trout sipping mayflies in this 30-foot-wide spring creek. A number of sporting clubs operate in these parts.

As the population increased and fishing became more popular, it became necessary in the early 20th century to establish laws to conserve the supply of fish. The size of fish caught was regulated and the state of Pennsylvania built fish hatcheries where young fish are maintained until they are large enough to be released into streams. Several hundred trout hatchlings could fit in a pail to be released into nature.

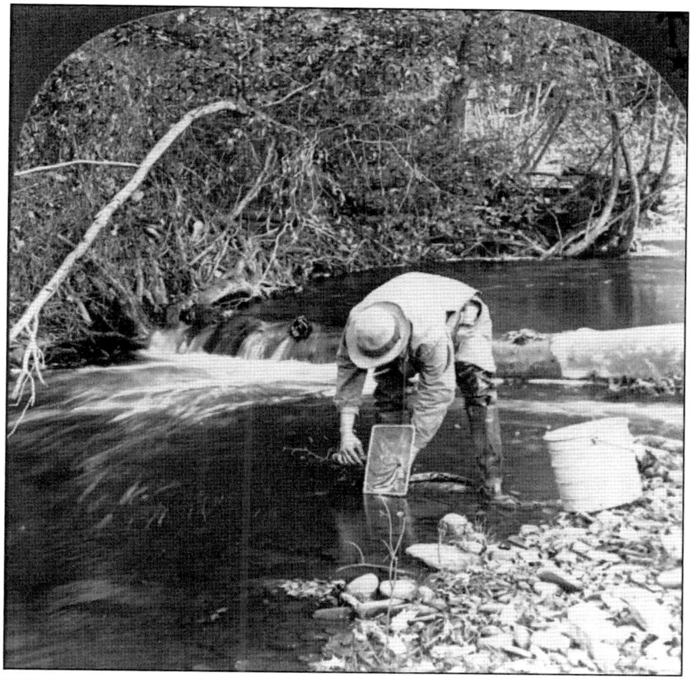

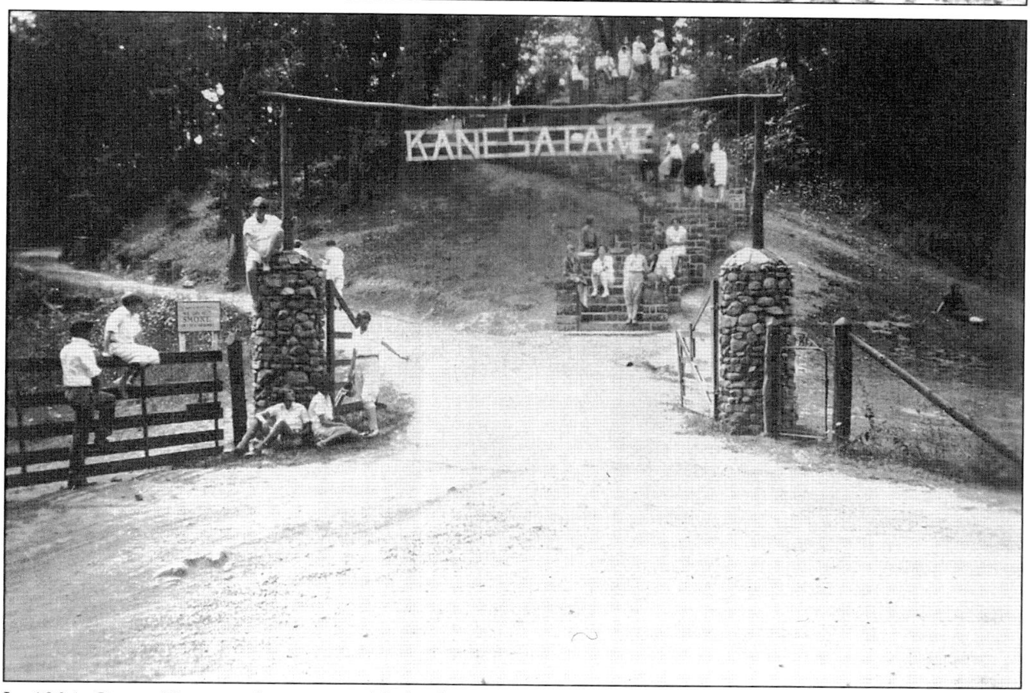

In 1924, Camp Kanesatake was established on 135 acres of wooded land near Huntingdon Furnace. A Mohawk settlement in Quebec lent its poetic name to this retreat of winding trails with cabins perched on hillsides. There are playing fields and an Olympic-sized swimming pool on the lower grounds. Since its inception, Boy Scouts, 4H Clubs, church groups, and band encampments have enjoyed this unique place in nature.

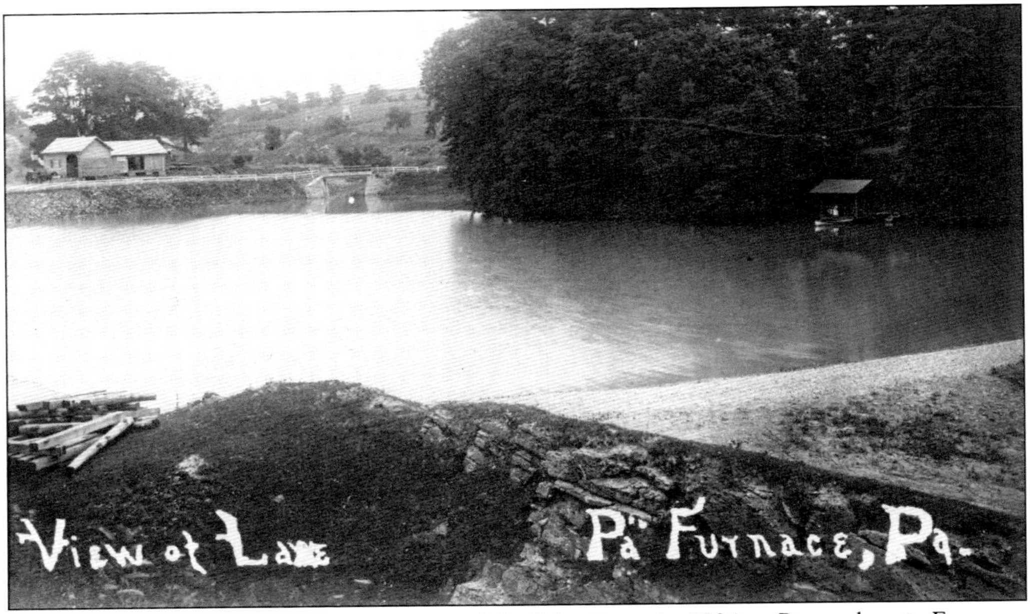

This ironmaster's mansion was constructed for John Lyon in 1834 at Pennsylvania Furnace. Water powered by Spruce Creek operated one of the most successful iron operations in central Pennsylvania at this location. A plantation surrounded this home, with workers' houses and operational buildings. Lyon owned a considerable amount of land. His enterprise plotted the nearby borough of Tyrone in 1851. In 1910, after three generations of Lyons in residence, the family home was sold. It became a country retreat known as the Tyrone Country Club, or Fairbrook. When it returned to private residency in 1944, the 28-room Lyon house played host to many visitors who came to fish. Pres. Dwight D. Eisenhower stayed here as a guest in 1953 while visiting his brother Milton, president of Penn State University. While in office, Pres. Jimmy Carter discovered the area and has been a frequent visitor over the years, staying on the grounds with his family.

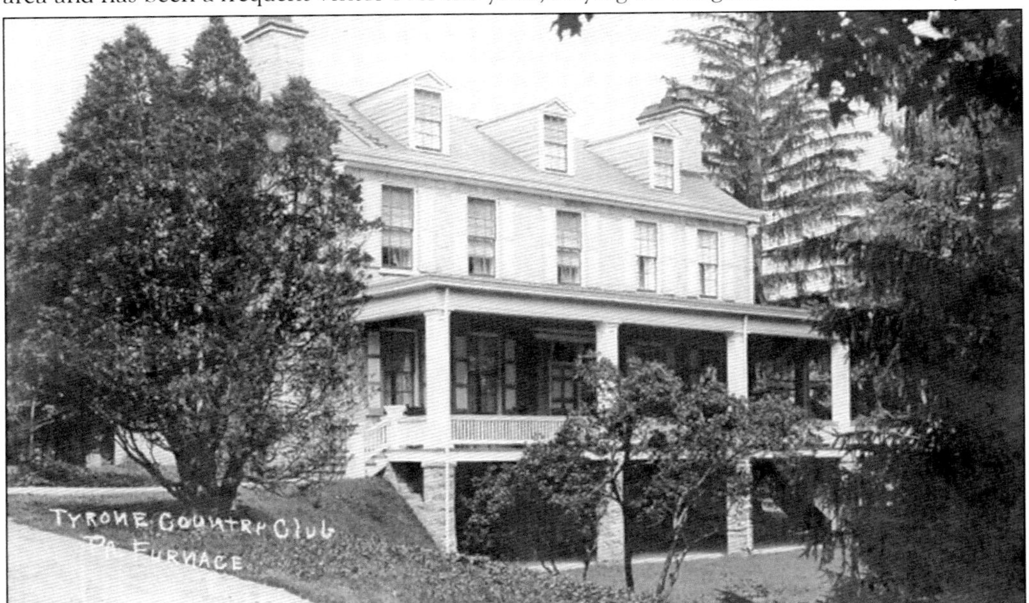

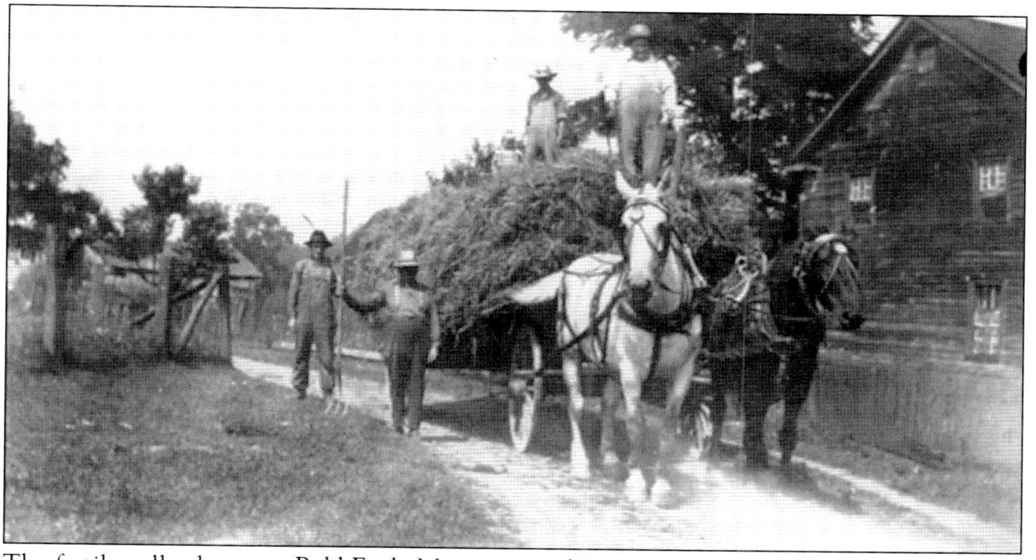

The fertile valley between Bald Eagle Mountain and Tussey Mountain was home to a number of villages and crossroads. Between the villages, farmland stretched in all directions. On the farm roads that connected the towns, a frequent sight were wagons piled high with hay for farm animals. Other wagons hauled wheat that was to be made into flour at one of the local mills. Pictured is the Harpster family near Warriors Mark.

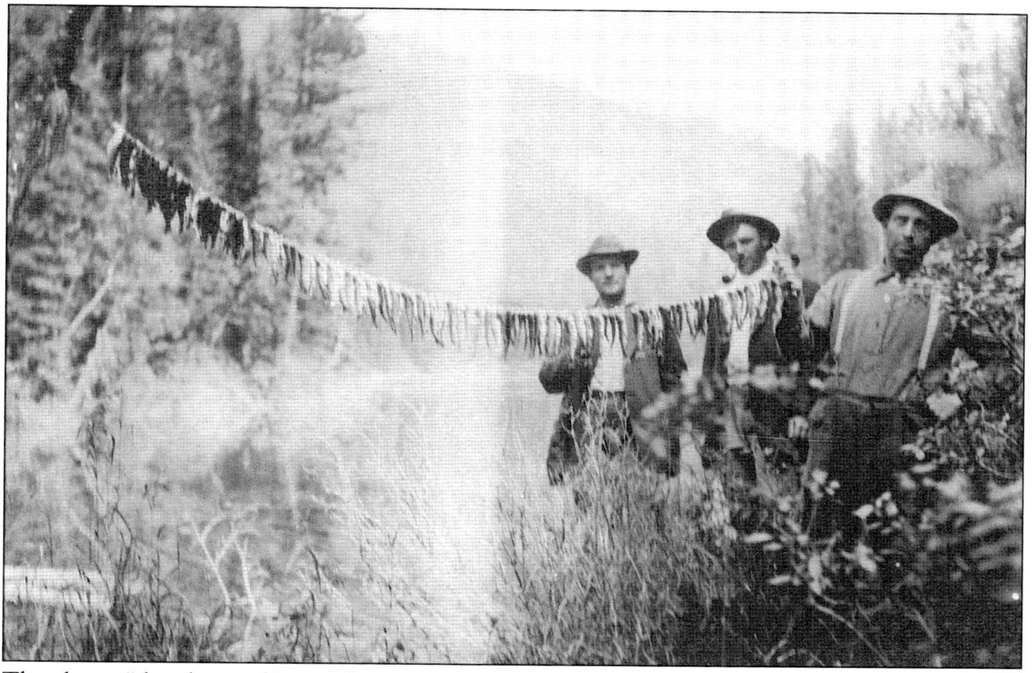

The phrase "the plenty of Pennsylvania" might come to mind with this image. These three buddies on a fishing weekend were able to bring in more than a few weeks' supply of fish on their Juniata River excursion. In the days before refrigeration, fish not eaten on the trip would be salt cured and then hardwood would be gathered. Experienced fishermen could build a nice steady fire and smoke their catch for packing and carrying home.

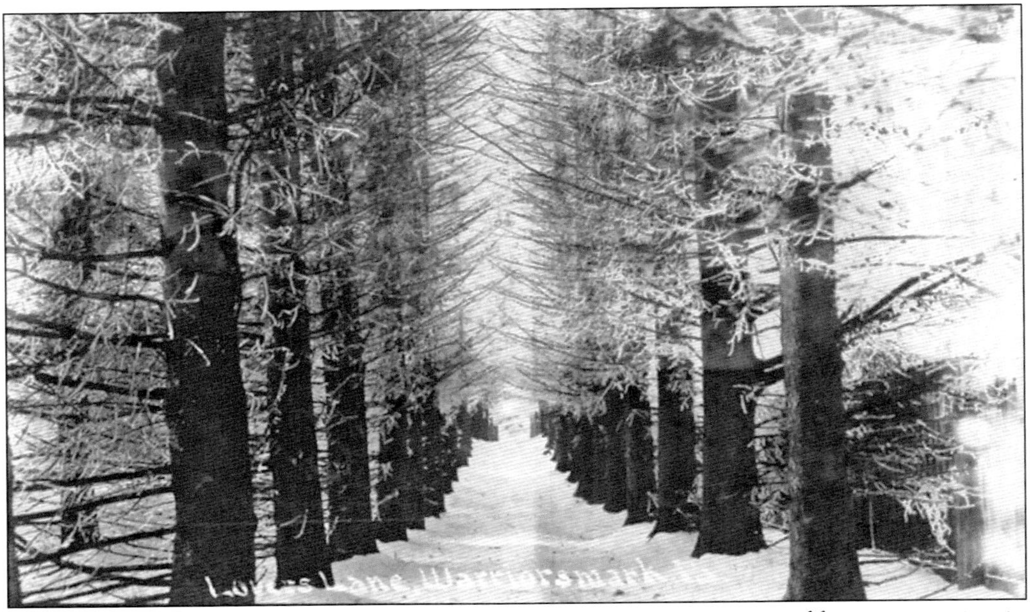

Before roadways were regulated, it was necessary for landowners or groups of farmers to maintain routes between villages and farms. Some went one step further and planned the plantings that went with the route. An unusual grove of identical trees once lined the road at Lovers Lane near Warriors Mark.

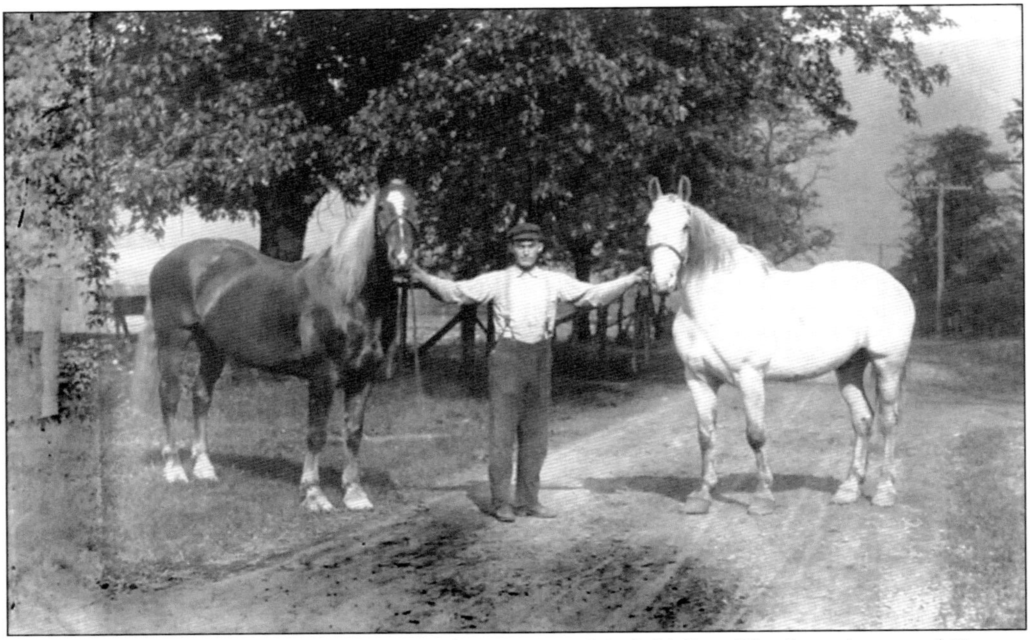

L. Allie Reigh ran an express wagon in the Warriors Mark Valley. The Lewisburg and Tyrone railroad had 12 stops between Tyrone and Scotia. Regular freight and passenger service was scheduled along this route. Reigh kept busy delivering packages from the small depots. He was also known in the valley for his ability to raise fine horses.

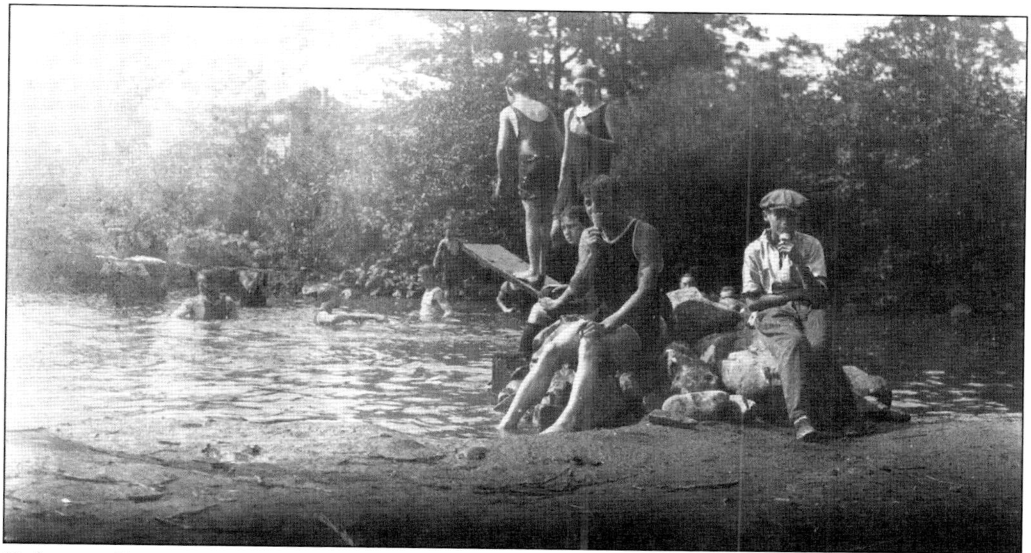

Coleraine Forge was in operation from about 1814 to 1860. When it ceased operation, the land was eventually converted into a public park. A large lake and wooded trails can be found there. This group of neighbors from Northwood, Blair County, spent the day enjoying their two favorite things: swimming and ice cream.

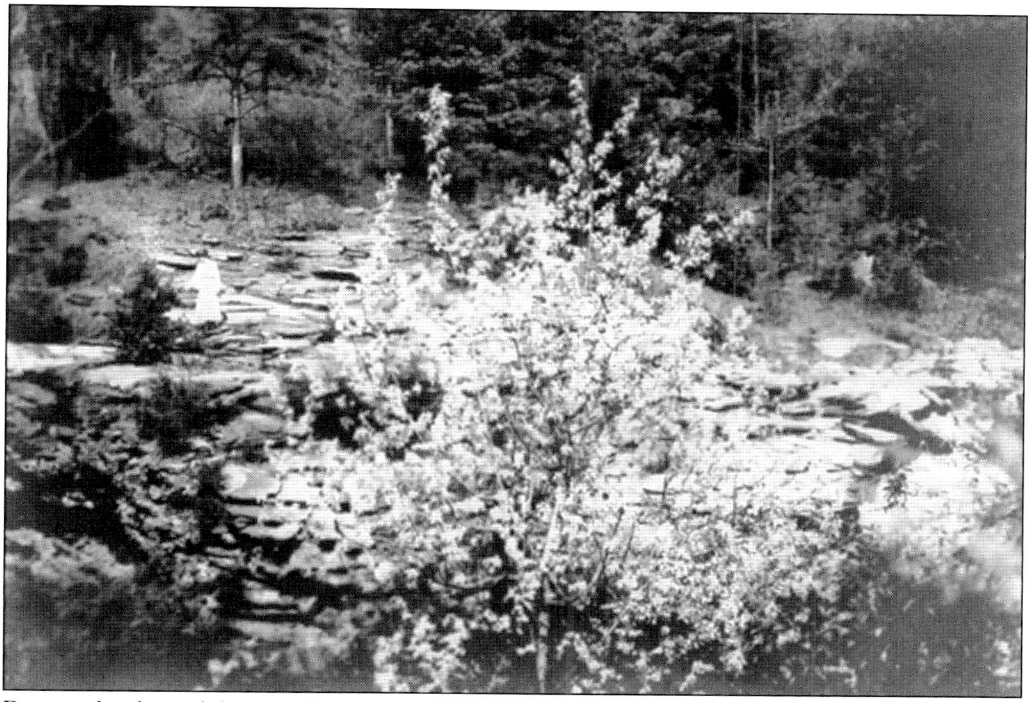

During the days of the iron furnaces and forges, lime was a necessary component in processing ore. Vast deposits of pure limestone were found in northeastern Huntingdon County. A number of stone companies had offices in Tyrone and millions of tons were hauled by rail out of this region. Some abandoned quarries from the early years became popular hiking areas. Here a woman strolls on the rocks beyond the tree.

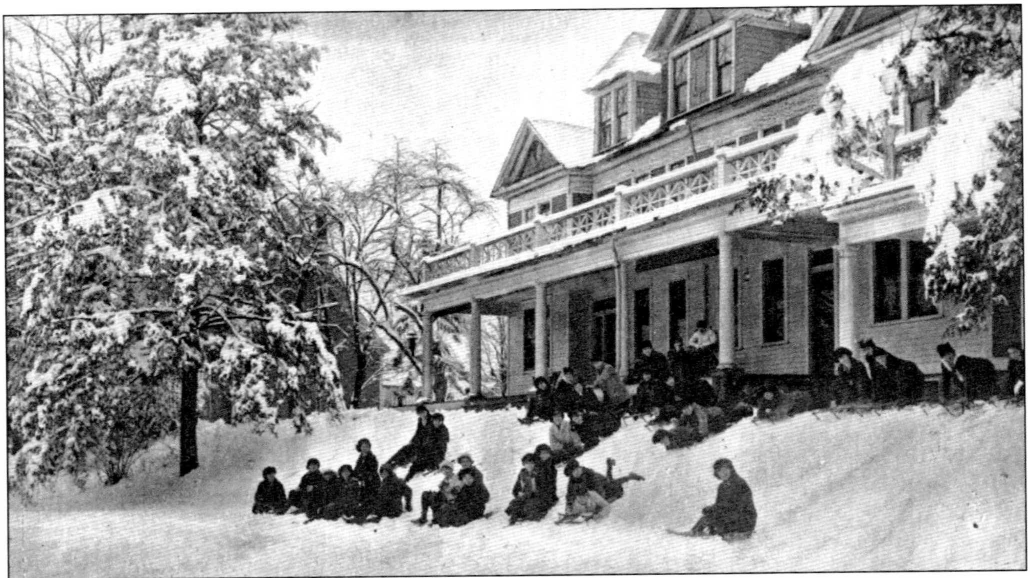

In 1853, the internationally known Grier School was opened as the Mountain Female Seminary outside of Tyrone at Birmingham. Founded by local investors, the growing campus was acquired by the Grier family that had in recent years established the Grier Foundation. The school provides a well-rounded education in a verdant setting. The Little Juniata River rolls directly below the campus.

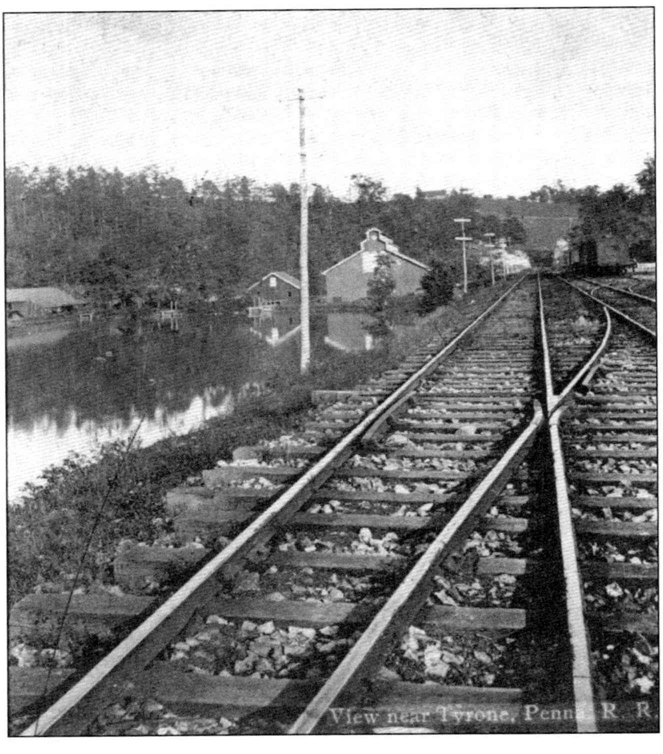

The Pennsylvania Railroad (PRR) rolled right past the forge and rolling mill below Tyrone. A large holding dam was built off the Little Juniata River for industrial use. Iron manufacturing began here around 1805. The iron produced in this region from two dozen furnaces and forges was known as "Juniata iron." The iron and stone nearby is perhaps the reason the PRR decided to take this hilly route across the region.

The Stereoscopic Emporium of New York sent a photographer along the Pennsylvania Railroad in the 1860s to capture picturesque views. He found a group of women walking to town and asked them to pose for an image around a wheelbarrow. He entitled his photograph "Five Fair Ladies on the Juniata East of Tyrone City."

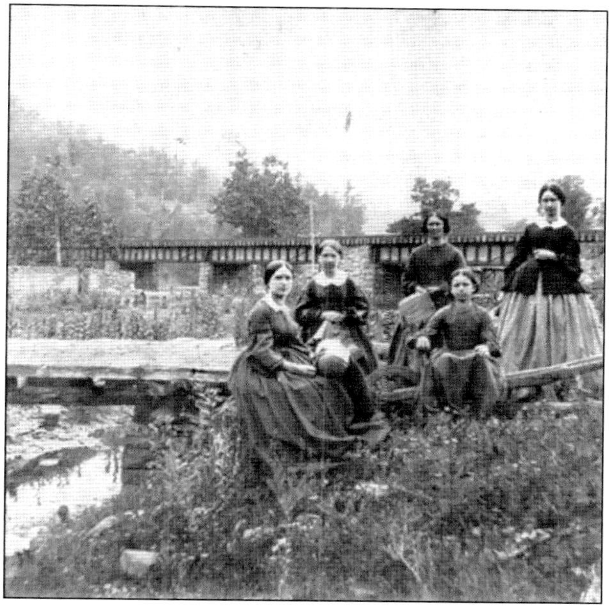

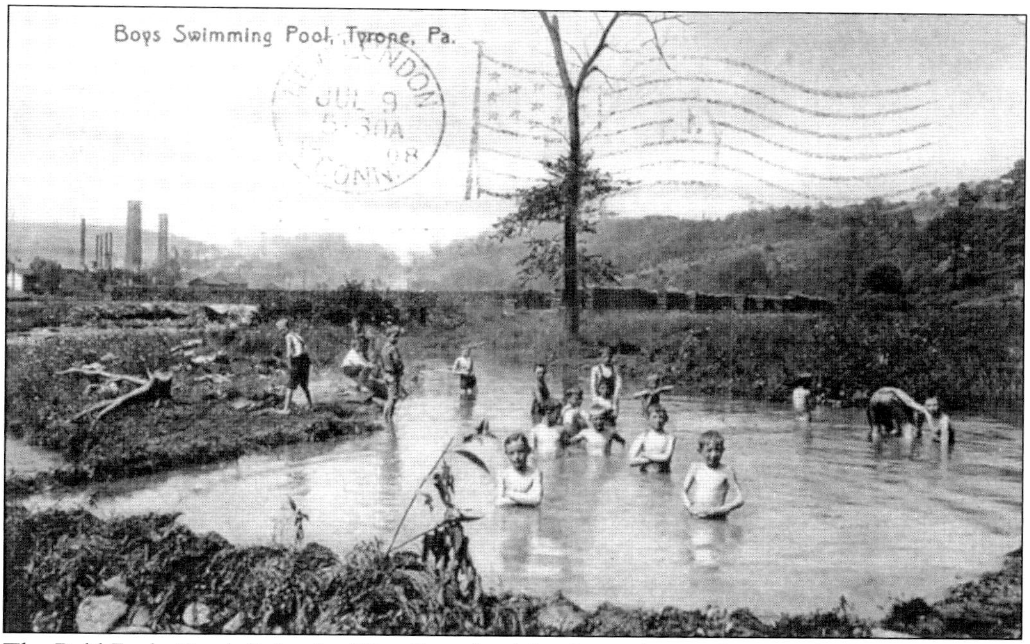

The Bald Eagle Creek links the West Branch of the Susquehanna River with the Little Juniata River. Swimming holes along the creek were once popular gathering places on a hot day. Stacked behind these boys are the "wood ranks." Acres of lumber for the paper company, Westvaco Corporation, were a constant presence on the northern end of Tyrone.

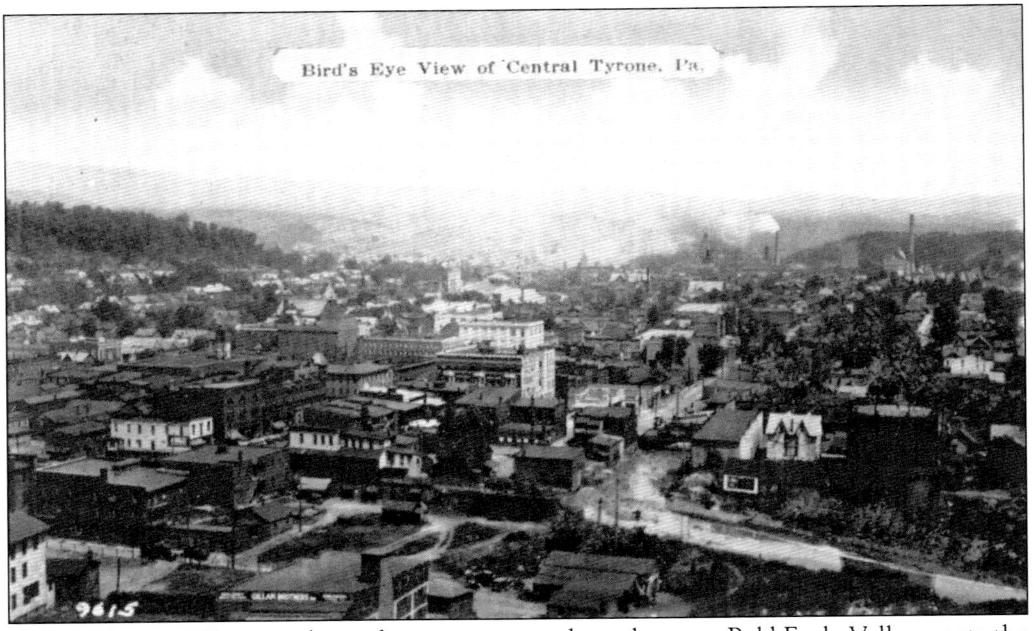

The small city of Tyrone is located at a water gap where the great Bald Eagle Valley meets the Logan Valley. It is here that the Bald Eagle Creek empties into the Little Juniata River. Because of its strategic position as a crossroads of commerce, Tyrone provided astounding profits for the railroad industry. This former iron center, first settled in 1851, was home to three national banks and a dozen hotels in its heyday.

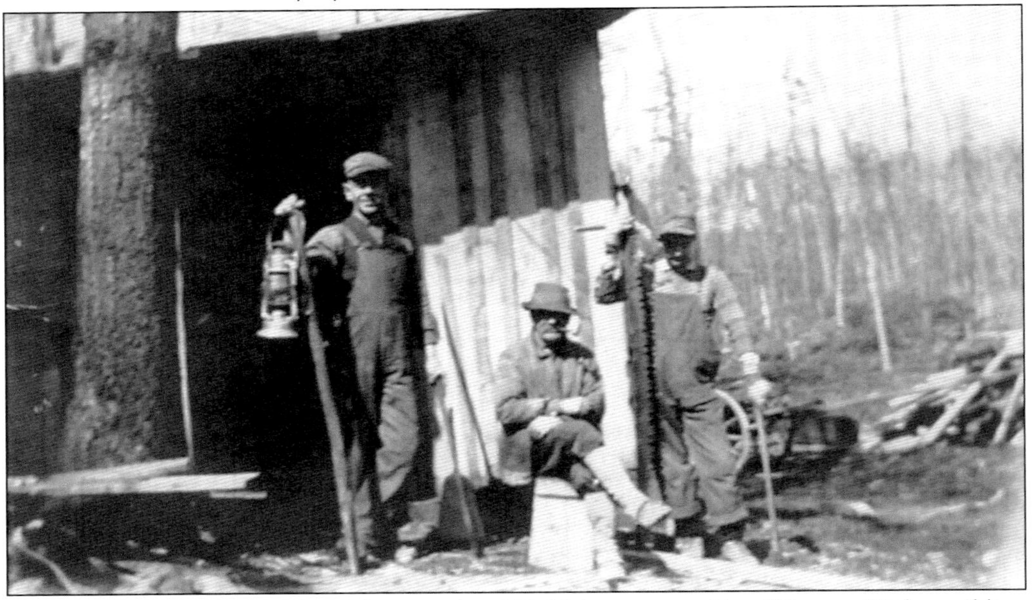

Three loggers pose for traveling photographer J.H. Holtzinger outside of Tyrone. With a rail line open in the Bald Eagle Valley to Pennsylvania's enormous forest region, Tyrone provided easy access to the main line of the Pennsylvania Railroad. Much of the lumber was used locally at a West Virginia paper company and at one of the four planing mills that operated here to provide finished building and decorative wood products.

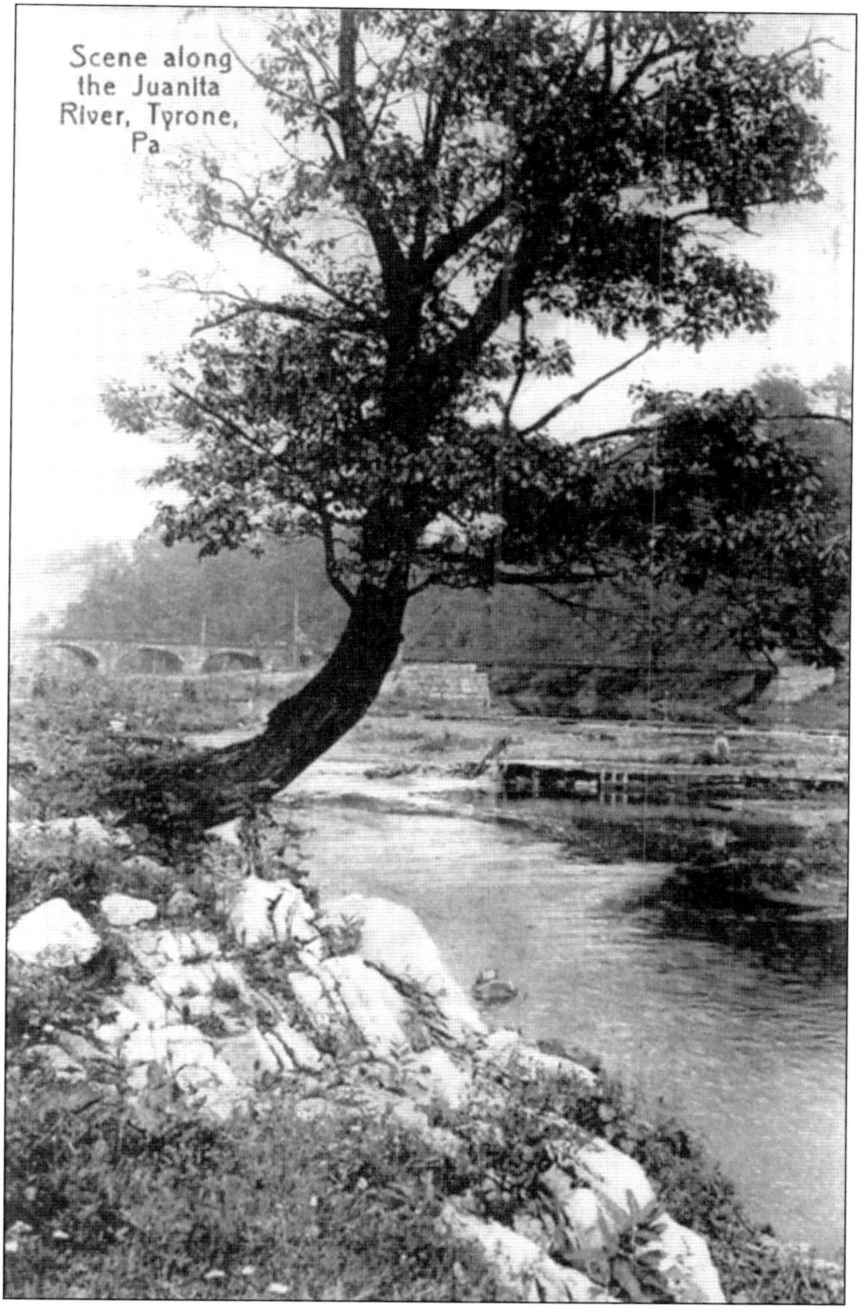

Between Spruce Creek and Birmingham, railroad bridges were needed to cross the Little Juniata River 12 times in a distance of only five miles. The 20-mile journey from Huntingdon to Tyrone required more bridge construction than the previous 100-plus miles from the Susquehanna River. At Tyrone, the bridges intensified. Railroads left town in three directions. A streetcar line operated, which had its own bridges, and there were two creeks that needed crossings. It is for this reason an old photograph may have three bridges of various building materials showing up in the background.

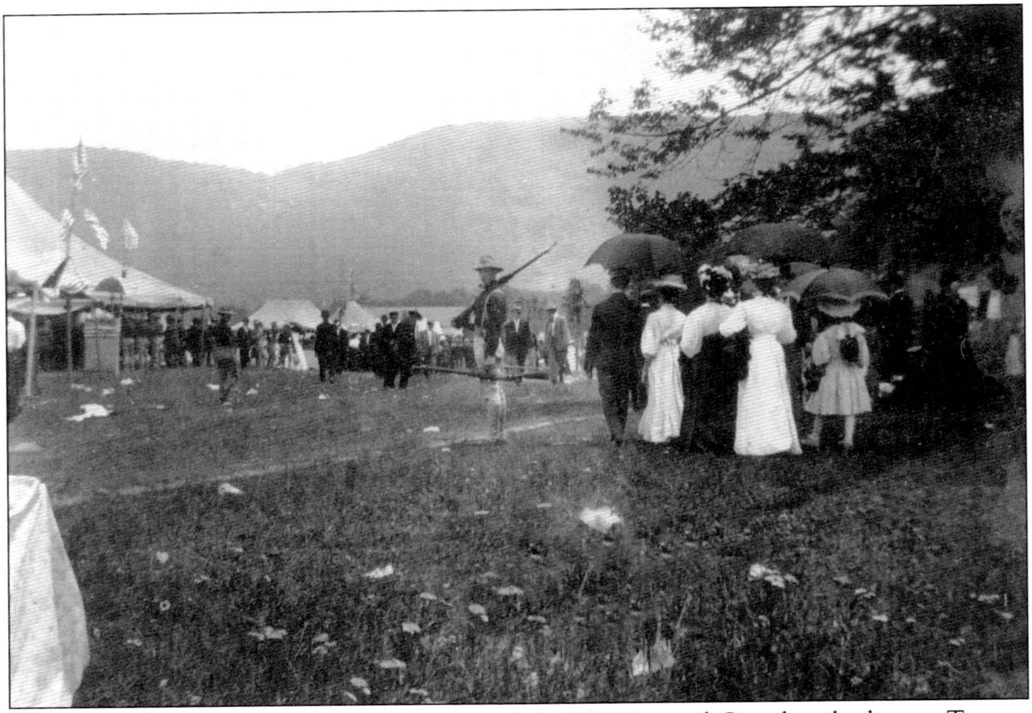

In 1907, Pennsylvania's largest encampment of the US National Guard took place at Tyrone. The Sheridan Troop, based in Tyrone, was given a directive to host the Western Division of the National Guard. Word was received that Gov. Edwin Stuart would arrive by train later in the week to review the troops. Known as Camp Lindsey, the temporary installation was under the command of General Wylie. From July 20–27, hundreds of tents were pitched and supplies were delivered by the carload. The men performed drills and weapon demonstrations. With Governor Stuart in attendance, an acrobatic rider and horse show was presented. Train stations were jammed with arrivals coming to view the camp. The activities took place at Tipton, just south of Tyrone Borough.

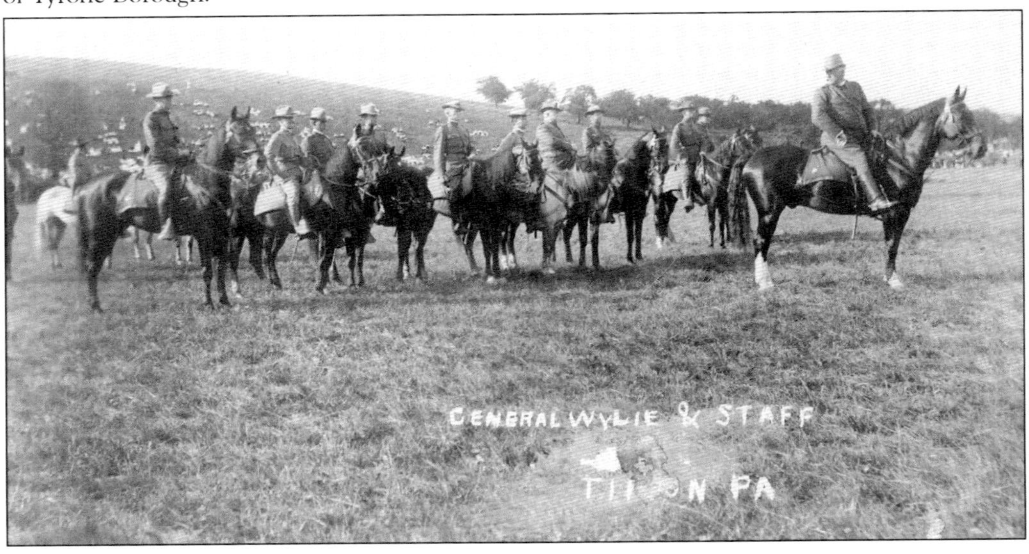

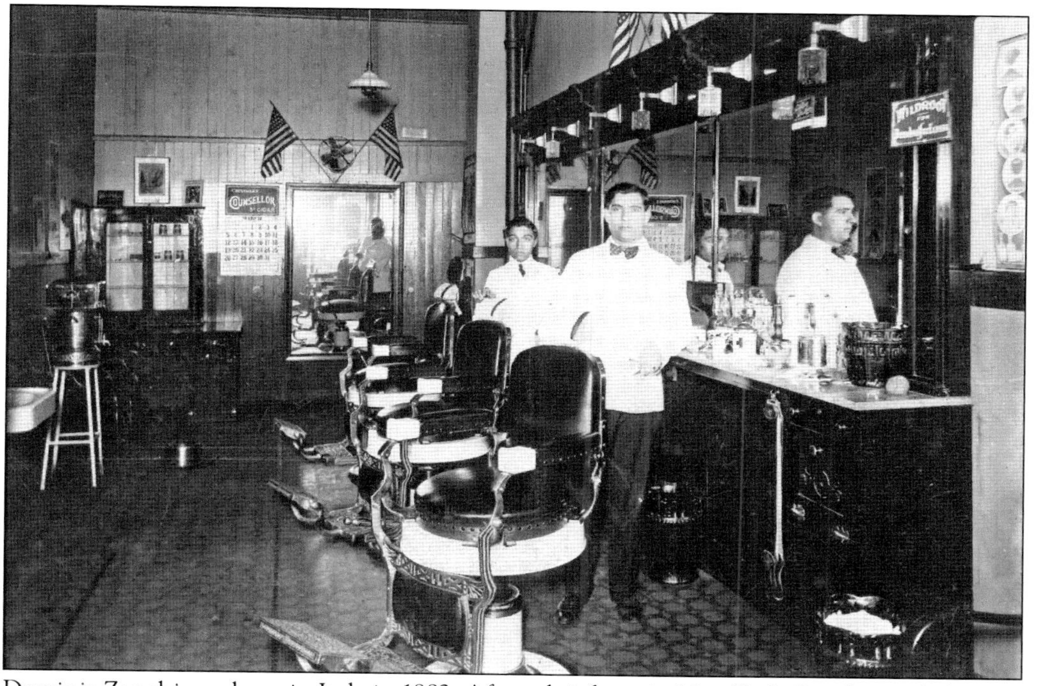

Dominic Zanghi was born in Italy in 1882. After a brief stay in New York City, he made his way to Tyrone where he was told business along the main line was brisk. Opening a barbershop near the depot, Zanghi, now known as "Mr. Zang," raised his son Joe Zang in the business. The Zang barbershop had a presence in the Tyrone business district for more than 80 years.

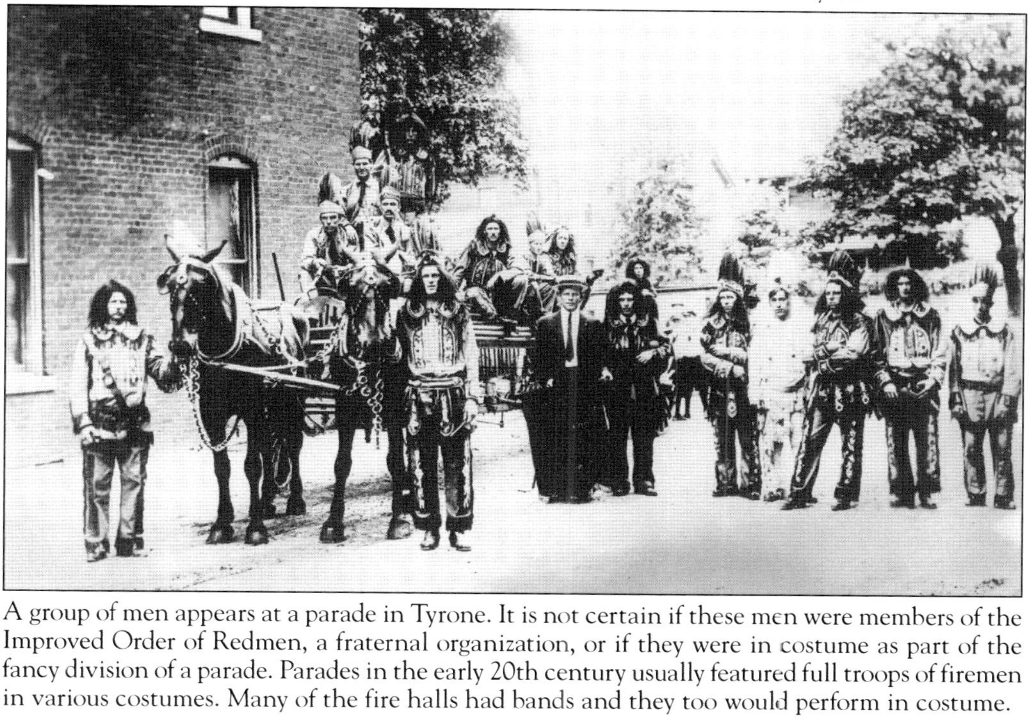

A group of men appears at a parade in Tyrone. It is not certain if these men were members of the Improved Order of Redmen, a fraternal organization, or if they were in costume as part of the fancy division of a parade. Parades in the early 20th century usually featured full troops of firemen in various costumes. Many of the fire halls had bands and they too would perform in costume.

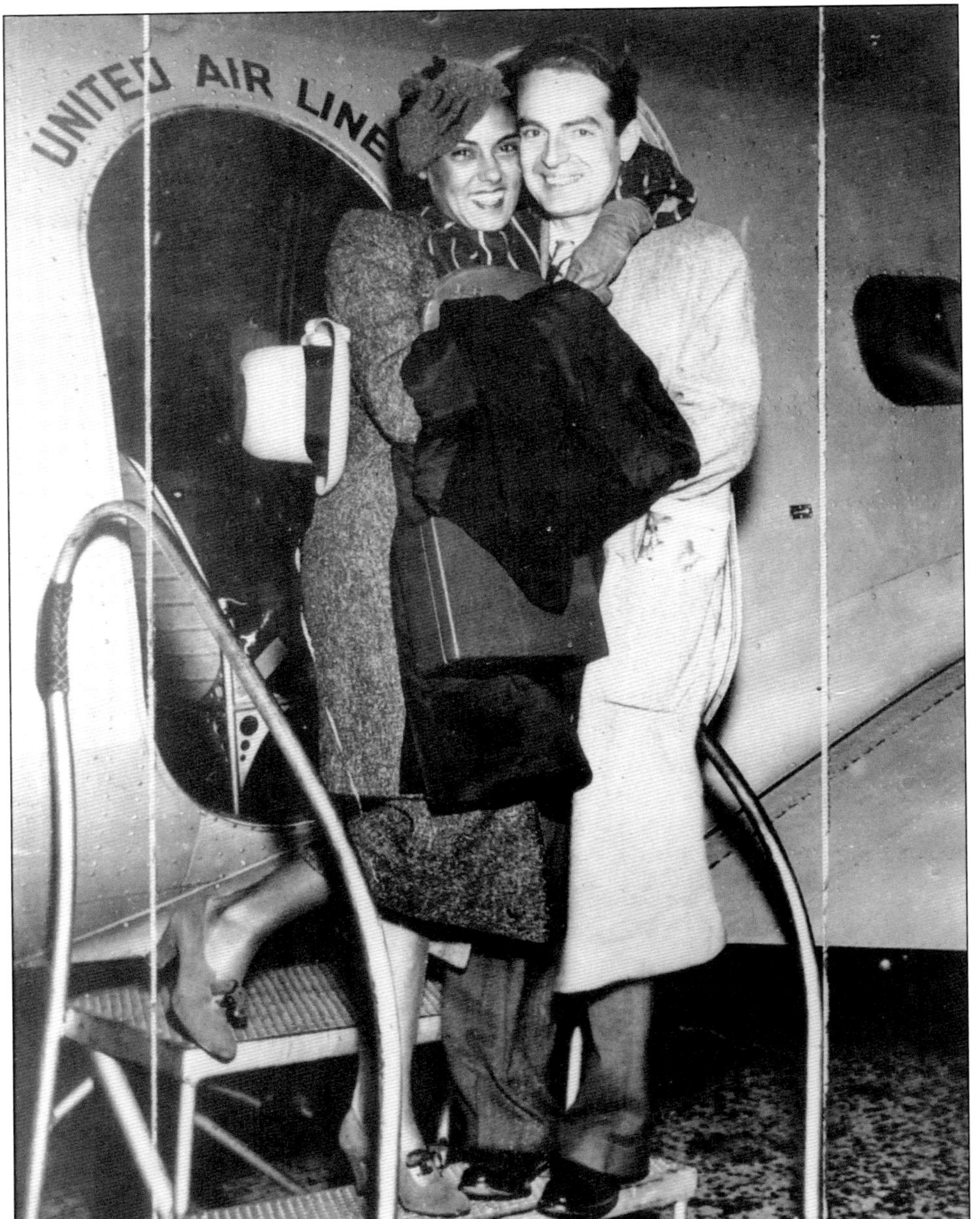

Internationally acclaimed entertainer Fred Waring was a Juniata native. Born in 1900 in Tyrone, he gained prominence in the early 1920s as the leader of Waring's Pennsylvanians. This talented musician and emcee formed one of the largest organizations in the entertainment industry. A broadcasting pioneer, Waring performed for more than 60 years and died at Penn State University in July 1984. During his extended career, he was responsible for a number of innovations that today are taken for granted. In 1939, his band appeared on the first television broadcast of a performing orchestra. Later, in the 1940s, Waring introduced America to the televised musical variety format. Pictured here, Waring poses for a pre-wedding photograph with dancer Evelyn Nair in 1933 at Chicago.

In the wilderness above Tyrone in the 1870s, a photographer recorded a fish camp on one of the smaller streams that eventually leads to the Juniata River. The fish camps of central Pennsylvania were non-permanent structures seen along the banks of streams. Constructed of sticks and rope, those who fished could find shelter from the elements in one of these structures. If the sportsman was lucky, it would still be standing when visiting that spot again.

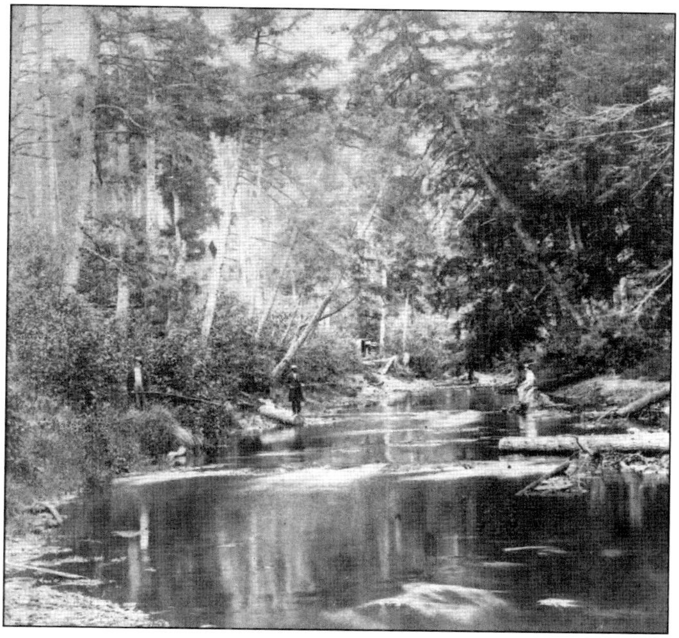

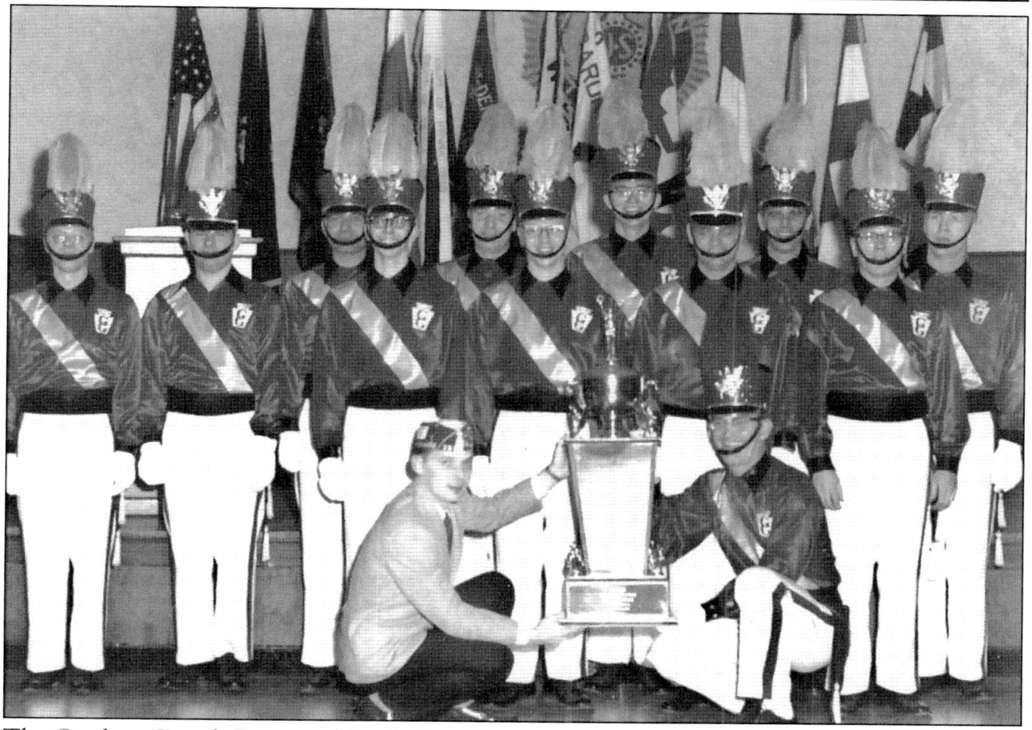

The Gardner Guards Drum and Bugle Corps are assembled after receiving a best in show trophy at the 1961 inaugural parade for Pres. John F. Kennedy. The group formed shortly after World War II. Many of the members had no training, but through discipline, they developed into one of the top parade units in the state. They appeared on the Ed Sullivan Show in 1957, and have brought much honor to Tyrone.

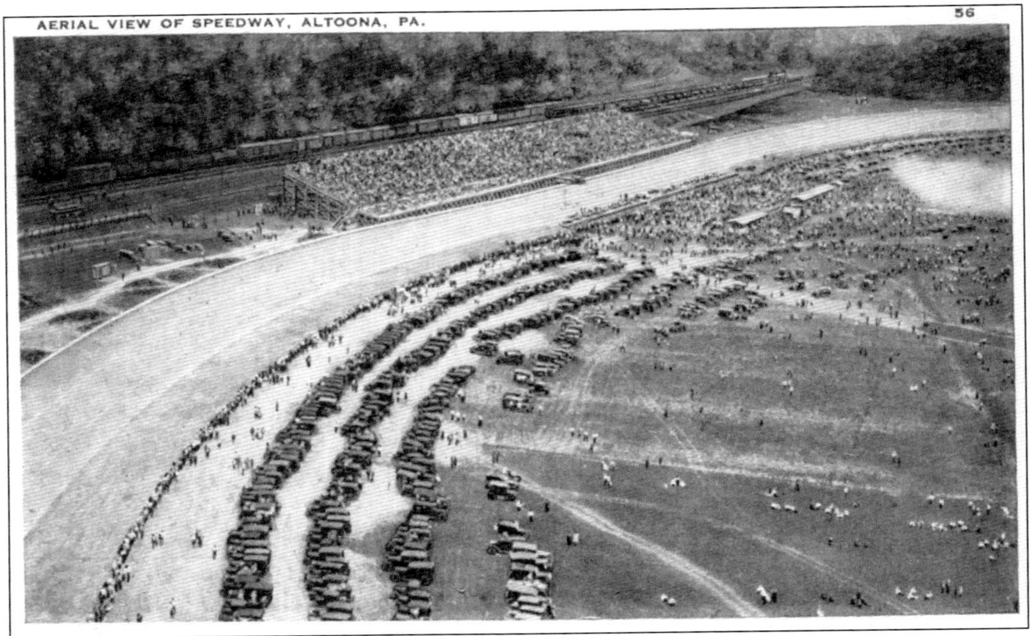

In the 1920s, the top race car drivers of the era converged on Tyrone to compete at "the mile-and-a-quarter bowl" constructed from lumber. The Altoona Tyrone Speedway board track attracted as many as 55,000 to some events. Races were held in June and September. Five world records were broken at the opening race in 1921. This track was on a circuit that included Daytona and Indianapolis.

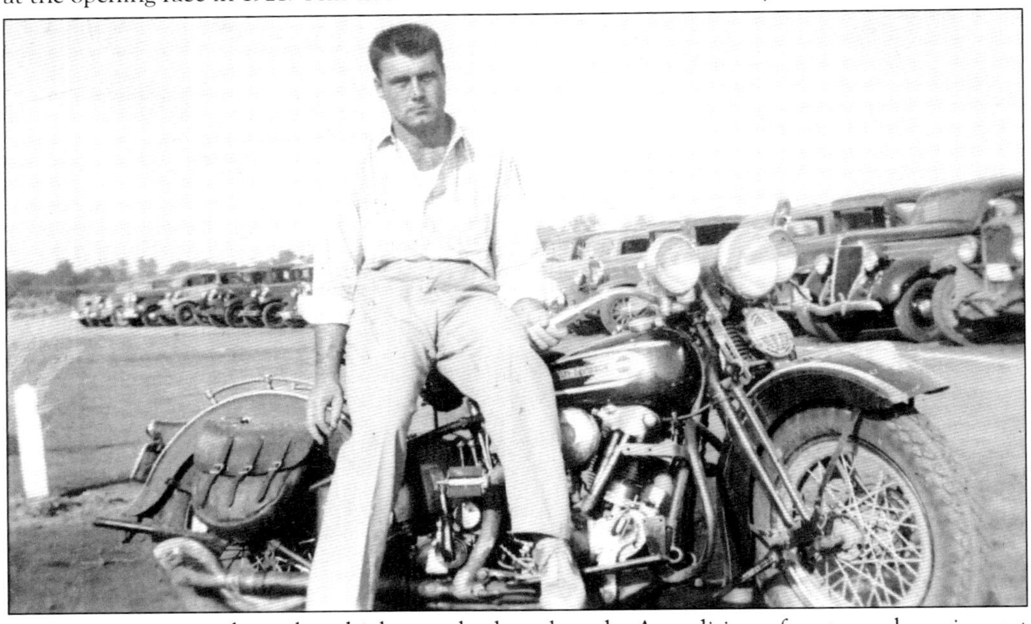

Race cars were not the only vehicles to ply these boards. A tradition of motorcycle racing got started here. Harley Davidson Company sponsored some of the meets. This gave the manufacturers a chance to test the limits of their new bikes. When the Great Depression ended professional races, the board track was dismantled. Motorcycles used the dirt path here for another 30 years. Stock cars competed also.

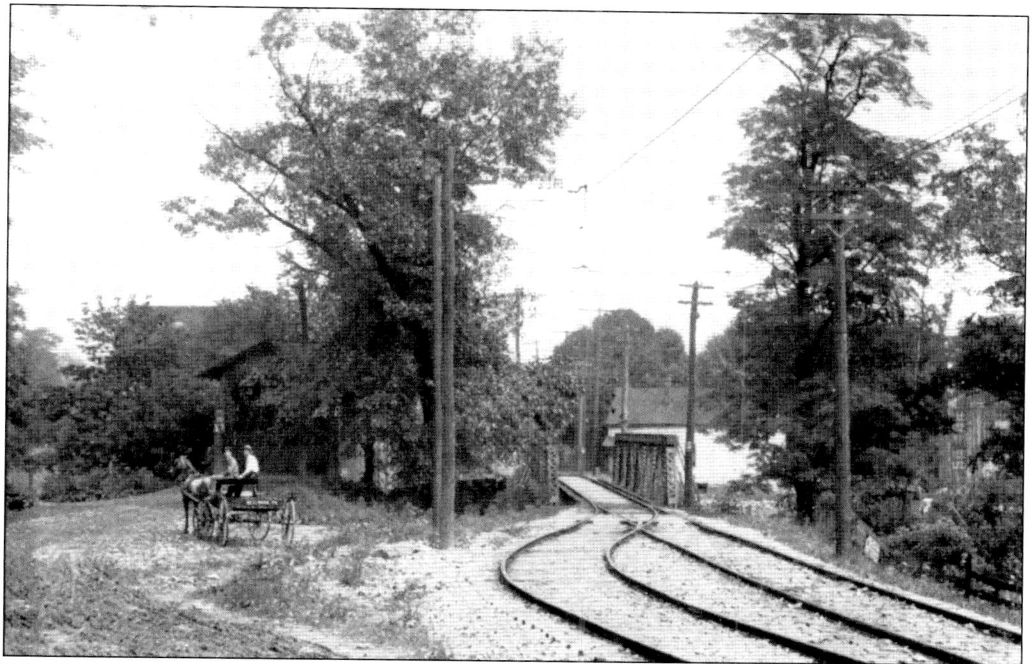

The double tracks of the Altoona and Logan Valley Electric Railway converged to a single track at White Bridge on the edge of Bellwood. White Bridge crosses the Little Juniata River on a small iron trestle. Bellwood was one of the last communities to be established in Blair County, in 1888. Bells Mills preceded the borough. The Pennsylvania and Northwestern Railroad, a subsidiary of the Pennsylvania Railroad, had repair shops in Bellwood.

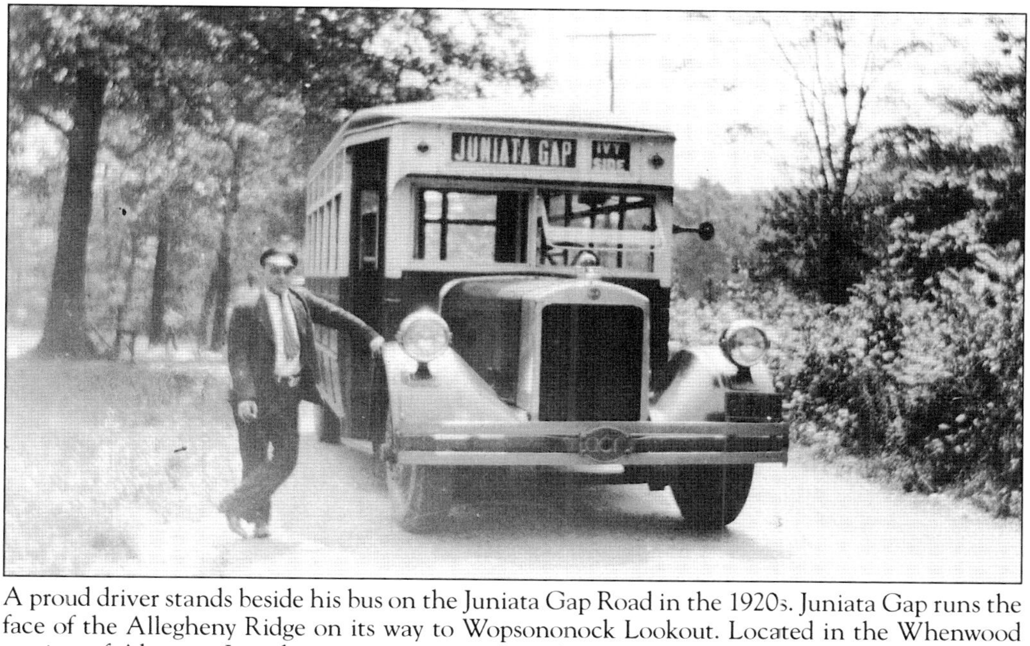

A proud driver stands beside his bus on the Juniata Gap Road in the 1920s. Juniata Gap runs the face of the Allegheny Ridge on its way to Wopsononock Lookout. Located in the Whenwood section of Altoona, Ivyside was an amusement park in generations past. In 1947, Penn State University bought 38 acres in Whenwood and moved its downtown facility to the former park.

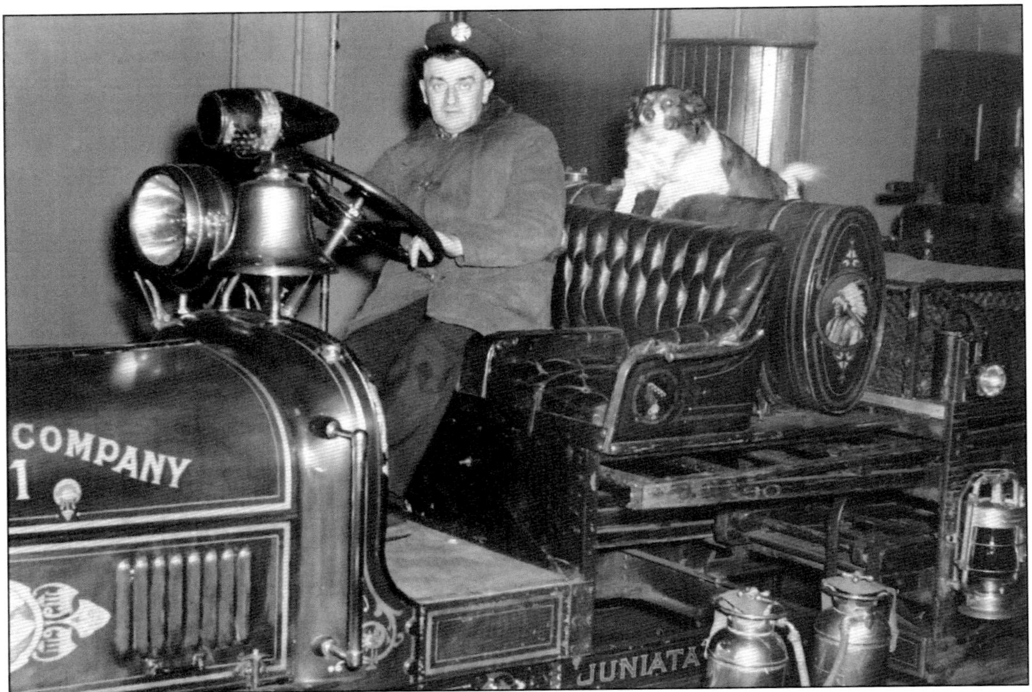

Juniata was at one time a town of its own before the quickly expanding city of Altoona consumed a number of independent neighborhoods. In this photograph, a fireman prepares to drive a very early fire engine out of the firehouse. His model has right-hand drive and is fitted with leather seats. Sparky the firehouse dog goes along for a ride.

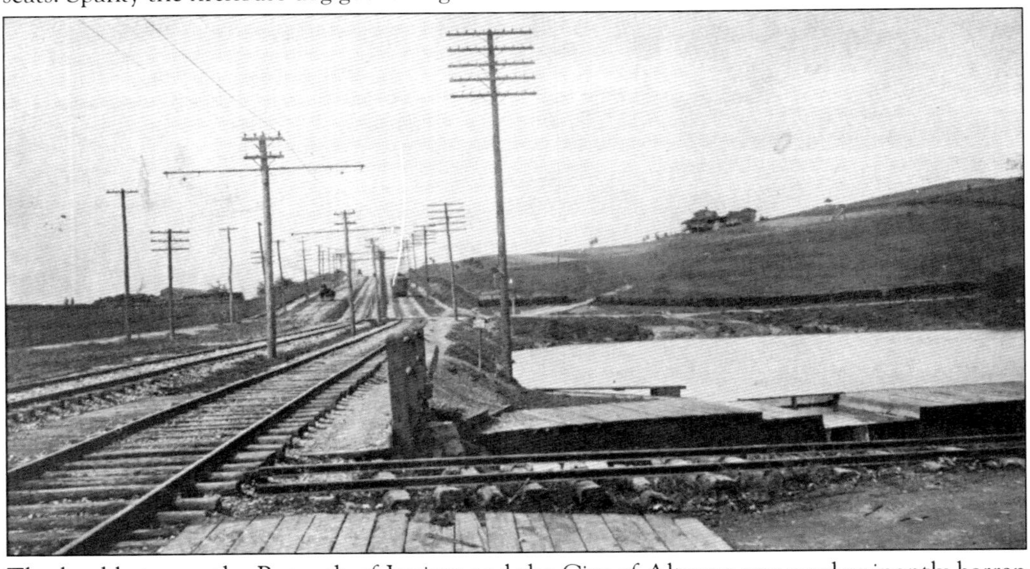

The land between the Borough of Juniata and the City of Altoona was predominantly barren at the start of the 20th century. The Altoona and Logan Valley Electric Railway maintained a double track here and was responsible for getting thousands of rail workers to their shops each day. The Pennsylvania Railroad constructed Cricket Field, seen in the distance. This sports complex drew athletes from all over the state for competitions.

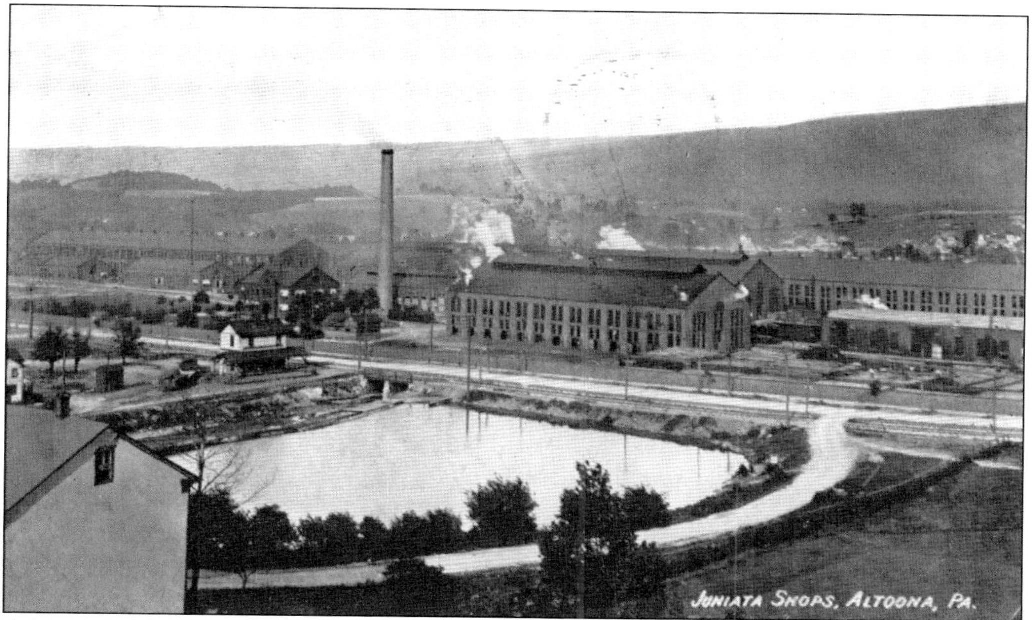

A large tract of land in the eastern section of Altoona known as Juniata was the choice for an ongoing expansion program of the Altoona Machine Shops. Pennsylvania Railroad officials found the old plant, built in1850, was overcrowded and could not accommodate the new breed of larger locomotives developed in the 1880s. Construction began here in 1888, with completion in 1890. A new assembly line process of engine construction streamlined the entire production process.

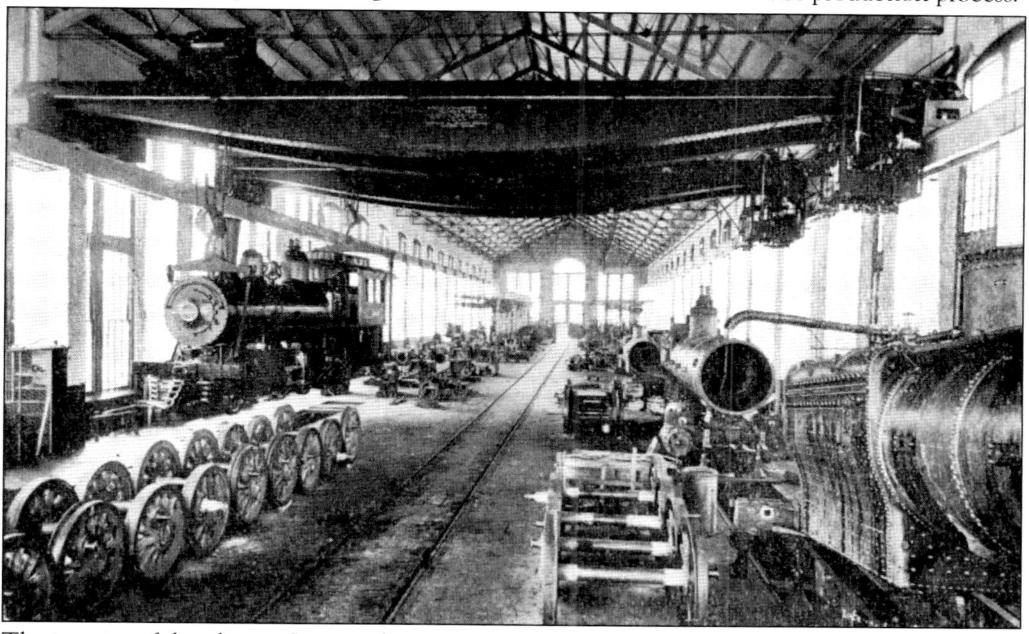

The interior of the plant at Juniata shows an inventory of completed wheels. As a locomotive was being built, the number of wheels was delivered to the staging area to be added to the engine. The wheels are actually known as tires. After thousands of miles of track contact, they are returned to the foundry, heated, and the band of steel on the surface slides off to be replaced.

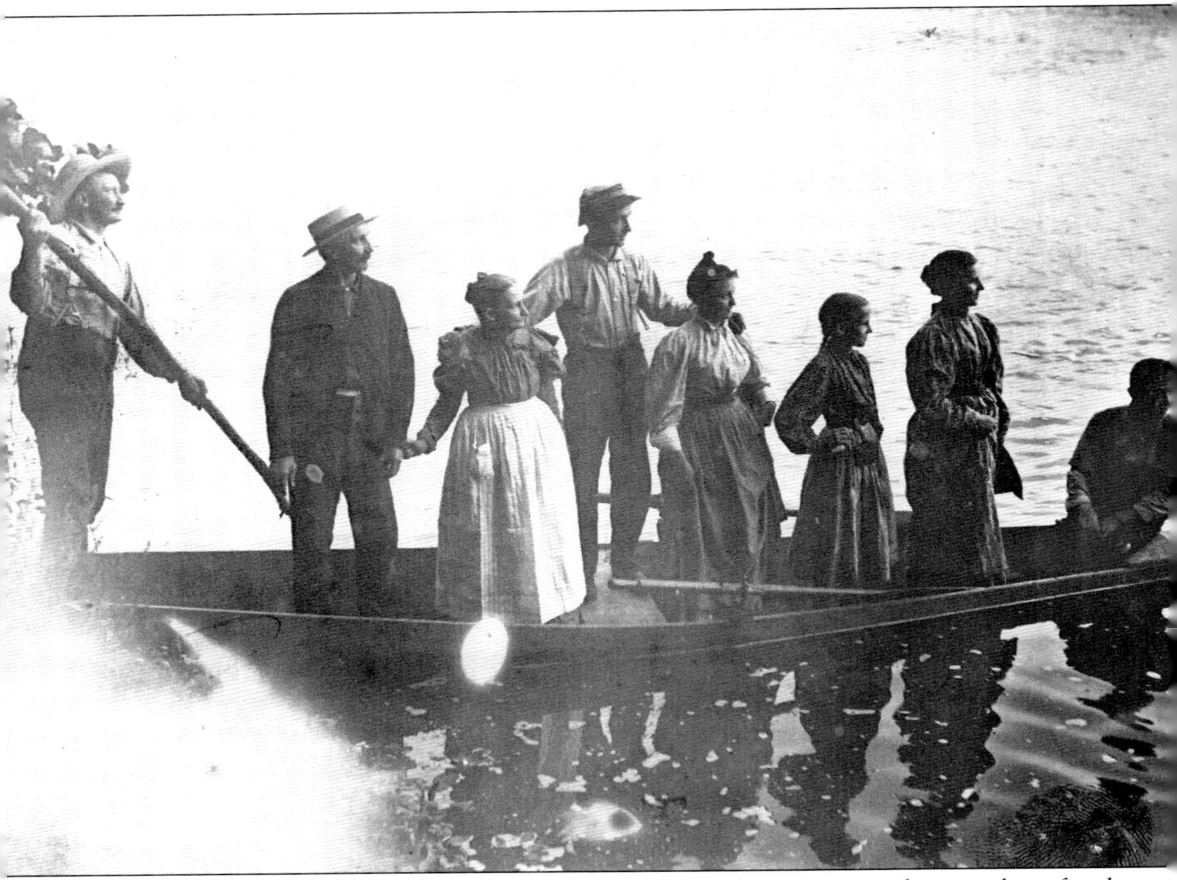

A family picnic at Altoona was an occasion to gather this group together in a boat for the photographer. The Little Juniata River finds its source outside of Altoona where numerous runs from the Allegheny Front form a stream. Winding its way north through the Logan Valley, the stream gains power at each gap and tributary. It merges with the Bald Eagle Creek at Tyrone where it exits the Logan Valley through a natural water gap between Bald Eagle Mountain and Brush Mountain.

Eight

The PRR, Juniata's Companion

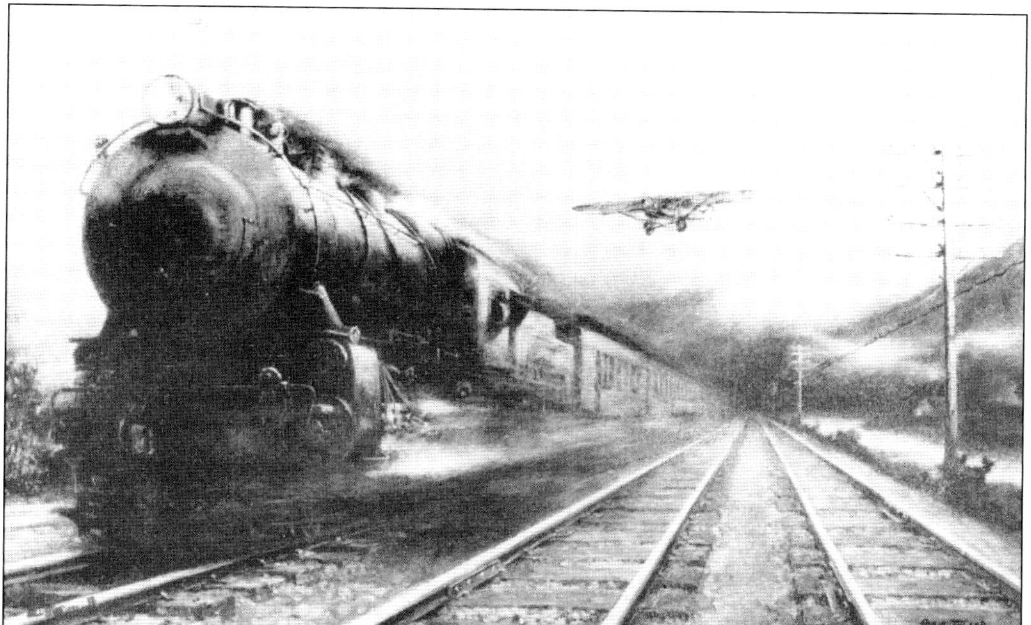

Artists working for the Pennsylvania Railroad (PRR) used the Juniata Valley as a backdrop in a great deal of their iconic advertising. The Broadway Limited was the premier PRR passenger train, operating one train daily between New York and Chicago via Philadelphia. The hills of Pennsylvania and the Juniata River were a reoccurring theme, making their appearance on office calendars and in magazines for generations to promote the world's greatest railway.

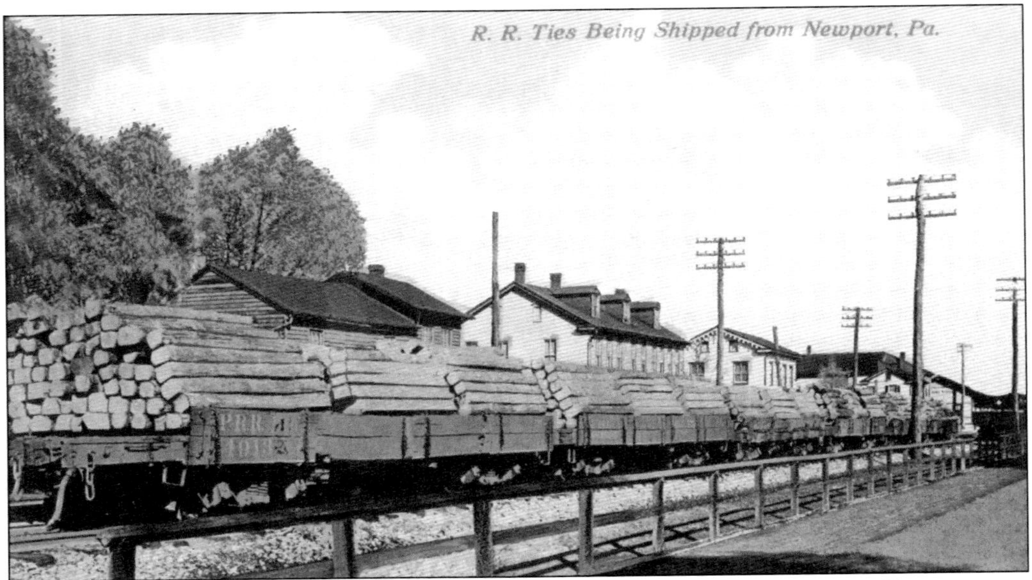

With the dramatic increase in rail usage in the late 1800s and the growing size of locomotives, the Pennsylvania Railroad announced plans for a monumental expansion of services. Magnificent stone arch viaducts replaced iron bridges and the enlargement of tunnels took place. The most noticeable upgrade was the addition of two more tracks to the whole system. The four-track operation required an unprecedented request for lumber. Flat cars laden with rail ties became a common sight.

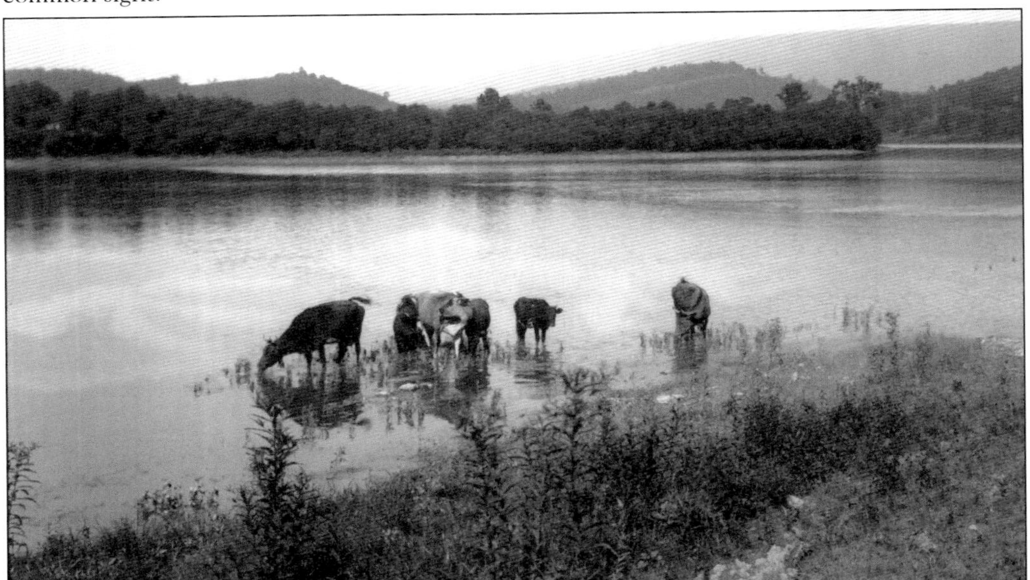

This 1891 photograph was taken along the Juniata River and was used in the promotion of ridership along the main line of the Pennsylvania Railroad. Special cameras were used that produced large format photographs that had striking detail. A custom-fitted railcar had a crow's nest on top so the photographer could take photographs from any angle as the train moved. A darkroom on board guaranteed completed photographs when the train reached its destination.

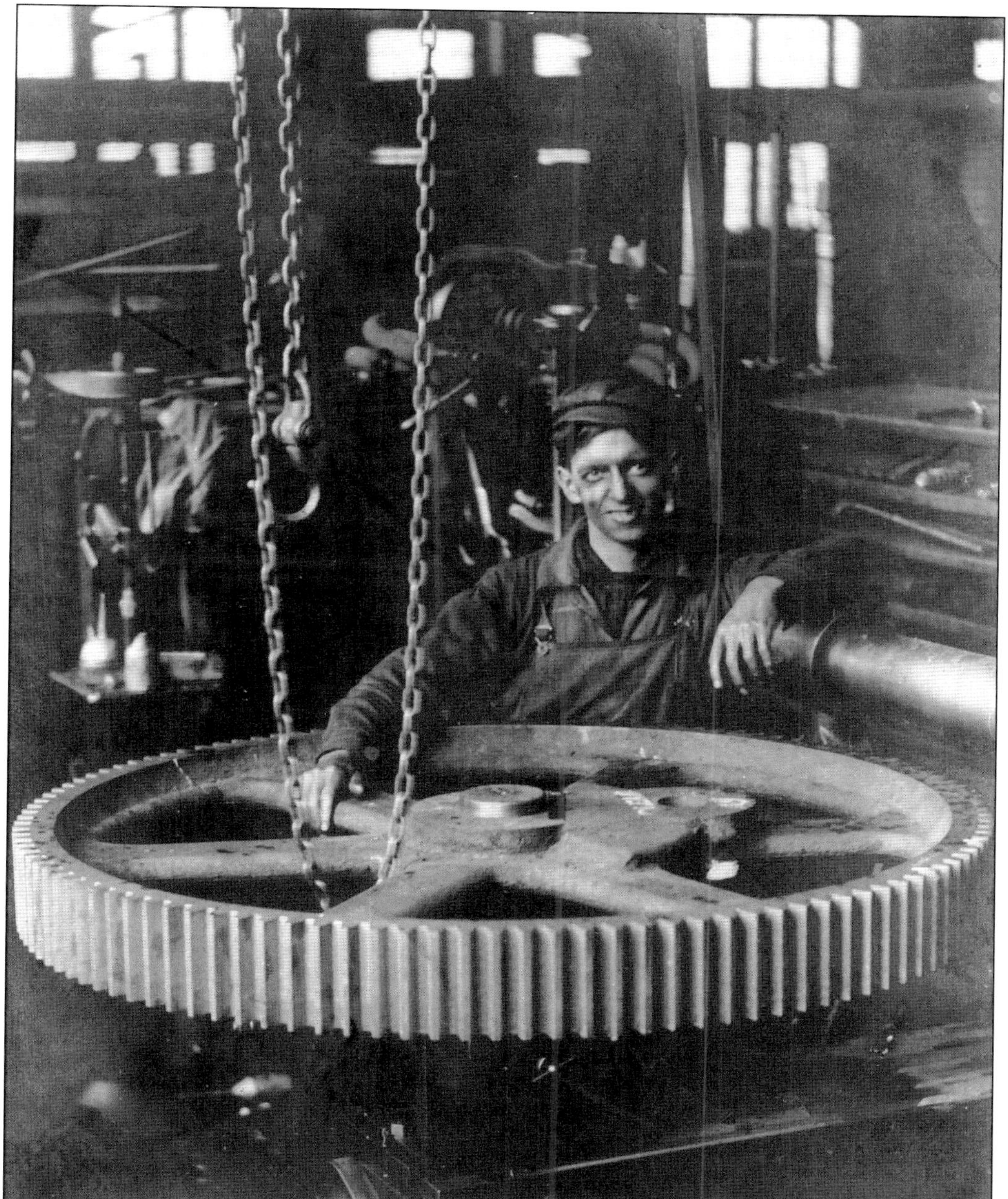

Dan poses in the Juniata Shops. He has just finished removing the filings from a gear that he is sending on its way to be fitted onto a locomotive. This was a project that Dan was assigned to follow from conception to finish. At the Pennsylvania Railroad foundry, Dan witnessed the sand casting of this key piece of machinery. Once cooled and inspected, it was returned for finishing. After polishing and oiling, it was ready for placement. This prototype gear was ordered for an engine that would produce a faster speed while utilizing the same amount of energy as previously used. Dan notes on the reverse of this photograph, "This is the largest gear ever made on the No. 3 universal milling machine and the largest ever made in the PRR shops . . . and, Dan made it!" Precision machinery and quality products were a standard at Juniata.

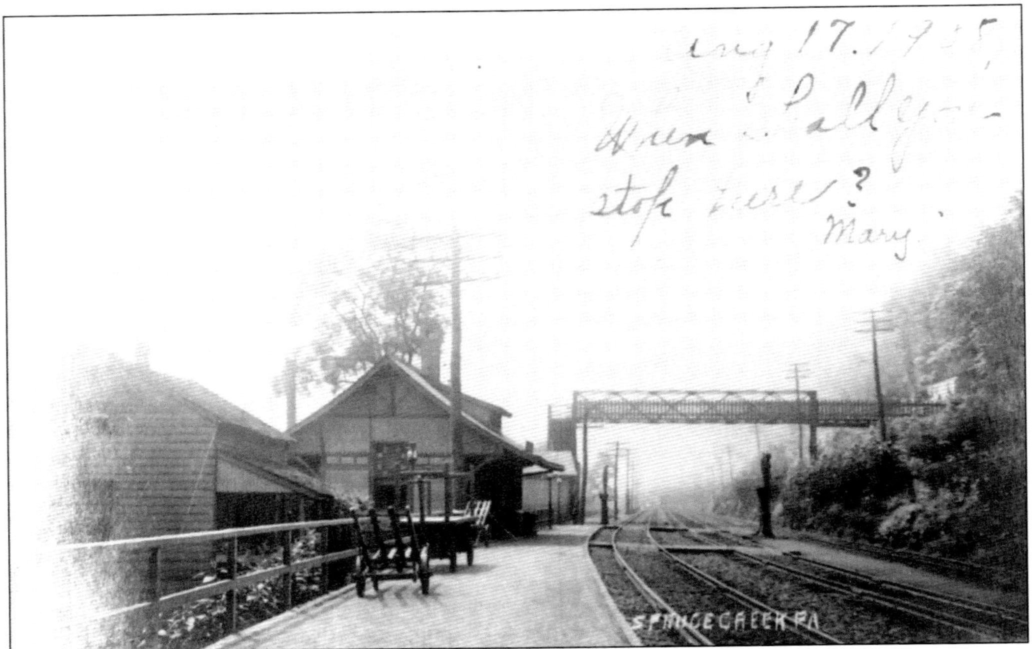

At Spruce Creek Station, the two-track system was still in place when this image was taken. The town had to be connected with a safety walkway above the tracks since the rail line skirted the town on a lower level. Spruce Creek is the first station after emerging from the tunnel. The next stop is Union Furnace, then Birmingham, before the train pulls into Tyrone City.

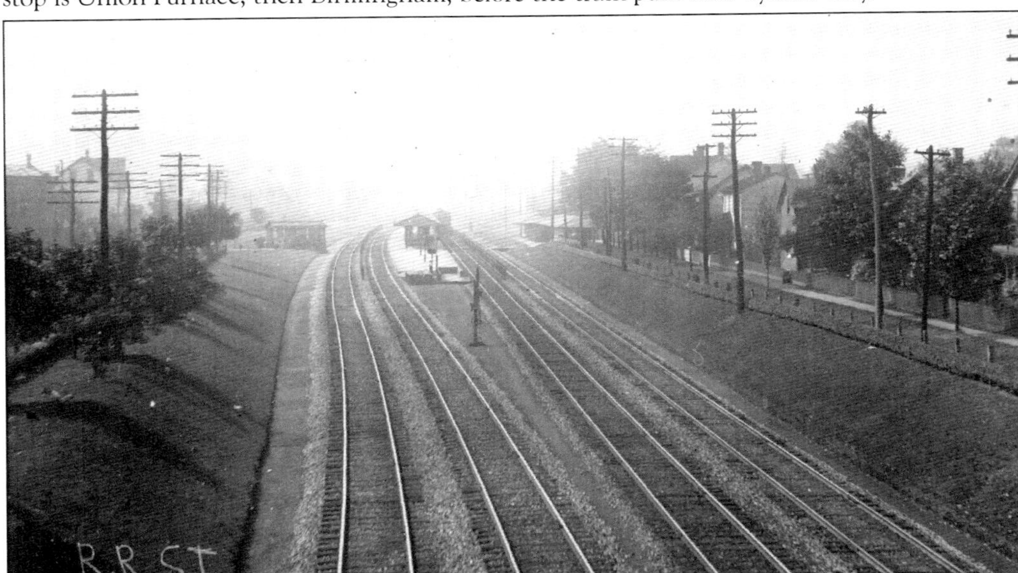

This is a fine example of the main line after the large scale rebuilding of the system. Four main tracks and branch lines for the Pennsylvania and Northwestern Railroad split the town of Bellwood. This gleaming broad width of track is what gave the Pennsylvania Railroad the idea to name its most prestigious locomotive the *Broadway Limited*. Many people mistakenly think the name refers to the New York City avenue.

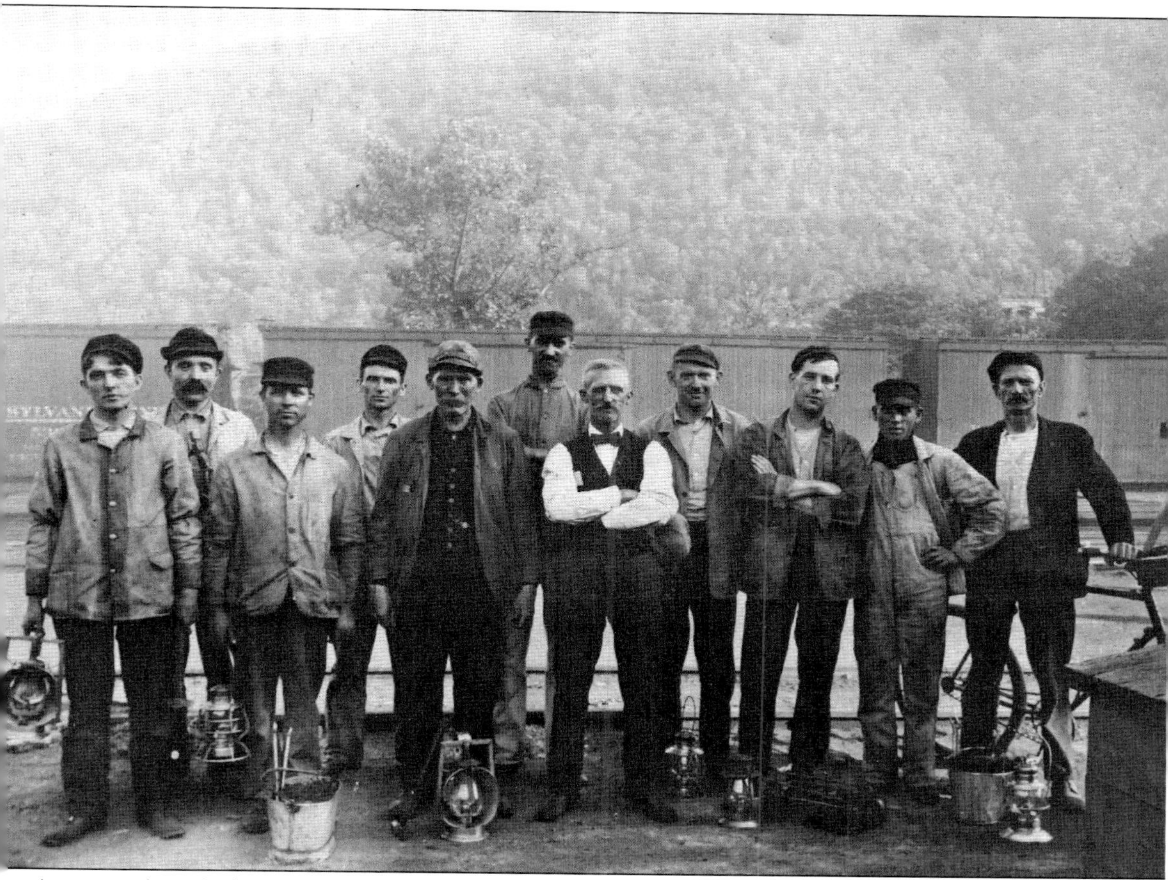

A group of gandy dancers and brakemen pause for the photographer while performing their rail inspections. Jacks Mountain appears to be in the distance. One fellow brought along his bicycle.

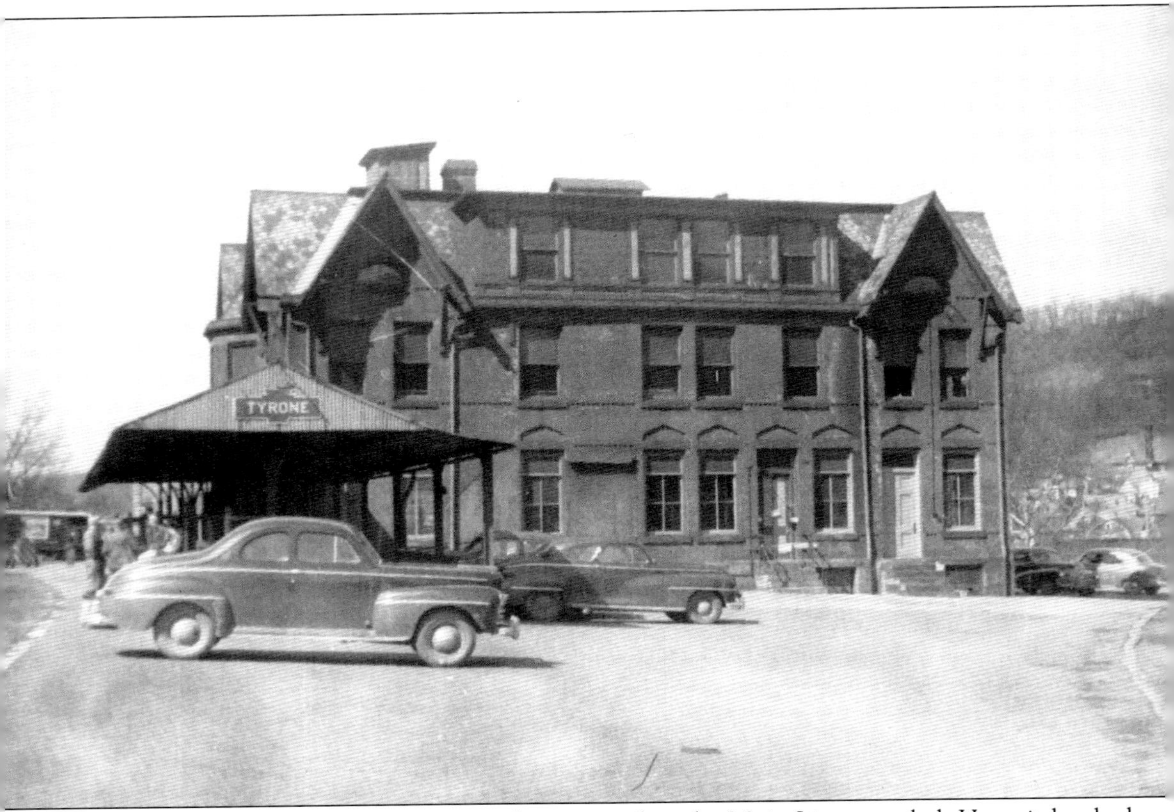

Tyrone Station sits at the most northern spot that the Main Line traveled. Here, it hooked south down the Logan Valley to Altoona. Due to its strategic location, it became one of the busiest depots on the Pennsylvania Railroad (PRR). Divisional offices were in this building for the Middle Division and the Tyrone Division. The Tyrone Division had its yards north of the town. An enormous tonnage of freight traveled through here from the far reaches of the state. Originally referred to as "Tyrone City" on maps, by 1900, most listings show it as simply "Tyrone." This depot served Penn State University students, countless troops leaving central Pennsylvania during wartime, and thousands of immigrants bound for Pennsylvania's heartland. Tyrone was the closest link from the mainline to the New York Central. When the PRR dissolved in 1968 and these two rival railroads became Penn Central, this once glorious station was destroyed.

Nine

POST SCRIPTS

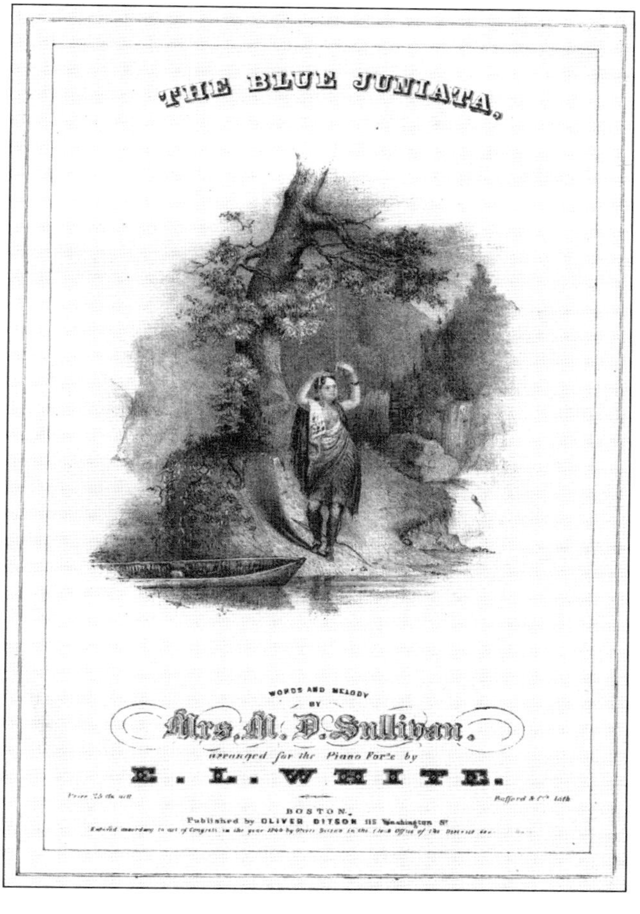

A mythical symbol of the Juniata region is Alfarata, an Indian princess. "The Blue Juniata" was written in 1841 by Marion Dix Sullivan. It became one of the most popular songs of that century. It was also the first successful song written by an American woman. Alfarata sings the praises of her warrior while she travels along the Juniata River. During General Sherman's march across the South in 1864–1865, his men sang "The Blue Juniata" for morale.

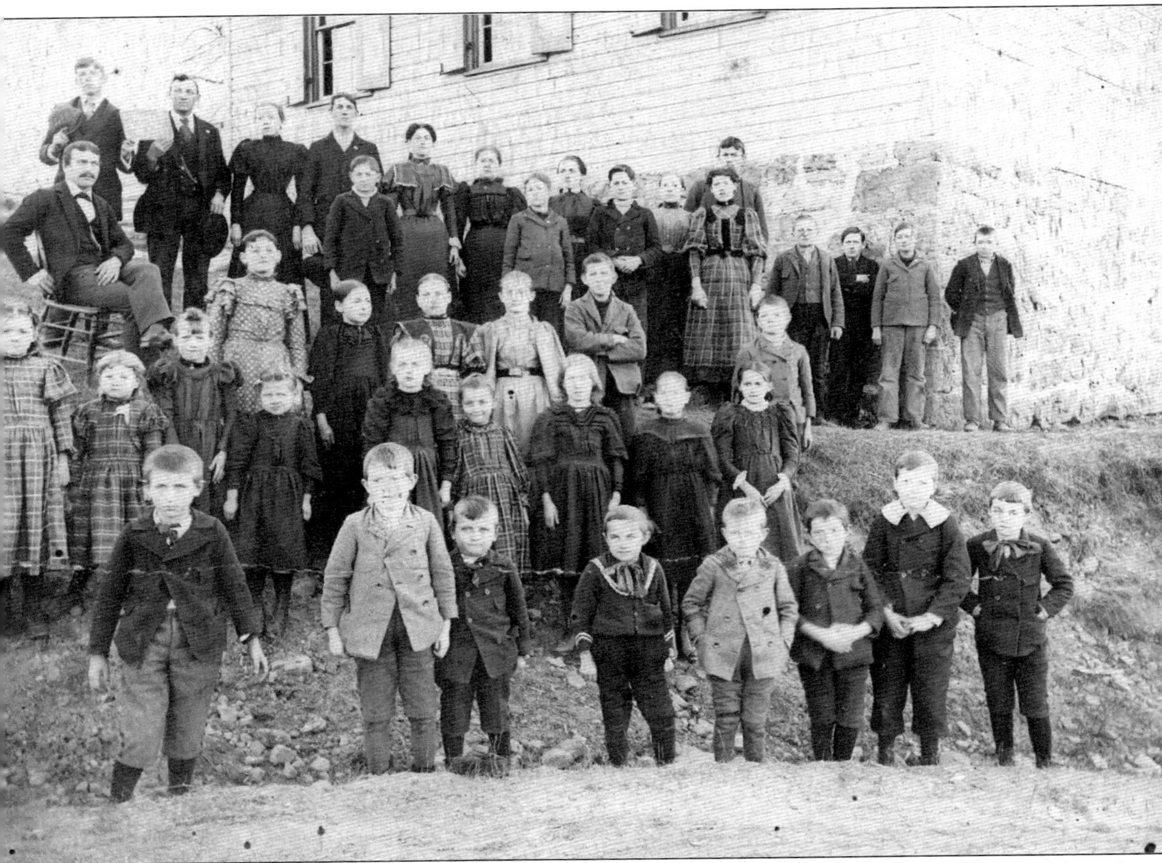

Martinsburg is located in the region the Native Americans called "the Great Cove." Although Martinsburg is in Blair County, prior to 1846 this borough appears on Bedford County maps. In 1860, the Juniata Collegiate Institute obtained its charter here. This unusual photograph produced in 1898 shows an assemblage of students at another building in Martinsburg known as Pleasant Valley School.

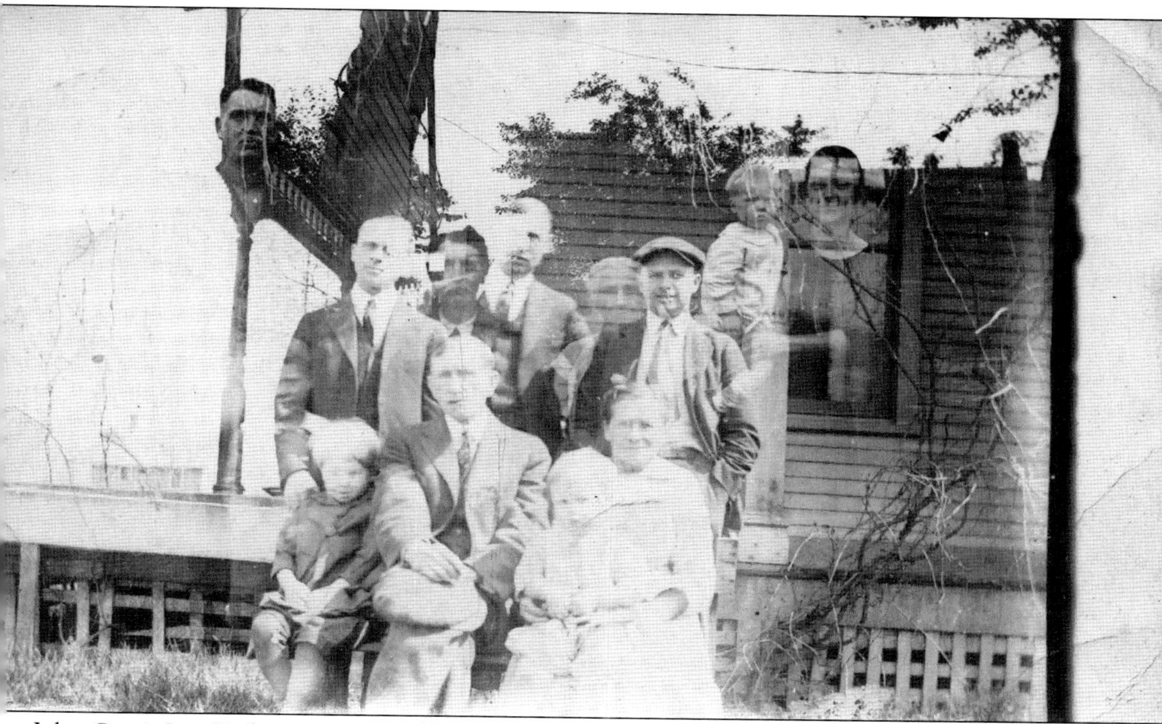

John Curtis Lee Tackett, great-grandfather of the author, was an itinerant photographer as well as a railroad engineer. He showed up at reunions, picnics, and gatherings with his large tripod camera equipped with its black bellows. Tackett developed and printed his own work at his home in Bellwood. He later switched to a duplex film camera, which was used for this image. Neglecting to wind between shots created this haunting double exposure. Usually, a photographer destroys photographs that are not presentable; however, he held on to this one. The author calls this photograph "The Spirit of the Juniata." It appears as if a past generation joins with its descendants. A postcard collection compiled by Tackett sparked an interest for ephemera in the author at a young age.

Discover Thousands of Local History Books Featuring Millions of Vintage Images

Arcadia Publishing, the leading local history publisher in the United States, is committed to making history accessible and meaningful through publishing books that celebrate and preserve the heritage of America's people and places.

Find more books like this at
www.arcadiapublishing.com

Search for your hometown history, your old stomping grounds, and even your favorite sports team.

Consistent with our mission to preserve history on a local level, this book was printed in South Carolina on American-made paper and manufactured entirely in the United States. Products carrying the accredited Forest Stewardship Council (FSC) label are printed on 100 percent FSC-certified paper.

MADE IN THE USA